Home Canning

By the Editors of Sunset Books and Sunset Magazine

Sunset Publishing Corporation ● *Menlo Park, California*

Research & Text
Barbara E. Goldman

Special Consultant
Kenneth N. Hall, Ph.D.
Extension Food Scientist and
Professor of Nutritional Sciences
University of Connecticut

Contributing Editor
Rebecca LaBrum

Coordinating Editors
Kathryn Lescroart Detzer
Deborah Thomas Kramer

Design
Susan Sempere

Illustrator
Liz Wheaton

Photographer
Tom Wyatt

Photo Stylist
Susan Massey

Easy Cherry-Amaretto Topping (page 125), Raspberry-Peach Topping (page 124), and Caramel Pecan Topping (page 125) add a special flourish to a banana split.

Home Canning & Preserving — in Step with the Times

Putting up preserves with fresh, distinctive flavors you just can't get in store-bought products is one of life's simple pleasures. ● And with the help of this updated book, you'll turn out the very best home-canned foods, from pantry basics like canned peaches and tomatoes to delectable treats such as Brandied Sweet Cherries, Spiced Apple Rings, and Jalapeño Jelly, just right for gift-giving or special meals at home. ● Whether you're a novice or an experienced cook, our thorough review of basic techniques and illustrated step-by-step instructions ensure rewarding results every time. And because all the canning instructions and recipes in these pages conform to the latest USDA guidelines, you can rest assured that your canned goods will be as safe to eat as they are delicious. ● Of course, canning isn't the only way to preserve foods. This book also includes all the information you need for successful freezing and drying. Our helpful guides tell you how to freeze and dry fruits, vegetables, herbs, and meats; you'll also find instructions for making crisp vegetable chips, flavorful dehydrated jams, rainbow-hued fruit ices, and more. ● We wish to thank Gerald D. Kuhn, Professor of Food Science, and Thomas S. Dimick, Senior Extension Aide, at the Pennsylvania State University for their assistance. We also thank Gloria Herbert, El Dorado County Program Coordinator for the Master Food Preservers Program of the University of California Cooperative Extension Service, for her valuable help. ● We extend our sincere appreciation to Fillamento and Beaver Brothers Antiques for props used in our photographs, and to Monterey Market, Whole Foods Market, and Schaub's Meat, Fish & Poultry for their special help. ● For our recipes, we provide a nutritional analysis (see page 128) prepared by Hill Nutrition Associates, Inc. of Florida. We are grateful to Lynne Hill, R.D., for her expert advice.

Cover
Our bounty of canned foods includes (from left) Lime-Mint Jelly (page 56), Cranberry-Apple Jelly (page 57), Easy Strawberry Jam (page 37), Raspberry-Plum Jam (page 41), Brandied Apricots (page 14), Papaya Butter (page 43), and Bread & Butter Pickles (page 61). Design by Susan Bryant. Photography by Tom Wyatt. Photo styling by Susan Massey. Food styling by Barbara E. Goldman.

About the recipes:
All of the recipes in this book were tested and developed in the Sunset test kitchens. **Senior Editor (Food and Entertaining), Sunset Magazine:** Jerry Anne Di Vecchio

Editorial Director, Sunset Books: Bob Doyle

Third printing June 1995

Contents

Basics of Canning

Easy techniques, equipment guide, safety tips

*N*o matter where you live—in the city or country, in a high-rise apartment or a home surrounded by gardens—you can reap the rewards of canning. ● If you don't grow your own fruits and vegetables, just start with best-of-season produce purchased from a nearby supermarket, roadside stand, or farmers' market. If you do have a thriving garden, you'll experience the special satisfaction of putting up the crops you've carefully nurtured to ripe, wholesome goodness. You can choose your favorite varieties, too; perhaps you prefer a certain kind of tomato or peach that's not always available in local markets. What's more, canning home-grown fruits and vegetables is economical: if you have too much to eat fresh, preserve it to enjoy later. ● Whether you start with home-harvested or store-bought produce, canning is easy. Once you've gathered the equipment you need and mastered the basic techniques described in this chapter, you'll quickly convert that top-quality produce into a whole range of mouthwatering foods to savor at home or give as gifts: sparkling jams and jellies, meal-brightening chutneys, relishes, and sauces, and fruits and vegetables seasoned just right.

How Canning Preserves Food

There's no special magic to canning: you simply pack food into a jar fitted with a self-sealing lid, then heat the bottled food to a temperature high enough to destroy any microorganisms that could cause spoilage. Heat also causes gases in both food and jar to expand, driving out air. As the jar cools, a vacuum forms, pulling the lid down against the mouth to make a tight seal. Air and microorganisms cannot enter unless this seal is broken.

Two Kinds of Food, Two Canning Methods

For home canning purposes, all foods are considered either *acid* or *low-acid*. Acidity is stated in terms of a pH value: the lower the pH, the higher the acidity. Acid foods have a pH of 4.6 or lower, while a low-acid food's pH is above 4.6. Each type of food requires a different processing method.

Acid foods may be safely processed in a boiling water canner. Foods in this group include almost all fruits, tomatoes acidified with bottled lemon juice or citric acid, pickles, relishes, chutneys, jams, jellies, and preserves. (Figs are the exception among fruits: they're low-acid. But if acidified before canning, they too may be safely processed in a boiling water canner.)

Low-acid foods must be processed in a pressure canner. Foods classed as low-acid include meats, poultry, seafood, milk, and all vegetables except tomatoes.

Botulism & Other Dangers

You've undoubtedly heard of botulism, a deadly form of food poisoning resulting from a toxin produced by spores of the bacterium *Clostridium botulinum*. This organism has some peculiar characteristics. It thrives without air in sealed jars at temperatures between 40° and 120°F, cannot be destroyed in a reasonable amount of time in a boiling water canner at 212°F, and cannot always be detected when a jar is opened. It doesn't grow well in an acid environment, but flourishes when acidity is low. For this reason, low-acid foods must be processed in a pressure canner at 240°F to eliminate the risk of botulism. As a further safeguard, it's wise to boil all such foods for 10 minutes before serving (to destroy any toxin that may be present), even if the food doesn't look in the least suspicious. Add an additional minute of boiling time for each 1,000 feet of altitude, starting at 1,000 feet above sea level.

"Boil before eating" is also the rule for tomatoes and tomato-vegetable mixtures such as chili sauce; though these are usually acidified before processing, boiling assures you that they're absolutely safe.

Other types of food spoilage, usually resulting from a poor or broken jar seal, are more easily detected. If food smells bad, looks discolored, is slimy-textured or topped with cottony mold, or if you see an unsealed or bulging lid, rising bubbles, or cloudy liquid in the jar, discard the food without tasting it. When in doubt, throw it out!

To can food safely, you must always use the proper canning method and adhere exactly to the research-based processing times in this book. For more safety information, see "Guarding against Botulism" (page 25).

Equipment You'll Need

For successful canning, it's essential to use the right equipment. If you're a beginner, consider sharing equipment expenses with a friend. Then take turns canning or, better still, work together.

Boiling water canner. This type of canner is recommended for processing fruits, tomatoes acidified with bottled lemon juice or citric acid, pickles, relishes, chutneys, jams, jellies, and preserves. It has a metal basket or rack that holds jars off the bottom of the kettle, allowing heat to circulate properly. Your canner should be no more than 4 inches wider than the burner on which it is placed, and it must be flat-bottomed if the burner is electric.

If you don't want to invest in a boiling water canner, it's possible to improvise. Just use any covered kettle large enough to let you surround the jars with water and cover them by 1 to 2 inches, while still leaving 1 to 2 inches of air space between water and lid. A large stockpot with a cake rack set in the bottom works well.

Pressure canner. This is the *only* canner to use for safe canning of vegetables, meats, poultry, and seafood. A heavy kettle with a cover that locks down steam-tight, it's mounted with a safety valve, vent, and pressure indicator.

There are two types of pressure indicators: weighted gauge and dial gauge. A dial gauge has a needle that indicates pressure on a numbered face; it should be checked each year (most Cooperative Extension offices will do this for you) and replaced if it reads high or low by more than 1 pound. A weighted gauge automatically limits pressure by a control preset for 5, 10, or 15 pounds; it need not be checked.

Before using your pressure canner, insert a pipe cleaner or string through the vent to make sure that it's unobstructed. Then follow the manufacturer's directions for your canner, and the exact instructions in this book for the particular food you are canning.

For safe operation and results using our recommended processing times, you must use a pressure canner large enough to hold at least four 1-quart jars.

Canning jars. Made of tempered glass that withstands heat shock and rough treatment, canning jars are sold along with other canning supplies in supermarkets and hardware stores. Available in quart, pint, and half-pint sizes, they require a two-piece closure: a vacuum **lid** with a rubber sealant and a metal **ring band.**

Bands are reusable (unless they're bent or rusty), but lids are not; if reused, they'll often fail to seal properly. Unused lids more than 3 years old may also fail, so it's best to buy only a single year's supply at a time.

Old-fashioned canning jars with zinc caps or glass lids are not recommended for canning, nor are newer glass-domed jars with gaskets (it's difficult to determine if you have a seal). Metric jars aren't recommended either, since adequate safety testing has not yet been completed. Finally, avoid reusing jars which contained purchased foods such as mayonnaise and peanut butter. These jars have a greater tendency to break during the home-canning process than do canning jars, since they may have been weakened by metal spoons or knives used to remove their contents: even tiny scratches in the glass can cause cracking or breakage during processing.

Wide, heavy pans. For cooking jams, jellies, preserves, pickles, and tomato sauces, you'll need wide, heavy-bottomed pans in 6- to 8-quart and 8- to 10-quart sizes.

Jar funnel. This wide-mouth funnel makes jars easier to fill and keeps the sealing surfaces clean.

Jar lifter. Available where canning supplies are sold. Some types have heat-resistant handles to protect hands, as well as a soft plastic coating to keep jars from slipping.

Narrow nonmetallic spatula. Use to release trapped air bubbles in filled jars before sealing. A plastic knife also works well. Don't use a metal spatula or knife, which could scratch—and thus weaken—the jar.

Tongs. Use these to remove canning lids from hot water and place them on filled jars.

Measuring cups & spoons. Cup measures (both liquid and dry) and measuring spoons are necessary for accurate measuring.

Long-handled spoons & ladle. Wooden and metal spoons, a long-handled slotted spoon, and a ladle are required for preparing foods and filling jars.

Knives. Sharp paring and chopping knives are essential.

Vegetable brush & peeler. A stiff-bristled brush helps clean vegetables thoroughly; a good, sharp peeler is essential for removing peel from carrots, potatoes, and other vegetables.

Food mill. This sturdy sieve has a hand-turned paddle that crushes vegetables and fruits; the pulp is pressed through, while any seeds, skin, and fiber remain behind. A food mill is especially useful when you're canning tomatoes or preparing jams, jellies, or sauces from fruits with small seeds.

Jelly or candy thermometer. An invaluable aid in cooking jellies and jams to the correct temperature.

Jelly bag. Use a jelly bag to strain juice from softened pulp during jelly making. A cheesecloth-lined colander may also be used.

Colander. For draining fruits and vegetables after washing, then holding them until needed.

Kitchen scale. Essential for reliable canning when ingredients are given by weight. It's helpful to have a scale with a capacity up to 25 pounds.

Timer. A good kitchen timer ensures accurate processing times. Before using your timer, be sure to check it with a reliable timepiece.

Equipment for successful canning includes:
1) Boiling water canner
2) Weighted gauge pressure canner
3) Dial gauge pressure canner
4) Jelly bag 5) Colander 6) Food mill
7) Wide, heavy-bottomed 8-quart pan
8) Kitchen scale 9) Jar funnel 10) Pot holder
11) Long-handled spoons 12) Long-handled ladles
13) Measuring cups 14) Measuring spoons
15) Canning jars, lids, and ring bands
16) Vegetable brush 17) Vegetable peelers 18) Timer
19) Narrow nonmetallic spatula 20) Long-handled
wooden spoon 21) Candy thermometer
22) Tongs 23) Jar lifter 24) Knives

Packing It Right

You may fill jars by either the hot-pack or raw-pack (formerly called "cold-pack") method.

The hot-pack method is preferred for most foods, especially acid types that you'll process in a boiling water canner. When you use this method, you bring food to a boil, simmer it for a few minutes, then pack it loosely into hot jars along with any required hot liquid. Hot-packing shrinks food, removes air from its tissues, helps keep it from floating in jars, and lengthens its shelf life.

The raw-pack method calls for packing unheated prepared food tightly into hot jars, then covering it with hot liquid. Raw-packing is more likely to result in floating food than is hot-packing. In addition, air will be trapped in both the food and the jars, causing the food to discolor during storage more rapidly than hot-packed products do.

Though popular in the past, the old-fashioned *open-kettle method*—filling jars with hot food without further processing—is no longer recommended, since jars often fail to seal properly. Other unsafe canning methods include processing in conventional and microwave ovens and in dishwashers. Avoid steam canners as well; safe processing times for newer models have not been established.

Leaving Headspace

When you fill jars with food, it's important to leave *headspace*: empty space between the top of the food (or liquid) and the jar lid. Headspace is required both to allow food to expand as the jar is heated and to form a vacuum as the jar seals.

Each recipe in this book tells you how much headspace to leave. In general, allow ¼ inch for jams and jellies, ½ inch for fruits and tomatoes processed in a boiling water canner, and 1 to 1½ inches for low-acid foods processed in a pressure canner.

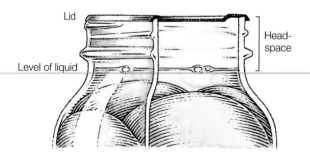

Lid

Headspace

Level of liquid

Testing the Seal

Once jars are processed, let them cool on a towel or rack for 12 to 24 hours. (Do not retighten ring bands after processing: seal failures may result.) After cooling, remove ring bands and check seals. You can do this in three ways (see illustrations on page 13).

- Press the center of the lid. If it stays down when you release your finger, the seal is good; if it springs back, there's no seal.

- Tap the lid with a spoon. A clear, high-pitched ringing sound indicates a good seal. If you hear a dull sound, either the lid is unsealed or you have a weak seal.

- Raise the jar to eye level and look across the lid. If it curves down slightly in the center, it's sealed. If it's flat or bulging, it has failed to seal.

Reprocessing Unsealed Jars

If a jar has failed to seal, you have two choices. You can either refrigerate it and use the food within 2 or 3 days (*if* the food looks and smells right); or you can reprocess it within 24 hours. To reprocess, remove the lid and check the sealing surface for tiny nicks. If the jar isn't flawed, just add a new lid. If it is flawed, reheat the food, pack it in a prepared, hot new jar, and apply a new lid. Then reprocess, using the *same* processing time. Keep in mind that the food may turn out softer, with inferior color and flavor.

Storing Canned Food

Once you remove the ring bands and determine that the cooled jars have sealed, wash each jar and lid to remove any food residue; rinse and dry. Label and date the jars, then store them (with ring bands left off to prevent rusting) in a clean, cool, dark, dry place. Don't store canned foods in an uninsulated attic or a damp area; dampness can corrode metal lids, break seals, and allow contamination. And make sure your storage spot is cooler than 95°F, out of sunlight, and away from hot pipes, your range, and your furnace.

Though properly canned foods with intact jar seals may be stored indefinitely, use them within 1 year for optimal flavor, texture, and nutritional value.

High-altitude Canning

Processing times given in the charts and recipes in this book are for canning at sea level. If you live at an altitude above 1,000 feet, you must adjust processing times or canner pressure: at higher altitudes, atmospheric pressure is lower, and water boils at a lower temperature.

If you don't know your altitude, ask your local Cooperative Extension office or contact your local District Conservationist with the Soil Conservation Service. Then calculate proper canning times and pressures by consulting the following charts.

Processing Times for Boiling Water Canner at High Altitude

Altitude (feet)	Increase in time
0 – 1,000	No increase
1,001 – 3,000	Add 5 minutes
3,001 – 6,000	Add 10 minutes
6,001 – 8,000	Add 15 minutes
8,001 – 10,000	Add 20 minutes

Pressures for Dial & Weighted Gauge Canners at High Altitude

Altitude (feet)	Dial Gauge (PSI)	Weighted Gauge (PSI)*
0 – 1,000	11	10
1,001 – 2,000	11	15
2,001 – 4,000	12	15
4,001 – 6,000	13	15
6,001 – 8,000	14	15
8,001 – 10,000	15	15

Above 1,000 feet, operate weighted gauge canners at 15 pounds only. They cannot correct incrementally for higher altitudes.

Glossary

Acid foods. Foods with enough natural acid, or with enough additional acid such as vinegar or lemon juice, to result in a pH of 4.6 or lower. Fruits, acidified tomatoes, pickles, relishes, chutneys, jams, jellies, and preserves fall into this category. (Figs are an exception among fruits; they must be acidified before processing.)

Ascorbic acid. The chemical name for vitamin C. A commercially available form is often used in canning to keep peeled light-colored fruits and vegetables from browning. (Lemon juice is frequently used for the same purpose.)

Botulism. A deadly form of food poisoning, caused by a toxin produced by spores of the bacterium *Clostridium botulinum*. For more on botulism and how to prevent it, see page 25.

Citric acid. An acid derived from citrus fruits. It can be added to canned foods to increase acidity or to improve color and flavor.

Headspace. The unfilled space between the top of the food (or liquid) in a jar and the top of the jar.

Hot-pack method. A canning method that involves filling hot jars with hot precooked food before processing. It's the preferred method for processing foods in a boiling water canner.

Low-acid foods. Foods that contain little natural acid and have a pH above 4.6. This group includes meats, poultry, seafood, milk, vegetables, and some varieties of tomatoes. These foods must be processed in a pressure canner or acidified to a pH of 4.6 or lower before processing in a boiling water canner.

pH. A measure of acidity or alkalinity. Values range from 0 to 14; a pH of 7 is neutral. The lower the pH, the more acid the food.

Pickling. Adding enough vinegar or lemon juice to a low-acid food to bring its pH down to 4.6 or below. Properly pickled foods may be safely processed in a boiling water canner.

Raw-pack method. A canning method that involves filling hot jars with raw, unheated food prior to processing.

Venting (also called "exhausting"). Permitting excess air inside a pressure canner to escape before closing the vent or putting on the weighted gauge.

Home-canned fruits let you enjoy summer flavors all year long. Shown below right is a dish of Brandied Apricots (page 14) with Blackberry-Peach Topping (page 124) and sour cream. Jars on the tabletop include blackberries, pears, peaches, and more topping; on the shelf are (left to right) Brandied Apricots, raspberries, pears, and Brandied Sweet Cherries (page 14).

Canning Fruits

Sweet summer flavors, homey sauces, brandied fruit

*Y*ou can easily and confidently preserve fresh fruit in a boiling water canner. The hot-pack method (see "Packing It Right," page 8) is best for most fruits, though some cooks feel that raw-packing is preferable for small or soft types such as berries, cherries, apricots, and plums, since it minimizes crushing. ● Adding some sweetening helps fruit hold its shape and maintain its color and flavor; a very light syrup approximates the natural sugar content of many fruits. If you'd rather not use syrup, you may also can fruit in juice. Unsweetened apple, pineapple, and white grape juices are all good packing liquids, but the best choice is juice from the fruit being canned (to prepare juice, crush soft fruit, then heat and strain it). ● Packing fruit in water is another option, but water-packed fruits fall short on flavor, color, and texture. If you want to sweeten such fruits with an artificial sweetener, add it just before serving. ● No matter which pack you choose, start with fruit that's fully ripened, yet still firm. Examine it carefully to make sure it's free from bruises or soft spots, then rinse it well with cool water to remove any dirt or residues. ● To keep fruits such as pears, peaches, nectarines, and apples from turning brown when cut, treat them with an antidarkening agent (see "Protecting Fruit Colors," page 12).

Step-by-Step Canning for Fruits

1. Read the information about canning fruit on the preceding page. Check the fruit chart (pages 16 and 17) for instructions on the specific fruit you're canning. Prepare an antidarkening solution, if needed (see "Protecting Fruit Colors," below).

2. Get out boiling water canner, jars, *new* lids, ring bands, and other equipment you'll need (see pages 5 and 6). Jars must be free of nicks or cracks that might prevent sealing; ring bands must not be rusty, dented, or scratched. Be sure all equipment is clean and ready to use.

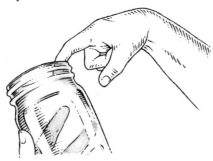

3. Wash jars; keep them hot in hot water to prevent breakage when filling with hot food. If jars will be processed for less than 10 minutes in the boiling water canner, you must sterilize them. To sterilize, cover with water and boil for 10 minutes; leave in hot water until filled.

   Prepare lids according to manufacturer's directions; keep them hot in hot water. Check the manufacturer's advice concerning the ring bands you're using, then follow any preparation instructions printed on the box.

4. Place basket or rack in canner. Half-fill canner with hot water. Cover; bring water to a simmer. In a large teakettle or another pan, heat additional water to add later.

5. Prepare only enough fruit for one canner load at a time, following chart instructions. If necessary, treat fruit to prevent darkening (see below). Prepare syrup of your choice as directed on facing page; or heat fruit juice or water. Keep hot until ready to use.

6. Remove a jar from hot water. Stand it upright on a cloth towel.

   To pack hot, bring syrup or other liquid to a boil. Add prepared fruit; cook briefly, or as directed. Pack hot fruit into prepared, hot jars (pack halves cavity side down, in overlapping layers); leave ½-inch headspace. Ladle or pour hot liquid over fruit, leaving directed headspace.

   To pack raw, fill prepared, hot jars with raw fruit (pack halves cavity side down, in overlapping layers); leave ½-inch headspace. Cover with hot liquid, leaving ½-inch headspace, or as chart directs.

7. Gently run a narrow nonmetallic spatula between fruit and jar sides to release air bubbles; add more liquid, if necessary.

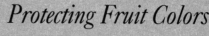

Protecting Fruit Colors

To keep apples, apricots, nectarines, peaches, and pears from darkening after cutting, drop the cut fruit into a commercial antidarkening mixture prepared according to the manufacturer's instructions; or use 1 teaspoon ascorbic acid (or enough crushed vitamin C tablets to equal 3,000 milligrams) to 1 gallon cold water.

8. Wipe jar rim and threads with a clean, damp cloth or paper towel to remove food particles that might prevent a seal. Lift a jar lid from hot water; place on jar, sealing side down. Firmly and evenly screw on ring band by hand; don't over-tighten. As each jar is filled, use jar lifter to place it on canner rack. Space jars so they don't touch each other or sides of canner. If needed, add more hot water to cover jars by at least 1 inch.

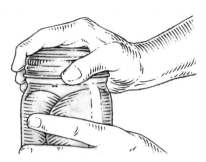

9. Cover canner; increase heat to high and bring water to a vigorous boil. Set timer for required processing time (see chart on pages 16 and 17); at altitudes above 1,000 feet, adjust times according to "Processing Times for Boiling Water Canner at High Altitude" (page 9). Reduce heat to maintain a gentle boil throughout processing. Add more boiling water, if needed, to keep water level above jars.

10. When processing time is up, turn off heat. Immediately remove jars with jar lifter. Place jars at least 1 inch apart on a towel or rack, out of drafts. *Do not retighten bands.* Let cool for 12 to 24 hours.

11. When jars are cool, remove ring bands. (To loosen a band that sticks, cover it with a hot, damp cloth for 1 to 2 minutes.) Test seal as directed on page 8 and shown below. If a jar fails to seal, refrigerate it and use the food within 2 or 3 days— *if* it looks and smells right. Or reprocess as directed on page 8.

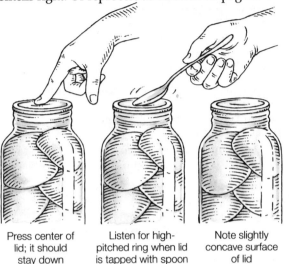

Press center of lid; it should stay down

Listen for high-pitched ring when lid is tapped with spoon

Note slightly concave surface of lid

12. Wash jars and lids to remove any food residue; rinse and dry. Label and date jars; store in a clean, cool, dark, dry place.

Syrups for Canning

Amounts make enough syrup to pack 8 or 9 pints or 4 quarts of fruit.

Type of Syrup	Water (Cups)	Sugar (Cups)
Very light	6½	¾
Light	5¾	1½
Medium	5¼	2¼
Heavy	5	3¼
Very heavy	4¼	4¼

To prepare syrup, combine sugar and water in a heavy-bottomed pan. Bring to a boil, stirring until sugar is dissolved; keep hot. You need ½ to ¾ cup syrup for each pint of fruit.

You may use a mild-flavored honey or light corn syrup in place of up to half the sugar, if you prefer. A higher proportion will mask the fruit flavor.

Many fruits, particularly sweeter varieties, are excellent when packed in lighter syrups. In general, use lighter syrups with sweeter fruits, heavier syrups with tarter fruits. Try a small amount of syrup first to see if you like it.

Home-style Applesauce

Pictured on facing page

Applesauce as *you* like it. Sweeten and spice it to taste, or leave it entirely plain. For a smoother sauce, whirl the cooked fruit in a food processor or blender before seasoning it and reheating to boiling. (For a new twist on this all-time favorite, don't pass up our winning pear and plum sauces.)

- 9 **pounds (about 27 medium-size) apples (such as Jonathan, McIntosh, Golden Delicious, or Gravenstein), peeled, cored, and sliced**
- 1½ **cups water**
- 1 **to 1½ cups sugar (optional)**
- 1 **to 2 teaspoons ground cinnamon (optional)**

Combine apples and water in a heavy-bottomed 8- to 10-quart pan. Bring to a boil over medium-high heat, stirring often. Reduce heat, cover, and simmer, stirring often, until apples are soft (about 30 minutes). Add sugar and cinnamon, if desired; bring to a boil. (Sauce will be slightly chunky; to remove larger lumps, whisk briefly with a wire whisk.)

Fill prepared, hot jars with hot sauce, leaving ½-inch headspace. Gently run a narrow nonmetallic spatula between sauce and jar sides to release air bubbles. Wipe rims and threads clean; top with hot lids, then firmly screw on bands. Process in boiling water canner for 15 minutes for pints, 20 minutes for quarts. Or omit processing and ladle sauce into freezer containers, leaving ½-inch headspace for pints, 1-inch headspace for quarts; apply lids. Let cool; freeze or refrigerate. Makes about 6 pints or 3 quarts.

Storage time. *Processed:* Up to 1 year. *Unprocessed:* Up to 1 week in refrigerator; up to 10 months in freezer.

Per ½ cup: 82 calories, 0 g protein, 21 g carbohydrates, 0 g total fat, 0 mg cholesterol, 0 mg sodium

Home-style Pear Sauce

Follow directions for **Home-style Applesauce,** but substitute 9 pounds **Bartlett pears** for apples, reduce water to 1 cup, and add 2 tablespoons **lemon juice.** After seasoning sauce, simmer, uncovered, until it thickens to the desired consistency. Makes about 4 pints or 2 quarts.

Per ½ cup: 139 calories, 1 g protein, 36 g carbohydrates, 1 g total fat, 0 mg cholesterol, 0 mg sodium

Home-style Plum Sauce

Follow directions for **Home-style Applesauce,** but substitute 9 pounds **plums** for apples. Rinse, pit, and slice; do not peel. Before seasoning sauce, whirl, a portion at a time, in a food processor or blender until smooth. Or put through a food mill or fine strainer. Makes about 6 pints or 3 quarts.

Per ½ cup: 88 calories, 1 g protein, 21 g carbohydrates, 1 g total fat, 0 mg cholesterol, 0 mg sodium

Brandied Apricots

Pictured on page 10

Fruits canned in brandy syrup have much the same heady flavor as those brandied in a stone crock. Serve the fruit plain or topped with vanilla yogurt, sour cream, or crème fraîche; or spoon it over ice cream or slices of pound cake.

- 3 **cups sugar**
- 2½ **cups water**
- 6 **pounds firm-ripe apricots**
- 1¼ **to 1½ cups brandy**

First, prepare syrup. Combine sugar and water in a heavy-bottomed 8- to 10-quart pan and bring to a boil over medium heat, stirring until sugar is dissolved. Keep hot.

Halve and pit apricots; treat to prevent darkening (see page 12). Drain apricots; add to hot syrup and bring to a boil. Pack (cavity side down, in overlapping layers) into prepared, hot pint jars.

Pour about ¼ cup hot syrup into each jar; then pour in 3 to 4 tablespoons brandy (the amount depends on your preference for a moderate or strong brandy flavor). Then fill jars with more hot syrup, leaving ½-inch headspace. Gently run a narrow nonmetallic spatula between fruit and jar sides to release air bubbles. Wipe rims and threads clean; top with hot lids, then firmly screw on bands. Process in boiling water canner for 20 minutes. Makes about 6 pints.

Storage time. Up to 1 year.

Per ½ cup: 177 calories, 1 g protein, 37 g carbohydrates, 0 g total fat, 0 mg cholesterol, 1 mg sodium

Brandied Sweet Cherries

Follow directions for **Brandied Apricots,** but substitute 6 pounds **dark sweet cherries** for apricots. Rinse, stem, and pit cherries. If desired, substitute **kirsch** for brandy. Process for 15 minutes. Makes about 6 pints.

Per ½ cup: 200 calories, 1 g protein, 42 g carbohydrates, 1 g total fat, 0 mg cholesterol, 0 mg sodium

Delicious fruit sauces add great flavor—and a pretty flourish—
to a variety of entrées. Here, pork tenderloin on a bed of noodles receives a
tangy assist from Home-style Plum Sauce. Home-style Applesauce (top left) is
another superb choice; or try making the same sauce with mellow pears.
All three sauce recipes are on the facing page.

Guide for Canning Fruits

You'll find recipes for syrups on page 13. Processing times are given for altitudes of 1,000 feet or below. Above 1,000 feet, you will need to increase times; see "Processing Times for Boiling Water Canner at High Altitude" (page 9). Before applying hot lids to filled jars, run a narrow nonmetallic spatula gently between fruit and jar sides to release trapped air bubbles.

Note: The suitable varieties noted for a number of fruits (apples, apricots, and peaches, for example) are meant only as general suggestions. The types listed are among the best choices for canning, but other kinds may also work well.

Fruit	Quantity to yield 1 pint	How to prepare	Processing time Pints	Quarts
Apples Golden Delicious, Granny Smith, Gravenstein, Jonathan, McIntosh, Newtown Pippin	1¼ to 1½ lbs.	Rinse, peel, and core; quarter or slice. Treat to prevent darkening (see page 12); drain. Prepare syrup or other packing liquid; add apples and boil gently for 5 minutes. Pack hot into prepared, hot jars; cover with hot liquid, leaving ½-inch headspace.	20 min.	20 min.
Apricots Castlebrite, Patterson, Royal-Blenheim, Tilton, Wenatchee	1 to 1¼ lbs.	You may leave apricots whole if tree-ripened (use varieties that hold their shape well); remove pits from apricots harvested before fully ripe. Rinse apricots; if desired, peel as directed for peaches. Halve or slice. Treat to prevent darkening (see page 12); drain. Prepare syrup or other packing liquid. ***To pack hot***, bring apricots and syrup (or other liquid) to a boil. Pack hot into prepared, hot jars (place halves cavity side down, in overlapping layers). Cover with hot liquid, leaving ½-inch headspace. ***To pack raw***, fill prepared, hot jars with apricots (place halves cavity side down, in overlapping layers). Cover with hot liquid, leaving ½-inch headspace.	20 min. 25 min.	25 min. 30 min.
Bananas		Canning not recommended.		
Berries (Except strawberries and cranberries, which are not recommended for canning)	¾ to 1½ lbs.	Rinse 1 to 2 quarts at a time. Drain, hull, and stem if necessary. For gooseberries, snip off tops and tails with scissors. Prepare syrup or other packing liquid and bring to a boil; pour ½ cup into each prepared, hot jar. ***To pack hot*** (for firm berries), heat berries in boiling water for 30 seconds; drain. Pack hot into jars. Cover with more hot liquid, leaving ½-inch headspace. ***To pack raw***, fill jars with berries, shaking down gently while filling. Cover with more hot liquid, leaving ½-inch headspace.	15 min. 15 min.	15 min. 20 min.
Cherries, all varieties *Sweet:* Bing, Black Tartarian, Lambert, Rainier, Royal Ann *Sour:* Early Richmond, English Morello, Montmorency	1 to 1½ lbs.	Rinse and stem; pit, if desired. If pitted, treat sour cherries and light-colored varieties of sweet cherries to prevent darkening (see page 12); drain. If left unpitted, prick skins on opposite sides with a clean needle to prevent splitting. Prepare syrup or other packing liquid. ***To pack hot***, bring cherries to a boil in syrup (or other liquid). Pack hot into prepared, hot jars. Cover with hot liquid, leaving ½-inch headspace. ***To pack raw***, pour ½ cup hot syrup (or other liquid) into each prepared, hot jar. Fill jars with cherries, shaking down gently while filling. Cover with more hot liquid, leaving ½-inch headspace.	15 min. 25 min.	20 min. 25 min.
Figs Black Mission, Celeste, Kadota, Brown Turkey	¾ to 1½ lbs.	Avoid overripe figs. Rinse; do not peel or stem. Cover figs with water; bring to a boil and boil for 2 minutes. Drain. Prepare light syrup or other packing liquid. Add figs; boil gently for 5 minutes. ***Add 2 tablespoons bottled lemon juice to each quart jar (1 tablespoon to each pint).*** Pack hot figs into prepared, hot jars. Cover with hot liquid, leaving ½-inch headspace.	45 min.	50 min.
Grapefruit	2 lbs.	Use thoroughly ripe fruit. Cut off peel, including white membrane. Run a thin knife between pulp and skin of each segment; lift out whole segment. Remove any seeds. Prepare syrup or other packing liquid. Fill prepared, hot jars with fruit. Cover with hot liquid, leaving ½-inch headspace.	10 min.	10 min.

Fruit	Quantity to yield 1 pint	How to prepare	Processing time Pints	Quarts
Grapes Any tight-skinned, slightly underripe seedless grapes, preferably harvested 2 weeks before reaching optimum eating quality	2 lbs.	Rinse and stem. Prepare light or medium syrup or other packing liquid. **To pack hot**, heat grapes in boiling water for 30 seconds; drain. Pack hot into prepared, hot jars. Cover with hot liquid, leaving 1-inch headspace. **To pack raw**, fill prepared, hot jars with grapes. Cover with hot liquid, leaving 1-inch headspace.	10 min. 15 min.	10 min. 20 min.
Lemons/Limes		Canning not recommended.		
Loquats	1½ to 2 lbs.	Rinse; remove stem and blossom ends. Halve and remove seeds. Prepare light syrup or other packing liquid; add loquats and boil gently for 3 to 5 minutes. Pack hot loquats into prepared, hot jars. Cover with hot liquid, leaving ½-inch headspace.	15 min.	20 min.
Melons		Freezing recommended (balls, cubes, or slices); see page 85.		
Nectarines Firebrite, Flavortop, Gold Mine, Panamint, Stanwick	1 to 1½ lbs.	Rinse; do not peel. Pit; halve or slice. Treat to prevent darkening (see page 12); drain. Prepare syrup or other packing liquid. **To pack hot**, bring fruit and syrup (or other liquid) to a boil. Pack hot into prepared, hot jars (pack halves cavity side down, in overlapping layers). Cover with hot liquid, leaving ½-inch headspace. **To pack raw**, fill prepared, hot jars with nectarines (pack halves cavity side down, in overlapping layers). Cover with hot liquid, leaving ½-inch headspace.	20 min. 25 min.	25 min. 30 min.
Oranges		Can as directed for grapefruit. Flavor is best when canned with equal parts grapefruit.		
Peaches Elberta, Halford, J.H. Hale, O'Henry, Redglobe, Redhaven, Rio Oso Gem	1 to 1½ lbs.	Rinse. To peel, dip firm-ripe peaches in boiling water for 1 to 1½ minutes to loosen skins. Dip in cold water; drain. Slip off skins. Pit, then halve or slice. Treat to prevent darkening (see page 12); drain. Prepare syrup or other packing liquid. **To pack hot,** follow hot-pack directions for nectarines. **To pack raw,** follow raw-pack directions for nectarines. (Note: Hot-packed peaches will generally be higher in quality than raw-packed fruit.)	20 min. 25 min.	25 min. 30 min.
Pears Bartlett	1 to 1½ lbs.	Rinse, peel, cut into halves or quarters, and remove cores. Treat to prevent darkening (see page 12); drain. Prepare syrup or other packing liquid; add pears and boil gently for 5 minutes. Pack hot into prepared, hot jars (pack halves cavity side down, in overlapping layers). Cover with hot liquid, leaving ½-inch headspace.	20 min.	25 min.
Pineapple	1 to 1½ lbs.	Rinse and peel; remove eyes and core. Slice or cube. Prepare syrup or other packing liquid; add pineapple and simmer for 10 minutes. Pack hot into prepared, hot jars. Cover with hot liquid, leaving ½-inch headspace.	15 min.	20 min.
Plums & fresh prunes Casselman, French Prune, Friar, Italian Prune, Laroda, Nubiana, Santa Rosa	1 to 1½ lbs.	Rinse and stem. Freestone varieties may be halved and pitted. If plums are left whole, prick skins on opposite sides with a clean needle to prevent splitting. Prepare syrup or other packing liquid. **To pack hot**, boil plums in syrup (or other liquid) for 2 minutes. Remove from heat, cover pan, and let stand for 20 to 30 minutes. Pack plums into prepared, hot jars (pack halves cavity side down, in overlapping layers). Cover with hot liquid, leaving ½-inch headspace. **To pack raw**, fill prepared, hot jars with plums, packing firmly (pack halves cavity side down, in overlapping layers). Cover with hot liquid, leaving ½-inch headspace.	20 min. 20 min.	25 min. 25 min.
Rhubarb	⅔ to 1 lb.	Rinse unpeeled stalks; cut into ½-inch lengths. Place in a large pan. Add ½ cup sugar for each 4 cups fruit; let stand for 3 to 4 hours. Heat gently just to a boil. Pack hot into prepared, hot jars; cover with hot cooking liquid, leaving ½-inch headspace.	15 min.	15 min.

Capture the robust flavor of red, ripe tomatoes by canning the fruit whole, halved, or crushed; or use your tasty crop as a base for zesty sauces. Surrounding a bowl of Meatless Pasta Sauce (page 24) are, from left, Barbecue Sauce (page 24), canned tomatoes (page 20), Salsa (page 22), and more Meatless Pasta Sauce.

Canning Tomatoes

Succulent tomatoes, spicy condiments, savory sauces

W hen the tomatoes in your garden ripen all at once, capture their sunny, full-bodied flavor with home canning. You can preserve the fruit whole or crushed, or use it in sauces, salsa, or spicy homemade catsup. ● Because some modern varieties are less acidic than older types, it's especially important to acidify tomatoes to minimize the risk of botulism. Just add bottled lemon juice or citric acid to each jar, in the amounts the recipe directs. Be aware that acidification is necessary even if you use a pressure canner (see basic tomato pack instructions, page 20), since the pressure canning times for tomatoes do not provide protection against botulism. ● When you prepare the recipes in this chapter, follow all instructions *explicitly*. If only pressure canning instructions are given, you *must* process in a pressure canner. Do not change processing times, preparation methods, or ingredient proportions. If you wish to add other ingredients or seasonings, wait until just before serving. And remember—for safety's sake, boil all home-canned tomatoes and tomato-vegetable mixtures for 10 minutes before eating; boil very thick mixtures for 15 to 20 minutes. Add an additional minute of boiling for every 1,000 feet of altitude, starting at 1,000 feet above sea level.

Step-by-Step Canning for Tomatoes

1. Choose firm-ripe tomatoes. Don't use overripe tomatoes with soft or wrinkled skins, tomatoes from dead or frost-killed vines, or those ripened in the house; these are all lower in acidity than firm, vine-ripened fruit, and thus carry a greater risk for botulism. (You may, however, safely can green tomatoes picked near maturity; follow the instructions for ripe tomatoes.)

2. Check recipe or pack instructions. If you will be using a boiling water canner, follow steps 2 through 4 on page 12. If you will be using a pressure canner, follow steps 2 and 3 on page 28.

3. Prepare just one canner load at a time. Rinse tomatoes gently but thoroughly; don't use detergent. Dip in boiling water until skins split (30 to 60 seconds), then dip in cold water. Slip off skins; cut out cores and any bruised or discolored areas. Prepare tomatoes and any other ingredients according to recipe or pack instructions.

4. Remove a jar from hot water; place upright on a cloth towel.

For tomatoes, add 2 tablespoons bottled lemon juice or ½ teaspoon citric acid to each quart jar (1 tablespoon juice or ¼ teaspoon citric acid to each pint jar). Add a little sugar to offset the tartness, if you like; you may also add salt. Fill jar according to pack instructions, leaving recommended headspace.

For tomato-vegetable mixtures, fill jar as recipe directs, leaving recommended headspace.

Gently run a narrow nonmetallic spatula between food and jar sides to release air bubbles; add more liquid, if necessary.

5. **To process in a boiling water canner,** follow steps 8 through 12 on page 13.

To process in a pressure canner, follow steps 7 through 13 on pages 28 and 29.

Basic Tomato Packs

Whether you can your tomatoes whole, halved, or crushed, you'll need an average of 3 pounds per quart. Rinse, peel, and core tomatoes, following the step-by-step instructions above; then proceed as directed below for the pack you're preparing. Note that it's necessary to adjust processing times or canner pressure at elevations higher than 1,000 feet; see page 9.

Crushed Tomatoes

Quarter tomatoes, then place a sixth of them in a large, heavy-bottomed non-aluminum pan. Heat quickly over high heat, crushing to release juice and stirring constantly to prevent scorching. Bring to a boil; gradually add remaining tomato quarters (do not crush). Boil gently, uncovered, for 5 minutes, stirring often.

Add 2 tablespoons bottled lemon juice or ½ teaspoon citric acid to *each* prepared, hot quart jar (1 tablespoon juice or ¼ teaspoon citric acid to *each* pint). *Don't* use fresh lemon juice; the acidity varies too much. If you wish to add salt, place 1 teaspoon in each quart jar, ½ teaspoon in each pint jar (or season to taste). Fill jars with hot tomatoes, leaving ½-inch headspace.

Process tomatoes in boiling water canner for 35 minutes for pints, 45 minutes for quarts. Or process in pressure canner for 15 minutes for pints and quarts (at 11 pounds pressure on dial gauge; 10 pounds for weighted gauge).

Whole or Halved Tomatoes

Leave tomatoes whole or cut into halves. Place in a large, heavy-bottomed non-aluminum pan and add enough water to cover. Bring to a boil; boil gently, uncovered, for 5 minutes.

Add 2 tablespoons bottled lemon juice or ½ teaspoon citric acid to *each* prepared, hot quart jar (1 tablespoon juice or ¼ teaspoon citric acid to *each* pint). *Don't* use fresh lemon juice; the acidity varies too much. If you wish to add salt, place 1 teaspoon in each quart jar, ½ teaspoon in each pint jar (or season to taste). Fill jars with hot tomatoes, leaving ½-inch headspace. Add hot cooking liquid, leaving ½-inch headspace.

Process tomatoes in boiling water canner for 40 minutes for pints, 45 minutes for quarts. Or process in pressure canner for 10 minutes for pints and quarts (at 11 pounds pressure on dial gauge; 10 pounds for weighted gauge).

Tomato Sauce

Use this tasty tomato sauce much as you would commercially canned sauce—in stews, soups, and casseroles, and as a base for pasta sauces.

- 10 **pounds (about 20 large) firm-ripe tomatoes, peeled, cored, and quartered**
- ¼ **cup lightly packed chopped fresh basil**
- 2 **tablespoons chopped fresh oregano**
- 5 **cloves garlic, minced or pressed**
- 2 **to 4 tablespoons sugar**
- 2 **teaspoons salt (optional)**
- ½ **teaspoon freshly ground pepper**
  About 3 tablespoons bottled lemon juice (1 tablespoon per pint jar)

In a heavy-bottomed 8- to 10-quart non-aluminum pan, combine tomatoes, basil, oregano, garlic, sugar, salt (if used), and pepper. Bring to a boil over high heat, stirring almost constantly; reduce heat and simmer, uncovered, stirring often, for 20 minutes. Put through a food mill or fine strainer, a portion at a time.

Return purée to pan and bring to a boil over high heat, stirring often. Then reduce heat and simmer, uncovered, stirring often, until sauce is thickened and reduced to about 6 cups (about 1½ hours); as sauce thickens, reduce heat and stir more often to prevent sticking.

Add 1 tablespoon bottled lemon juice to *each* **prepared, hot pint jar.** Fill jars with hot sauce, leaving ¼-inch headspace. Gently run a narrow nonmetallic spatula between sauce and jar sides to release air bubbles. Wipe rims and threads clean; top with hot lids, then firmly screw on bands. Process in boiling water canner for 35 minutes or in pressure canner for 15 minutes (at 11 pounds pressure on dial gauge; 10 pounds for weighted gauge). Or omit processing and ladle sauce into pint freezer containers, leaving ½-inch headspace; apply lids. Let cool; freeze or refrigerate. Makes about 3 pints.

Storage time. *Processed:* Up to 1 year. *Unprocessed:* Up to 1 week in refrigerator; up to 6 months in freezer.

Per tablespoon: 11 calories, 0 g protein, 2 g carbohydrates, 0 g total fat, 0 mg cholesterol, 4 mg sodium

---

Peeling Tomatoes

To peel tomatoes, dip them in boiling water until the skins split (30 to 60 seconds). Dip in cold water, then peel; the skins will slip off easily.

Mild Chili Sauce

Mild green chiles add a suggestion of heat to a sauce that's great over grilled hamburgers, barbecued chicken, and even scrambled eggs. If you'd prefer a little more heat, substitute jalapeño or serrano chiles for some of the Anaheim chiles.

- 7 **pounds (about 14 large) firm-ripe tomatoes, peeled, cored, and quartered**
- ¾ **pound (about 4 large) fresh mild green chiles such as Anaheim, seeded (if desired) and chopped**
- ½ **pound onions, quartered**
- 2 **cloves garlic, halved**
- 1½ **cups sugar**
- 3 **cups cider vinegar (5% acidity)**
- 1½ **teaspoons** *each* **ground cinnamon and ground cloves**
- 1 **teaspoon ground ginger**
  Salt and freshly ground pepper

In a large bowl, combine tomatoes, chiles, onions, and garlic. Purée vegetables in a blender or food processor, a portion at a time. Pour purée into a heavy-bottomed 8- to 10-quart non-aluminum pan and stir in sugar, vinegar, cinnamon, cloves, and ginger. Bring to a boil over high heat, stirring. Then reduce heat and simmer, uncovered, stirring occasionally, until sauce is thickened and reduced to 2 quarts (about 2 hours); as sauce thickens, reduce heat and stir more often to prevent sticking. Season to taste with salt and pepper.

Fill prepared, hot pint jars with hot sauce, leaving ¼-inch headspace. Gently run a narrow nonmetallic spatula between sauce and jar sides to release air bubbles. Wipe rims and threads clean; top with hot lids, then firmly screw on bands. Process in boiling water canner for 15 minutes. Or omit processing and ladle sauce into pint freezer containers, leaving ½-inch headspace; apply lids. Let cool; freeze or refrigerate. Makes about 4 pints.

Storage time. *Processed:* Up to 1 year. *Unprocessed:* Up to 3 weeks in refrigerator; up to 6 months in freezer.

Per tablespoon: 17 calories, 0 g protein, 4 g carbohydrates, 0 g total fat, 0 mg cholesterol, 2 mg sodium

Spicy Tomato Catsup

When you're overwhelmed with ripe tomatoes, try putting up a batch of homemade catsup. This version is seasoned with herbs, chiles, and sweet spices.

- 12 **pounds (about 24 large) firm-ripe tomatoes, coarsely chopped**
- 2 **large onions, quartered**
- 1 **medium-size red bell pepper, seeded and cut into pieces**
- 1 **tablespoon *each* mustard seeds, whole black peppercorns, and dry basil**
- 2 **teaspoons whole allspice**
- 2 **small dried hot red chiles**
- 1 **large dry bay leaf**
- 1 **cinnamon stick (about 3 inches long)**
- 1½ **cups firmly packed brown sugar**
- 1 **tablespoon paprika**
- 1 **cup cider vinegar (5% acidity)**
  Salt

In a large bowl, combine tomatoes, onions, and bell pepper. Smoothly purée vegetables in a blender or food processor, a portion at a time. Put through a food mill or fine strainer; you should have 6 quarts purée. Discard pulp left in food mill or strainer.

Pour purée into a heavy-bottomed 8- to 10-quart non-aluminum pan. Bring to a boil over medium-high heat; then boil gently, uncovered, stirring often, until reduced by about half (about 1 hour).

Tie mustard seeds, peppercorns, basil, allspice, chiles, bay leaf, and cinnamon stick in a washed square of cheesecloth. Add spice packet to purée. Add sugar and paprika; stir until well blended. Continue to boil gently over medium-high heat, uncovered, stirring occasionally, until catsup is very thick and reduced to 2 quarts (1½ to 2 hours); as catsup thickens, reduce heat and stir more often to prevent sticking. Stir in vinegar during last 10 to 15 minutes of cooking. Discard spice packet. Season to taste with salt.

Fill prepared, hot pint jars with hot catsup, leaving ¼-inch headspace. Gently run a narrow nonmetallic spatula between catsup and jar sides to release air bubbles. Wipe rims and threads clean; top with hot lids, then firmly screw on bands. Process in boiling water canner for 20 minutes. Or omit processing and ladle into pint freezer containers, leaving ½-inch headspace; apply lids. Let cool; freeze or refrigerate. Makes about 4 pints.

Storage time. *Processed:* Up to 1 year. *Unprocessed:* Up to 3 weeks in refrigerator; up to 6 months in freezer.

Per tablespoon: 20 calories, 0 g protein, 5 g carbohydrates, 0 g total fat, 0 mg cholesterol, 4 mg sodium

Salsa

Pictured on page 18 and on facing page

This red salsa is medium hot; if you prefer a tamer or more fiery sauce, you can adjust the proportions of mild and hot chiles (just be sure not to exceed 2 pounds of chiles *total*). Wear rubber gloves while handling chiles; or, if you work without gloves, wash your hands with soap and water before touching your face.

- 5 **pounds (about 10 large) firm-ripe tomatoes, peeled, cored, and chopped**
- 1 **pound onions, chopped**
- 1 **pound (about 6 large) fresh mild green chiles such as Anaheim, seeded and chopped**
- 1 **pound (about 35) fresh green or red jalapeño chiles, seeded and chopped**
- 1¼ **cups cider vinegar (5% acidity)**
- 2 **teaspoons salt**

In a heavy-bottomed 6- to 8-quart non-aluminum pan, combine tomatoes, onions, mild and jalapeño chiles, vinegar, and salt. Bring to a boil over high heat, stirring often; then reduce heat and simmer, uncovered, stirring occasionally, until thickened (about 15 minutes).

Fill prepared, hot pint jars with hot salsa, leaving ½-inch headspace. Gently run a narrow nonmetallic spatula between sauce and jar sides to release air bubbles. Wipe rims and threads clean; top with hot lids, then firmly screw on bands. Process in boiling water canner for 20 minutes. Or omit processing and ladle into pint freezer containers, leaving ½-inch headspace; apply lids. Let cool; freeze or refrigerate. Makes about 6 pints.

Storage time. *Processed:* Up to 1 year. *Unprocessed:* Up to 3 weeks in refrigerator; up to 6 months in freezer.

Per tablespoon: 5 calories, 0 g protein, 1 g carbohydrates, 0 g total fat, 0 mg cholesterol, 24 mg sodium

Take advantage of juicy summer tomatoes and mild and hot chiles to create your own signature salsa (facing page). Here, the lively sauce perks up a quesadilla stuffed with cheese, black beans, sliced green onion—and more salsa. By varying the chiles you use, you can make the sauce as tame or fiery as you like.

Meatless Pasta Sauce

Pictured on page 18

This robust sauce is wonderful as is, but if you like, you can stir in cooked ground meat just before serving. Do *not* increase the proportion of mushrooms, onion, or celery.

- 30 pounds (about ½ bushel) firm-ripe tomatoes, peeled, cored, and quartered
- 2 tablespoons olive oil
- 1 pound mushrooms, sliced
- 1 cup *each* chopped onion and chopped celery
- 6 cloves garlic, minced or pressed
- 2 tablespoons *each* dry basil, dry oregano, and parsley flakes
- ¼ cup firmly packed brown sugar
  Salt and freshly ground pepper

Place tomatoes in a heavy-bottomed 16-quart non-aluminum pan and bring to a boil over medium-high heat, stirring often. Then reduce heat and simmer, uncovered, for 20 minutes, stirring often. Put through a food mill or fine strainer; return to pan.

Heat oil in a wide frying pan over medium-high heat. Add mushrooms, onion, celery, and garlic; cook, stirring often, until onion is soft (about 10 minutes).

Add mushroom mixture, basil, oregano, parsley flakes, and sugar to tomato purée. Bring to a boil over medium-high heat. Then reduce heat and simmer, uncovered, stirring occasionally, until sauce is thickened and reduced by about half (about 6 hours); as sauce thickens, reduce heat and stir more often to prevent sticking. Season to taste with salt and pepper.

Fill prepared, hot jars with hot sauce, leaving 1-inch headspace. Gently run a narrow nonmetallic spatula between sauce and jar sides to release air bubbles. Wipe rims and threads clean; top with hot lids, then firmly screw on bands. Process in pressure canner for 20 minutes for pints, 25 minutes for quarts (at 11 pounds pressure on dial gauge; 10 pounds for weighted gauge). Or omit processing and ladle sauce into freezer containers, leaving ½-inch headspace for pints, 1-inch headspace for quarts; apply lids. Let cool; freeze or refrigerate. Makes about 10 pints or 5 quarts.

Storage time. *Processed:* Up to 1 year. *Unprocessed:* Up to 1 week in refrigerator; up to 6 months in freezer.

Per ½ cup: 83 calories, 3 g protein, 17 g carbohydrates, 2 g total fat, 0 mg cholesterol, 32 mg sodium

Barbecue Sauce

Pictured on page 18

Spicy-sweet barbecue sauce is great for slathering over grilled ribs, steak, or chicken.

- 12 pounds (about 24 large) firm-ripe tomatoes, peeled, cored, and quartered
- 2 cups chopped onions
- 2 cups chopped green bell peppers
- 1½ cups chopped celery
- 2 fresh hot red or green chiles (such as jalapeño or Fresno), seeded and minced
- 4 cloves garlic, minced or pressed
- 1½ cups firmly packed brown sugar
- 2½ cups cider vinegar (5% acidity)
- 1 tablespoon *each* dry mustard and paprika
- 1½ teaspoons ground red pepper (cayenne)
  About 1 teaspoon liquid hot pepper seasoning
  Salt

In a heavy-bottomed 8- to 10-quart non-aluminum pan, combine tomatoes, onions, bell peppers, celery, chiles, and garlic. Cook over medium-high heat, uncovered, stirring occasionally, until vegetables are soft (about 30 minutes). Put through a food mill or fine strainer, a portion at a time.

Return vegetable purée to pan and bring to a boil over medium-high heat; then boil gently, uncovered, stirring often, until reduced by about half (about 1 hour). Add sugar, vinegar, mustard, paprika, and red pepper. Continue to cook gently, uncovered, stirring often, until sauce is very thick and reduced to about 2½ quarts (about 1½ hours); as sauce thickens, reduce heat and stir more often to prevent sticking. Add hot pepper seasoning; season to taste with salt.

Fill prepared, hot pint jars with hot sauce, leaving ¼-inch headspace. Gently run a narrow nonmetallic spatula between sauce and jar sides to release air bubbles. Wipe rims and threads clean; top with hot lids, then firmly screw on bands. Process in boiling water canner for 20 minutes. Or omit processing and ladle into pint freezer containers, leaving ½-inch headspace; apply lids. Let cool; freeze or refrigerate. Makes about 5 pints.

Storage time. *Processed:* Up to 1 year. *Unprocessed:* Up to 3 weeks in refrigerator; up to 6 months in freezer.

Per tablespoon: 17 calories, 0 g protein, 4 g carbohydrates, 0 g total fat, 0 mg cholesterol, 5 mg sodium

Guarding against Botulism

Botulism is an especially dangerous form of food poisoning, caused by a toxin produced by spores of the bacterium *Clostridium botulinum.* Because these spores are extremely resistant to heat and favor a low-acid environment, they can thrive in improperly processed low-acid foods—often without producing discoloration or an "off" odor. Even a taste of food containing the botulinum toxin can prove fatal. Symptoms of botulism, usually appearing within 12 to 36 hours after contaminated food is consumed, include double vision, inability to swallow, and speech and respiratory difficulties. Medical treatment should be sought immediately; there are antitoxins.

How can you guard against botulism?

First, remember that for low-acid foods, safe processing means pressure canning: this is the only method to use for canning vegetables (see pages 30 through 33), meats, poultry, and seafood. Unlike processing in a boiling water canner, pressure canning at the correct time and pressure (temperature) destroys *C. botulinum* spores.

Second, keep in mind that though botulism rarely occurs in fruits or tomatoes, some tomato varieties have pH values in the low-acid range, slightly above 4.6 (as do figs). To can these foods safely in a boiling water canner, you must first acidify them with bottled lemon juice or citric acid. Likewise, be sure you follow recipes for pickles and relishes meticulously, always adding the proper amount of vinegar; if insufficiently acidified, these foods may not be safe to eat.

Third, always err on the side of caution. Do not even taste foods from jars that show signs of gas—a bulging lid, oozing from under the lid, or tiny upward-moving bubbles. Nor should you taste food that looks mushy or moldy, or gives off a disagreeable odor when the jar is opened.

Dispose of suspect food very carefully. If the jars are unopened (and no leakage has occurred), wrap them in a heavy garbage bag, then discard in the trash or bury in a landfill.

Unsealed, open, or leaking jars of low-acid foods or tomatoes must be detoxified before disposal. Carefully place both the jars and their lids in an 8-quart or larger pan; then wash your hands thoroughly. Slowly add enough water to the pan to cover the contents by 1 inch; avoid splashing as you pour. Cover the pan, bring the water to a boil, and boil for 30 minutes. Let the water and bottled food cool; then dispose of jars, lids, and food in the trash or bury them in the ground. Thoroughly scrub all equipment and counters. Wrap used sponges or dishcloths and discard them in the trash. Wash your hands thoroughly.

Fourth, as an additional safeguard, boil all home-canned low-acid foods, tomatoes, and tomato-vegetable mixtures (such as pasta sauce) for 10 minutes before eating; boil very thick mixtures for 15 to 20 minutes. Add an additional minute of boiling time for each 1,000 feet of altitude (starting at 1,000 feet above sea level).

And remember—

- Don't experiment or take shortcuts in home canning. Use only tested, approved methods.
- Use fresh, firm (not overripe), thoroughly washed vegetables. Can vegetables as soon as possible after you pick them.
- Use jars and lids made especially for home canning; discard cracked or nicked jars.
- Don't overpack foods. Putting too much food in a jar may result in underprocessing and spoilage.
- Never use lids a second time. Once the sealant on the lids has been through the processing stage, it may be ineffective for sealing again.
- Use only a pressure canner with an accurate gauge (have dial gauges tested annually). Process for the full required time at the correct pressure (temperature). Follow directions exactly, and make adjustments for high altitude (see "High-altitude Canning," page 9).
- Test each jar's seal before storing.
- Never use—or even taste—canned food that shows signs of spoilage.

Select fresh vegetables at peak quality, then can them to enjoy throughout the year.
The gleaming jars shown here contain (clockwise from right) sliced carrots,
roasted peppers (in a combination of red, yellow, and green), baby carrots, peas,
asparagus, beets, roasted red peppers, green beans, and whole-kernel corn.

Canning Vegetables

Garden-fresh, economical goodness

When your garden overflows with more produce than you and your family can eat fresh, put your canner to work and preserve that summertime bounty to enjoy later in the year. ● Fresh vegetables are easy to can — with nutritious, good-tasting results. But because these are low-acid foods, you do need to take special care: can all vegetables in a pressure canner under specific amounts of pressure, for specific times. *Never* can vegetables by the boiling water method; the processing temperature isn't high enough to kill botulism spores. ● Ready to begin? Start by choosing the best, freshest vegetables you can find. Rinse them well and scrub them with a vegetable brush. Then follow the instructions for the specific vegetable you're canning in our "Guide for Canning Vegetables," pages 30 through 33. You may season vegetables with salt, if you like, but it's not necessary for safety purposes. If you use a salt substitute, add it shortly before serving. ● And remember — for safety's sake, always boil home-canned vegetables for at least 10 minutes before eating; boil very thick mixtures for 15 to 20 minutes. Add an extra minute of boiling for each 1,000 feet of altitude, starting at 1,000 feet above sea level.

Step-by-Step Canning for Vegetables

1. Read the information about canning vegetables on the preceding page. Check the vegetable chart (see pages 30 through 33) for instructions on the specific vegetable you're canning.

2. Get out pressure canner, jars, *new* lids, ring bands, and other equipment you'll need (see pages 5 and 6). Jars must be free of nicks or cracks that might prevent sealing; ring bands must not be rusty, dented, or scratched. Be sure all equipment is clean and ready to use. Insert a pipe cleaner or string through your canner's vent to make sure that it's unobstructed.

3. Wash jars; keep hot in hot water to prevent breakage when filling with hot food. Prepare lids according to manufacturer's directions; keep hot in hot water. Check the manufacturer's advice concerning the ring bands you're using; then follow any preparation instructions printed on the box.

4. Prepare only enough vegetables for one canner load at a time, following chart instructions. If chart offers precooking as a choice (the hot-pack method), consider that precooking allows you to pack more food into jars and reduces the likelihood of floating food. If you run short of cooking liquid, you can use fresh boiling water to finish filling the jars. In general, you don't need to can vegetables with salt, but artichokes do require an acid-brine solution (see chart).

5. Pour 2 to 3 inches of hot water into pressure canner.

Remove a jar from hot water; stand it upright on a cloth towel. Fill with vegetables as instructed in chart, packing loosely enough for water to circulate between pieces without wasting space (a slotted spoon makes filling jars easier). Cover with hot

cooking liquid, dividing it among jars (or cover with fresh boiling water); leave 1-inch headspace, or as chart directs.

6. Gently run a narrow nonmetallic spatula between vegetable and jar sides to release air bubbles; add more liquid, if necessary.

7. Wipe jar rim and threads with a clean, damp cloth or paper towel to remove food particles that might prevent a seal. Lift a jar lid from hot water; place on jar, sealing side down. Firmly and evenly screw on ring band by hand; don't overtighten. As each jar is filled, use jar lifter to place it on canner rack. Space jars so they don't touch each other or sides of canner.

8. Before processing, you must vent pressure canner to eliminate air inside. To do this, fasten canner lid securely, following manufacturer's instructions. Turn heat to high, leaving petcock open or weight off vent. Allow steam to escape steadily for 10 minutes. (If canner isn't vented in this way, trapped air could prevent the temperature from rising as high as necessary, resulting in underprocessing.)

After venting, close petcock or place weight over vent; bring canner to required pressure level. Start counting processing time. (For altitudes above 1,000 feet, see "Pressures for Dial & Weighted Gauge Canners at High Altitude," page 9.) Keep pressure steady for entire processing time by adjusting heat source. If pressure falls below required level, record the time it takes to return to the proper level; then add that many minutes to the total processing time.

9. When time is up, simply turn off heat if you are processing over a gas burner. If you are processing on an electric range, remove canner to an unheated range element—not to a cold surface. Canner will be heavy, but don't tilt it; toppled jars may not seal.

10. Let pressure fall to zero on its own. This will take 30 to 45 minutes. Cooling time is figured into safe processing times, so never try to speed the process by running the canner under cold water or opening the vent. When the dial gauge registers zero—or a gentle prodding of the weight produces no steam—slowly open petcock or remove weight. Open lid away from you to avoid steam burns. Remove jars with jar lifter.

11. Place jars at least 1 inch apart on a towel or rack out of drafts. *Do not retighten bands.* Let cool for 12 to 24 hours.

12. When jars are cool, remove ring bands. (To loosen a band that sticks, cover it with a hot, damp cloth for 1 to 2 minutes.) Test seal as directed on page 8 and shown on page 13. If a jar fails to seal, refrigerate it and use the food within 2 or 3 days—*if* it looks and smells right. Or reprocess as directed on page 8.

13. Wash jars and lids to remove any food residue; rinse and dry. Label and date jars; store in a clean, cool, dark, dry place.

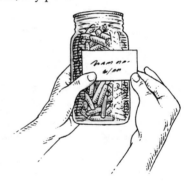

Guide for Canning Vegetables

Processing pressures for weighted and dial gauge canners are given for altitudes of 1,000 feet or below. If you live above 1,000 feet, you'll need to increase processing pressures; see "Pressures for Dial & Weighted Gauge Canners at High Altitude" (page 9).

You may add salt for flavor, if you like, but it's not necessary for safety. As a general rule, add ½ teaspoon per pint, 1 teaspoon per quart.

Before applying hot lids to the jars, don't forget to run a narrow nonmetallic spatula gently between the vegetable and the sides of the jar to release any trapped air bubbles.

Note: Not all vegetables are recommended for canning. Those not recommended include broccoli, Brussels sprouts, cabbage, cauliflower, cucumbers, eggplant, parsnips, rutabagas, and turnips.

Vegetables	Quantity to yield 1 quart	How to prepare	Processing time* Pints	Quarts
Small artichokes	35 to 40 (1¼-inch) or 20 to 30 (2-inch) trimmed whole small artichokes	Cut off thorny tops and stem ends. Remove coarse outer leaves, leaving only tender inner leaves. Precook for 5 minutes in boiling water to which you've added ¾ cup vinegar per gallon. Drain and discard cooking liquid. Fill prepared, hot jars with hot artichokes, leaving 1-inch headspace. Cover with boiling brine (¾ cup vinegar or lemon juice and 3 tablespoons salt per gallon water), leaving 1-inch headspace.	35 min.	40 min.
Asparagus	3 lbs.	Remove tough ends and scales. Rinse and drain. Cut stalks into lengths 1 inch shorter than jar; or cut stalks into 1- to 2-inch pieces. **To pack hot,** cover asparagus with boiling water. Bring to a boil; boil for 2 to 3 minutes. Loosely fill prepared, hot jars with hot asparagus. Cover with hot liquid, leaving 1-inch headspace; add salt, if desired. **To pack raw,** tightly fill prepared, hot jars with asparagus; don't crush pieces. Cover with boiling water, leaving 1-inch headspace; add salt, if desired.	30 min.	40 min.
Beans, fresh lima	4 lbs. (unshelled)	Shell and rinse beans. **To pack hot,** cover beans with boiling water; bring to a boil. Loosely fill prepared, hot jars with hot beans. Cover with hot liquid, leaving 1-inch headspace; add salt, if desired. **To pack raw,** loosely fill prepared, hot jars with beans; do not shake or press down. Cover with boiling water, leaving 1-inch headspace for pints. For quarts, leave 1½-inch headspace if beans are small, 1¼-inch headspace if they are large. Add salt, if desired.	40 min.	50 min.
Beans, snap Green, wax, Italian	2 lbs.	Rinse beans and trim ends; remove strings, if necessary. Leave whole, or cut into 1- to 1½-inch pieces. **To pack hot,** cover beans with boiling water. Bring to a boil; boil for 5 minutes. Loosely fill prepared, hot jars with hot beans. Cover with hot liquid, leaving 1-inch headspace; add salt, if desired. **To pack raw,** tightly fill prepared, hot jars with beans. Cover with boiling water, leaving 1-inch headspace; add salt, if desired.	20 min.	25 min.
Beets	3 lbs.	To keep color from bleeding, leave root ends and 1 inch of tops on beets. Scrub well; don't peel. Cover with boiling water; boil until skins slip off easily (about 15 minutes). Dip in cold water. Remove skins; trim off stems and roots. Discard woody beets. Small beets (1 to 2 inches in diameter) may be left whole; cut medium-size or large beets into ½-inch cubes or ¼- to ½-inch-thick slices. Halve or quarter very large slices. Fill prepared, hot jars with beets. Cover with boiling water, leaving 1-inch headspace; add salt, if desired.	30 min.	35 min.

* 10 pounds pressure (weighted gauge canner)
11 pounds pressure (dial gauge canner)

Canned roasted peppers add a bright, delicious finishing touch to a sandwich of
turkey, salami, and cheese on crusty bread. You'll find canning instructions for
both bell peppers and chiles on page 33.

Vegetables	Quantity to yield 1 quart	How to prepare	Processing time*	
			Pints	Quarts
Carrots	2½ lbs.	Rinse and peel. Leave baby carrots whole; slice or dice regular carrots. **To pack hot,** cover carrots with boiling water. Bring to a boil; boil gently for 5 minutes. Fill prepared, hot jars with hot carrots, leaving 1-inch headspace; add salt, if desired. **To pack raw,** tightly fill prepared, hot jars with carrots. Cover with boiling water, leaving 1-inch headspace; add salt, if desired.	25 min.	30 min.
Corn, cream style	Pints only; 2¼ lbs. (in husks) per pint	Discard husks and silk; rinse corn. Dip ears in boiling water for 4 minutes; then dip in cold water until cool enough to handle. With a sharp knife, cut corn from cob at about center of kernel. Then scrape cob, being careful not to scrape off any cob material. Add 2 cups boiling water to every 4 cups corn and scrapings. Bring to a boil. **Using pint jars only,** fill prepared, hot jars with hot corn mixture. Leave 1-inch headspace; add salt, if desired.	85 min.	
Corn, whole kernel	4½ lbs. (in husks)	Discard husks and silk; rinse corn. Dip ears in boiling water for 3 minutes; then dip in cold water until cool enough to handle. With a sharp knife, cut corn from cob at about three-fourths the depth of kernel. **Do not scrape cob.** **To pack hot,** add 1 cup of hot water to every 4 cups of kernels. Bring to a boil; boil gently for 5 minutes. Fill prepared, hot jars with hot corn and cooking liquid, leaving 1-inch headspace; add salt, if desired. **To pack raw,** loosely fill prepared, hot jars with raw kernels, leaving 1-inch headspace. Do not shake or press down. Cover with boiling water, leaving 1-inch headspace; add salt, if desired.	55 min.	85 min.
Greens (including spinach) Beet, collard, kale, mustard, spinach, turnip	4 lbs.	Rinse carefully, working with small amounts at a time. Drain; continue to rinse until water is clear and free of grit. Cut tough stems and midribs from leaves, then heat leaves in boiling water until wilted. Loosely fill prepared, hot jars with wilted leaves; cover with boiling water, leaving 1-inch headspace; add salt, if desired.	70 min.	90 min.
Mushrooms	Pints only; 2 lbs. per pint	Use small to medium-size commercial (button) mushrooms only. Trim off stems; cut out discolored parts. Soak in cold water for 10 minutes, then rinse. Leave small mushrooms whole; halve or quarter larger ones. Cover with water; bring to a boil and boil gently for 5 minutes. **Using pint jars only,** fill prepared, hot jars with hot mushrooms. Cover with fresh boiling water, leaving 1-inch headspace; add salt, if desired. For better color, add ⅛ teaspoon ascorbic acid or a 500-milligram tablet of vitamin C (crushed) to each jar.	45 min.	
Okra	1½ lbs.	Rinse tender young pods; trim ends. Leave whole or cut into 1-inch pieces. Cover okra with hot water and bring to a boil; boil gently for 2 minutes. Fill prepared, hot jars with hot okra. Cover with hot cooking liquid, leaving 1-inch headspace; add salt, if desired.	25 min.	40 min.
Peas, green	4½ lbs. (unshelled)	Shell and rinse tender young peas. **To pack hot,** cover peas with boiling water. Bring to a boil; boil for 2 minutes. Loosely fill prepared, hot jars with hot peas. Cover with hot liquid, leaving 1-inch headspace; add salt, if desired. **To pack raw,** loosely fill prepared, hot jars with raw peas. Do not shake or press down. Cover with boiling water, leaving 1-inch headspace; add salt, if desired.	40 min.	40 min.

* 10 pounds pressure (weighted gauge canner)
11 pounds pressure (dial gauge canner)

Vegetables	Quantity to yield 1 quart	How to prepare	Processing time*	
			Pints	Quarts
Peppers, bell or chile	Pints only; 1 lb. per pint	Select your favorite green, red, or yellow peppers—either bell, mild or hot chile, or a mix. Choose firm peppers, never soft or bruised ones; rinse well. Leave small peppers whole; remove stems and seeds from large peppers. Cut 2 slits in each pepper. Place in a shallow pan and broil, turning as needed, until skins blister. To make peeling easier, cover tightly with foil or place in a plastic bag and close bag. Let stand for about 10 minutes, then peel. Quarter large peppers; flatten small whole peppers. **Using pint jars only,** add 1½ teaspoons bottled lemon juice to each prepared, hot jar. Fill jars loosely with peppers. Cover peppers with boiling water, leaving 1-inch headspace; add salt, if desired.	35 min.	
Potatoes, sweet	2½ lbs.	Choose small to medium-size potatoes. Rinse well; boil or steam until partially softened (15 to 20 minutes). Remove skins. Leave small potatoes whole; cut larger ones into pieces. **Do not mash or purée.** Fill prepared, hot jars with hot sweet potatoes; cover with boiling water or syrup of your choice (see "Syrups for Canning," page 13). Leave 1-inch headspace; add salt, if desired.	65 min.	90 min.
Potatoes, white	5 lbs.	Choose small to medium-size potatoes (1- to 2-inch diameter for canning whole). Rinse well. Peel; cut into ½-inch cubes, if desired. To prevent discoloration, place in an antidarkening solution (see page 12) as peeled or cut. Drain potatoes; cover with boiling water and bring to a boil. **For cubed potatoes,** boil for 2 minutes and drain; **for whole potatoes,** boil for 10 minutes and drain. Fill prepared, hot jars with hot potatoes. Cover with fresh boiling water, leaving 1-inch headspace; add salt, if desired.	35 min.	40 min.
Spinach *See* Greens (including spinach)				
Squash, summer Crookneck, zucchini, pattypan	1½ lbs.	Rinse squash and trim ends; do not peel. Cut into ½-inch-thick slices. Steam or boil for 2 to 3 minutes. Fill prepared, hot jars with hot squash. Cover with hot cooking liquid or fresh boiling water, leaving 1-inch headspace; add salt, if desired.	30 min.	40 min.
Squash, winter (including pumpkin) Banana, butternut, Hubbard, pumpkin	2¼ lbs.	Rinse squash and cut into halves or large pieces; scrape out all seeds and fibrous material. Peel. Cut into 1-inch-wide strips; then cut into 1-inch cubes. Cover with boiling water; bring to a boil and boil for 2 minutes. **Do not mash or purée.** Fill prepared, hot jars with hot squash cubes. Cover with hot liquid, leaving 1-inch headspace.	55 min.	90 min.

* 10 pounds pressure (weighted gauge canner)
11 pounds pressure (dial gauge canner)

The variety of preserves you can make is limited only by the size of your cupboard. Pictured here (clockwise from bottom right) are Raspberry-Plum Jam (page 41), Cranberry-Apple Jelly (page 57), Jalapeño Jelly (page 56), Apple Butter (page 43), Lime-Mint Jelly (page 56), and Citrus Marmalade (page 46).

Jams, Jellies & Preserves

Sparkling jams & jellies, fragrant butters, tangy marmalades

*I*t's one of life's simple pleasures: "putting up" preserves with distinctively fresh flavors you just can't get in store-bought products. Despite their different names, all fruit spreads—jams, jellies, marmalades, conserves, preserves, and butters—are pretty much alike. They're all just cooked fruit or juice, thickened to some degree and preserved with sugar. ● *Jellies* are clear, sparkling spreads made from strained fruit juice; they're tender, yet firm enough to hold their shape when turned out of the jar. *Marmalades* are soft jellies, generally containing suspended slivers of citrus peel or fruit. To make *jam*, you start with crushed or chopped fruit, then cook it until thick enough to spread, but not as stiff as jelly. *Preserves* are made with larger fruit pieces or small whole fruits, suspended in a clear, slightly jelled syrup. *Conserves* are much like jam, but they usually contain two or more fruits and often include raisins and nuts. *Butters* are simply fruit pulp and sugar, thickened to a good spreading consistency by long, slow cooking. ● The easy-to-make spreads on the following pages get their extra-special flavors from interesting fruit combinations—and from fresh, best-of-season produce you pick out yourself. Both sweet and savory, they'll shine on your table and delight the friends lucky enough to receive them as gifts.

Before You Begin

For success with jams, jellies, and preserves, start by reviewing the basic information below.

Ingredients & Techniques

Fruit. In general, use fresh, just-ripe fruit. If your recipe contains no added pectin, though, a fourth of the fruit should be slightly underripe; natural pectin content—and jelling ability—decrease as fruit ripens.

Pectin. Many recipes call for added pectin, in either liquid or dry form. *The two types require different procedures,* so always use the kind the recipe specifies. Buy fresh pectin yearly, since old pectin may result in poor jelling.

Sugar. Don't cut the sugar in recipes: you're likely to end up with syrup, not jam! If you'd like to make less-sweet preserves, try our reduced-sugar spreads (page 48) and dehydrated jams (page 108).

Recipe yields. Always prepare recipes just as they're written. *Don't* double recipes: larger volumes take longer to heat, and since heat destroys pectin, your jam may fail to jell.

Cooking times. Depending on your altitude, the cooking pan you use, and the humidity, your cooking times may differ from those in the recipe. For this reason, it's important to pay close attention to the doneness tests given in the instructions.

Sealing & processing. Paraffin is no longer recommended for sealing jars, since paraffin-sealed jam is more likely to spoil than processed jam. Always process preserves in a boiling water canner, *unless* you plan to freeze or refrigerate them. (For no-cook freezer jams, see "Quick-fix Jams," page 44.)

A Word about Proportions

Though all fruits except figs are considered acid foods (see page 5), the degree of acidity varies. Some kinds have enough acid and pectin to jell when cooked with sugar. Others are lower in pectin and acid; to make jams and jellies from these, you'll need to add pectin or an acid such as lemon juice (or both). In some recipes, fruits low in acid or pectin are combined with others that supply them in the right amounts. Follow directions exactly: for good flavor and consistency, you need the correct balance of fruit, sugar, acid, and pectin. Proper proportions are especially crucial when you're preparing jelly (see page 52).

Step-by-Step Canning for Jams

To can jams, preserves, conserves, butters, and marmalades, follow these steps.

1. Assemble and prepare equipment and sterilize jars, following steps 2 through 4 on page 12.

2. Rinse and sort fruit; do not use any that is overripe. Chop, slice, or crush fruit, or leave it whole, as the recipe directs. To crush berries, use a potato masher and crush just 1 to 2 cups at a time. To chop fruit with a food processor, use brief pulses, taking care not to purée fruit (purées may add too much liquid and fruit for a good jell).

3. In a large, heavy-bottomed pan, prepare jam according to recipe instructions, one batch at a time. *Do not double recipes;* it doesn't work. Bring fruit and any liquid to a boil over high heat, stirring frequently or constantly, as the recipe directs.

For jams (or other spreads) without added pectin, cook to the desired thickness, following recipe directions. Remember that jam will continue to thicken as it cools. (To find the jell point, see page 52.)

When added pectin is required, the type of pectin and the precise cooking time will be specified. Follow directions *exactly.* If the recipe tells you to bring a fruit mixture to a "full rolling boil," you're aiming for a hard boil that does not stop when the fruit is stirred.

When jam is done, remove it from the heat and skim off any foam. Remove a sterilized jar from the hot water. Place on a cloth towel. Ladle hot jam into hot, sterilized jar, leaving ¼-inch headspace.

4. Seal and process jars as directed in steps 8 through 12 on page 13, using the processing time specified in your recipe. At high altitudes, add an extra minute for each 1,000 feet above sea level.

5. If you choose not to process your jam, ladle it into clean freezer jars or freezer containers; rinse jars with hot water before filling them to prevent the hot jam from cracking the glass. Before refrigerating or freezing filled jars or containers, let them stand for 12 to 24 hours at room temperature; this gives the jam time to jell completely.

Classic Strawberry Jam

This old-fashioned strawberry jam is a breakfast-time classic. For a change, you might use half raspberries, half strawberries.

> 4 **cups crushed strawberries (about 2 quarts whole berries)**
>
> 4 **cups sugar**

Place crushed strawberries in a heavy-bottomed 8- to 10-quart pan. Stir in sugar until well blended. Bring to a boil over high heat, stirring constantly. Continue to boil, uncovered, stirring often, until mixture thickens and reaches the jell point (220°F)—10 to 15 minutes. As mixture thickens, reduce heat and stir more often to prevent sticking. Remove from heat and skim off any foam.

Ladle hot jam into hot, sterilized half-pint jars, leaving ¼-inch headspace. Wipe rims and threads clean; top with hot lids, then firmly screw on bands. Process in boiling water canner for 5 minutes. Or omit processing and ladle jam into freezer jars or freezer containers, leaving ½-inch headspace; apply lids. Let stand for 12 to 24 hours at room temperature; freeze or refrigerate. Makes about 4 half-pints.

Storage time. *Processed:* Up to 1 year. *Unprocessed:* Up to 1 month in refrigerator; up to 1 year in freezer.

Per tablespoon: 54 calories, 0 g protein, 14 g carbohydrates, 0 g total fat, 0 mg cholesterol, 0 mg sodium

Easy Strawberry Jam

Fresh-tasting and easy to prepare, this bright spread is bound to become a favorite.

> 4 **cups crushed strawberries (about 2 quarts whole berries)**
>
> 2 **tablespoons lemon juice**
>
> 1 **box (1¾ or 2 oz.) dry pectin**
>
> 6 **cups sugar**

In a heavy-bottomed 8- to 10-quart pan, mix strawberries, lemon juice, and pectin. Bring to a full rolling boil over high heat, stirring constantly. Quickly add sugar, still stirring. Return to a full rolling boil; then boil, stirring, for 1 minute. (If using a 2-oz. box of pectin, boil for 2 minutes.) Remove from heat and skim off any foam.

Ladle hot jam into hot, sterilized half-pint jars, leaving ¼-inch headspace. Wipe rims and threads clean; top with hot lids, then firmly screw on bands. Process in boiling water canner for 5 minutes. Or omit processing and ladle jam into freezer jars or freezer containers, leaving ½-inch headspace; apply

lids. Let stand for 12 to 24 hours at room temperature; freeze or refrigerate. Makes about 6 half-pints.

Storage time. *Processed:* Up to 1 year. *Unprocessed:* Up to 1 month in refrigerator; up to 1 year in freezer.

Per tablespoon: 54 calories, 0 g protein, 14 g carbohydrates, 0 g total fat, 0 mg cholesterol, 0 mg sodium

Easy Strawberry-Peach Jam

Follow directions for **Easy Strawberry Jam,** but add ¼ cup **water** and substitute 2 cups peeled, pitted, crushed **peaches** (about 1½ lbs. peaches) for 2 cups of the strawberries. Makes about 6 half-pints.

Per tablespoon: 53 calories, 0 g protein, 14 g carbohydrates, 0 g total fat, 0 mg cholesterol, 0 mg sodium

Strawberry-Rhubarb Jam

Popular partners in pie fillings, sweet ripe strawberries and tart rhubarb are delicious together in jam.

> 1 **pound rhubarb**
>
> ¼ **cup water**
>
> **About 4 cups strawberries**
>
> 6 **cups sugar**
>
> 1 **pouch (3 oz.) liquid pectin**

Thinly slice unpeeled rhubarb stalks and place in a medium-size pan. Add water; bring to a boil over high heat. Reduce heat, cover, and simmer until rhubarb is limp (about 2 minutes), stirring once or twice. Drain rhubarb; then measure. Thoroughly crush strawberries; add enough crushed berries to rhubarb to make 3½ cups (pack fruit solidly into cup to measure). Turn fruit into a heavy-bottomed 8- to 10-quart pan. Stir in sugar until well blended.

Bring to a full rolling boil over high heat, stirring constantly; boil, stirring, for 1 minute. Remove from heat and stir in pectin all at once. Skim off any foam.

Ladle hot jam into hot, sterilized half-pint jars, leaving ¼-inch headspace. Wipe rims and threads clean; top with hot lids, then firmly screw on bands. Process in boiling water canner for 5 minutes. Or omit processing and ladle jam into freezer jars or freezer containers, leaving ½-inch headspace; apply lids. Let stand for 12 to 24 hours at room temperature; freeze or refrigerate. Makes about 8 half-pints.

Storage time. *Processed:* Up to 1 year. *Unprocessed:* Up to 1 month in refrigerator; up to 1 year in freezer.

Per tablespoon: 38 calories, 0 g protein, 10 g carbohydrates, 0 g total fat, 0 mg cholesterol, 0 mg sodium

Sweet Cherry Jam

Pictured on facing page

Here's a beautiful jam that's a superb choice for gift giving. A little kirsch adds complexity to the sweet cherry flavor.

- 4 **cups pitted, finely chopped sweet cherries (about 3 lbs. cherries)**
- ¼ **cup** *each* **lemon juice and kirsch**
- ½ **teaspoon ground cinnamon**
- 1 **box (1¾ or 2 oz.) dry pectin**
- 4½ **cups sugar**

In a heavy-bottomed 8- to 10-quart pan, mix cherries, lemon juice, kirsch, cinnamon, and pectin. Bring to a full rolling boil over high heat, stirring constantly. Quickly add sugar, still stirring. Return to a full rolling boil; then boil, stirring, for 2 minutes. (If using a 2-oz. box of pectin, boil for 4 minutes.) Remove from heat and skim off any foam.

Ladle hot jam into hot, sterilized half-pint jars, leaving ¼-inch headspace. Wipe rims and threads clean; top with hot lids, then firmly screw on bands. Process in boiling water canner for 5 minutes. Or omit processing and ladle jam into freezer jars or freezer containers, leaving ½-inch headspace; apply lids. Let stand for 12 to 24 hours at room temperature; freeze or refrigerate. Makes about 5 half-pints.

Storage time. *Processed:* Up to 1 year. *Unprocessed:* Up to 1 month in refrigerator; up to 1 year in freezer.

Per tablespoon: 59 calories, 0 g protein, 15 g carbohydrates, 0 g total fat, 0 mg cholesterol, 0 mg sodium

Peach-Orange Jam

Pictured on facing page

Aromatic ripe peaches combine with orange and lemon in a sprightly jam that's a perfect filling for jam tarts.

- 6 **cups peeled, pitted, crushed peaches (about 4 lbs. peaches)**
- ½ **cup frozen orange juice concentrate, thawed**
- ¼ **cup lemon juice**
- 5 **cups sugar**

In a heavy-bottomed 8- to 10-quart pan, mix peaches, orange juice concentrate, and lemon juice. Stir in sugar until well blended. Bring to a boil over high heat, stirring constantly. Continue to boil, uncovered, stirring often, until mixture thickens and reaches the jell point (220°F)—about 30 minutes. As mixture thickens, reduce heat and stir more often to prevent sticking. Remove from heat and skim off any foam.

Ladle hot jam into hot, sterilized half-pint jars, leaving ¼-inch headspace. Wipe rims and threads clean; top with hot lids, then firmly screw on bands. Process in boiling water canner for 5 minutes. Or omit processing and ladle jam into freezer jars or freezer containers, leaving ½-inch headspace; apply lids. Let stand for 12 to 24 hours at room temperature; freeze or refrigerate. Makes about 7 half-pints.

Storage time. *Processed:* Up to 1 year. *Unprocessed:* Up to 1 month in refrigerator; up to 1 year in freezer.

Per tablespoon: 42 calories, 0 g protein, 11 g carbohydrates, 0 g total fat, 0 mg cholesterol, 0 mg sodium

Easy Raspberry Jam

Pictured on facing page

It's hard to beat homemade raspberry jam—but our blackberry and boysenberry variations come close!

- 5 **cups crushed raspberries (about 2 quarts whole berries)**
- 1 **tablespoon lemon juice**
- 1 **box (1¾ or 2 oz.) dry pectin**
- 6½ **cups sugar**

In a heavy-bottomed 8- to 10-quart pan, mix raspberries, lemon juice, and pectin. (If you prefer seedless jam, heat the crushed berries until soft, then press them through a sieve or food mill before adding to pan with the lemon juice and pectin.) Bring mixture to a full rolling boil over high heat, stirring constantly. Quickly add sugar, still stirring. Return to a full rolling boil; then boil, stirring, for 1 minute. (If using a 2-oz. box of pectin, boil for 2 minutes.) Remove from heat and skim off any foam.

Ladle hot jam into hot, sterilized half-pint jars, leaving ¼-inch headspace. Wipe rims and threads clean; top with hot lids, then firmly screw on bands. Process in boiling water canner for 5 minutes. Or omit processing and ladle jam into freezer jars or freezer containers, leaving ½-inch headspace; apply lids. Let stand for 12 to 24 hours at room temperature; freeze or refrigerate. Makes about 7 half-pints.

Storage time. *Processed:* Up to 1 year. *Unprocessed:* Up to 1 month in refrigerator; up to 1 year in freezer.

Per tablespoon: 50 calories, 0 g protein, 13 g carbohydrates, 0 g total fat, 0 mg cholesterol, 0 mg sodium

Easy Blackberry or Boysenberry Jam

Follow directions for **Easy Raspberry Jam**, but substitute **blackberries** or boysenberries for raspberries. Makes about 7 half-pints.

Per tablespoon: 52 calories, 0 g protein, 13 g carbohydrates, 0 g total fat, 0 mg cholesterol, 0 mg sodium

Sparkling jam tarts are a lovely dessert—and they're easy to prepare, too. Start with dainty shells made from homemade or purchased pastry and baked in mini-muffin pans; then fill them with your favorite jams. We chose Sweet Cherry Jam, Peach-Orange Jam, and Easy Raspberry Jam (recipes on facing page).

Microwave Jams

Making jam in your microwave oven is quick and easy. You can even whip up a batch fresh in the morning to serve warm for breakfast. Just remember to store your jam in the refrigerator or freezer, since microwaving doesn't actually process jam the way a boiling water canner does.

To avoid boil-over, use an oversized container. We prefer a 2-quart glass measure; it's easy to remove from the oven, and the handle and spout simplify pouring the bubbly jam into jars. You can also use a 2½- to 3-quart ceramic or glass casserole, but this will get hot, so keep oven mitts handy.

Our basic recipe tells you how to make nine different fresh fruit jams. If you have an abundance of fruit, consider making several batches (don't multiply quantities; the recipe won't turn out properly). Or prepare measured amounts of fruit with sugar and flavorings, then freeze them. Later, thaw a portion and make fresh jam any time.

Because microwave ovens vary in power and wattage, your cooking times may differ somewhat from those given below.

Basic Microwave Jam

Fruit and flavorings (directions follow)
1½ cups sugar

Prepare fruit and flavorings; place in a 2-quart glass measure or 2½- to 3-quart casserole. Add sugar. Let stand until juices form (about 30 minutes).

Microwave, uncovered, on **HIGH (100%)** for 6 minutes or until mixture begins to boil. Stir well. Microwave on **HIGH (100%)** for 10 to 13 more minutes, stirring every 2 to 3 minutes. Spoon 1 tablespoon jam into a custard cup and refrigerate for 15 minutes; test consistency. For thicker jam, reheat jam to boiling, then microwave on **HIGH (100%)** for 2 more minutes; retest. Makes about 2 cups.

Storage time. Up to 1 month in refrigerator; up to 1 year in freezer.

Per tablespoon (approximate): 44 calories, 0 g protein, 11 g carbohydrates, 0 g total fat, 0 mg cholesterol, 0 mg sodium

Apricot. Rinse, pit, and chop about 1 pound **apricots** (you should have 2 cups). Add 2 tablespoons **lemon juice.**

Apricot-pineapple. Rinse, pit, and chop about ¾ pound **apricots** (you should have 1½ cups). Combine with ½ cup **crushed pineapple packed in its own juice** or ½ cup finely chopped fresh pineapple. Add 1 tablespoon **lemon juice.**

Berry. Rinse and crush 3½ cups **raspberries,** blackberries, boysenberries, or olallieberries; or use half raspberries and half of any of the blackberries. You should have 2 cups. Add 1 tablespoon **lemon juice.**

Blueberry. Rinse and slightly crush about 3 cups **blueberries** (you should have 2 cups). Add ¼ cup **lemon juice,** ½ teaspoon **grated lemon peel,** and ¼ teaspoon **ground cinnamon.**

Strawberry. Rinse and crush about 3½ cups hulled **strawberries** (you should have 2 cups). Add 1½ tablespoons **lemon juice.**

Cherry (sweet varieties). Rinse, pit, and quarter about 1 pound **cherries** (you should have 2 cups). Add ¼ cup **lemon juice** and ½ teaspoon each **grated lemon peel** and **ground cinnamon.**

Spiced fig-orange. Rinse 8 to 10 **figs;** clip off stems, then chop fruit (you should have 1½ cups). Combine with ½ cup peeled, seeded, chopped **orange.** Add 1½ teaspoons **grated orange peel,** 3 tablespoons **lemon juice,** and ¼ teaspoon *each* **ground cloves** and **ground cinnamon.**

Peach or nectarine. Rinse, peel, pit, and chop about 1⅓ pounds **peaches** or nectarines (you should have 2 cups). Add 1 tablespoon **lemon juice.** If desired, stir in 2 drops **almond extract** after cooking.

Peach-plum marmalade. Rinse, pit, and chop about ½ pound *each* **peaches** and **plums** (you should have 1½ cups *total*). Combine with ½ cup seeded, finely chopped unpeeled **orange.**

Raspberry-Plum Jam

Pictured on page 34

For pennywise raspberry jam, mix the berries—fresh or frozen—with more plentiful (and less expensive) plums. If you dice the plums with a food processor, be careful not to purée them.

> 2 **cups pitted, finely diced plums (about 1¼ lbs. plums)**
>
> 1½ **cups fresh raspberries; or 1½ cups unsweetened frozen raspberries, thawed**
>
> 5 **cups sugar**
>
> ¼ **cup lemon juice**
>
> 1 **pouch (3 oz.) liquid pectin**

In a heavy-bottomed 8- to 10-quart pan, mix plums and raspberries. Stir in sugar and lemon juice until well blended. Bring to a full rolling boil over high heat, stirring constantly. Stir in pectin all at once. Return to a full rolling boil; then boil, stirring, for 1 minute. Remove from heat and skim off any foam.

Ladle hot jam into hot, sterilized half-pint jars, leaving ¼-inch headspace. Wipe rims and threads clean; top with hot lids, then firmly screw on bands. Process in boiling water canner for 5 minutes. Or omit processing and ladle jam into freezer jars or freezer containers, leaving ½-inch headspace; apply lids. Let stand for 12 to 24 hours at room temperature; freeze or refrigerate. Makes about 6 half-pints.

Storage time. *Processed:* Up to 1 year. *Unprocessed:* Up to 1 month in refrigerator; up to 1 year in freezer.

Per tablespoon: 44 calories, 0 g protein, 11 g carbohydrates, 0 g total fat, 0 mg cholesterol, 0 mg sodium

Plum Jam

If you relish a touch of tart along with sweet, then use your favorite red- or purple-skinned plums to prepare this marvelous jam.

> 4 **cups pitted, finely diced plums (about 2½ lbs. plums)**
>
> 3½ **cups sugar**

Place plums in a heavy-bottomed 8- to 10-quart pan. Stir in sugar until well blended. Let stand for 1 hour, then bring to a boil over medium-high heat, stirring often. Continue to boil, uncovered, stirring often, until mixture thickens and reaches the jell point (220°F)—about 20 minutes. As mixture thickens, reduce heat and stir more often to prevent sticking. Remove from heat and skim off any foam.

Ladle hot jam into hot, sterilized half-pint jars, leaving ¼-inch headspace. Wipe rims and threads clean; top with hot lids, then firmly screw on bands. Process in boiling water canner for 5 minutes. Or omit processing and ladle jam into freezer jars or freezer containers, leaving ½-inch headspace; apply lids. Let stand for 12 to 24 hours at room temperature; freeze or refrigerate. Makes about 4 half-pints.

Storage time. *Processed:* Up to 1 year. *Unprocessed:* Up to 1 month in refrigerator; up to 1 year in freezer.

Per tablespoon: 51 calories, 0 g protein, 13 g carbohydrates, 0 g total fat, 0 mg cholesterol, 0 mg sodium

Cranberry-Orange Jam

Tangy, thick, orange-accented cranberry jam is just the thing to serve with your favorite roast poultry. For best flavor, store it for at least 1 week before using. (If you prefer a smooth and glistening jelly, pour the hot jam through a small sterilized metal strainer when you fill the jars.)

> 4 **cups (about 1 lb.) fresh or frozen cranberries**
>
> 3 **cups water**
>
> ¾ **cup orange juice**
>
> ¼ **cup lemon juice**
>
> 4 **cups sugar**
>
> 2 **pouches (3 oz. *each*) liquid pectin**

Place cranberries and water in a heavy-bottomed 8- to 10-quart pan. Bring to a boil over high heat; reduce heat and simmer, uncovered, until berries begin to pop (about 10 minutes). Drain well, reserving liquid. Place cranberries in a blender or food processor and whirl until smooth; add enough of the reserved liquid to berries to make 4 cups.

Return berry purée to pan. Stir in orange juice, lemon juice, and sugar until well blended. Bring to a full rolling boil over high heat, stirring constantly; then boil, stirring, for 1 minute. Remove from heat and stir in pectin all at once. Skim off any foam.

Ladle hot jam into hot, sterilized half-pint jars, leaving ¼-inch headspace. Wipe rims and threads clean; top with hot lids, then firmly screw on bands. Process in boiling water canner for 5 minutes. Or omit processing and ladle jam into freezer jars or freezer containers, leaving ½-inch headspace; apply lids. Let stand for 12 to 24 hours at room temperature; freeze or refrigerate. Makes about 6 half-pints.

Storage time. *Processed:* Up to 1 year. *Unprocessed:* Up to 1 month in refrigerator; up to 1 year in freezer.

Per tablespoon: 36 calories, 0 g protein, 9 g carbohydrates, 0 g total fat, 0 mg cholesterol, 0 mg sodium

Fresh bread spread with homemade preserves is an old-fashioned treat that will never go out of style. Our bread is topped with luscious, golden Papaya Butter; just as fragrant and delicious are Apple Butter (center) and Apricot Butter (right). All three recipes are on the facing page.

Apple Butter

Pictured on page 34 and facing page

Slow, even cooking is the secret of this aromatic butter's full flavor. If sweet Golden Delicious apples aren't available, you can use a tarter variety such as McIntosh, Jonathan, or Granny Smith, but you may want to add about ¼ cup more sugar.

- **4 cups bottled unsweetened apple juice or apple cider**
- **4 pounds (about 12 medium-size) Golden Delicious apples, peeled, cored, and sliced**
- **1½ cups sugar**
- **2 teaspoons ground cinnamon**

In a heavy-bottomed 8- to 10-quart pan, bring apple juice to a boil over high heat. Add apples; reduce heat to medium-low, cover, and simmer, stirring occasionally, until apples are soft enough to mash easily (about 30 minutes).

Stir in sugar and cinnamon until well blended. Cook, uncovered, mashing apples and stirring often, until mixture is thickened and reduced to 5 cups (about 1 hour); as mixture thickens, reduce heat and stir more often to prevent sticking.

Ladle hot apple butter into hot, sterilized half-pint jars, leaving ¼-inch headspace. Wipe rims and threads clean; top with hot lids, then firmly screw on bands. Process in boiling water canner for 5 minutes. Or omit processing and ladle into freezer jars or freezer containers, leaving ½-inch headspace; apply lids. Let stand for 12 to 24 hours at room temperature; freeze or refrigerate. Makes about 5 half-pints.

Storage time. *Processed:* Up to 1 year. *Unprocessed:* Up to 1 month in refrigerator; up to 1 year in freezer.

Per tablespoon: 32 calories, 0 g protein, 8 g carbohydrates, 0 g total fat, 0 mg cholesterol, 0 mg sodium

Apricot Butter

Pictured on facing page

Apples are doubtless the most popular choice for butters, but other fruits—apricots, in this case—are just as delicious.

- **3 pounds apricots, pitted**
- **¼ cup lemon juice**
- **3 cups sugar**

Whirl apricots, a portion at a time, in a blender or food processor until smoothly puréed; you should have about 4 cups. Pour purée into a heavy-bottomed 8- to 10-quart pan. Stir in lemon juice and sugar until well blended. Bring mixture to a boil over high heat, stirring constantly. Continue to boil, uncovered, stirring often, until thickened (15 to 18 minutes); as mixture thickens, reduce heat and stir more often to prevent sticking.

Ladle hot apricot butter into hot, sterilized half-pint jars, leaving ¼-inch headspace. Wipe rims and threads clean; top with hot lids, then firmly screw on bands. Process in boiling water canner for 5 minutes. Or omit processing and ladle into freezer jars or freezer containers, leaving ½-inch headspace; apply lids. Let stand for 12 to 24 hours at room temperature; freeze or refrigerate. Makes about 5 half-pints.

Storage time. *Processed:* Up to 1 year. *Unprocessed:* Up to 1 month in refrigerator; up to 1 year in freezer.

Per tablespoon: 37 calories, 0 g protein, 9 g carbohydrates, 0 g total fat, 0 mg cholesterol, 0 mg sodium

Papaya Butter

Pictured on facing page

Capture the tropical essence of golden papayas with this soft-spreading preserve. A hint of lime heightens the exotic flavor.

- **3 large ripe papayas (about 1¼ lbs. *each*)**
- **¼ cup lime juice**
- **1 teaspoon grated lime peel**
- **1½ cups sugar**

Peel and halve papayas; scoop out seeds, then cut fruit into small chunks. Whirl papayas and lime juice, a portion at a time, in a blender or food processor until smoothly puréed. Pour purée into a heavy-bottomed 8- to 10-quart pan. Stir in lime peel and sugar until well blended. Bring to a boil over high heat; then reduce heat, partially cover pan, and simmer, stirring occasionally, for 15 minutes. Uncover pan and continue to simmer, stirring often, until mixture is thickened (about 15 more minutes); as mixture thickens, reduce heat and stir more often to prevent sticking.

Ladle hot papaya butter into hot, sterilized half-pint jars, leaving ¼-inch headspace. Wipe rims and threads clean; top with hot lids, then firmly screw on bands. Process in boiling water canner for 5 minutes. Or omit processing and ladle into freezer jars or freezer containers, leaving ½-inch headspace; apply lids. Let stand for 12 to 24 hours at room temperature; freeze or refrigerate. Makes about 4 half-pints.

Storage time. *Processed:* Up to 1 year. *Unprocessed:* Up to 1 month in refrigerator; up to 1 year in freezer.

Per tablespoon: 25 calories, 0 g protein, 6 g carbohydrates, 0 g total fat, 0 mg cholesterol, 1 mg sodium

Quick-fix Jams

*F*or year-round giving, few gifts are better than homemade jam. And with our no-fuss methods, you can easily make plenty. The short-cook technique uses dry pectin and a 2-minute cooking time; fresh-tasting freezer jam, made with liquid pectin, requires no cooking.

Whichever procedure you use, keep two rules in mind: *you can't double jam recipes, and you can't reduce the amount of sugar.* If you do, you may end up with fruit syrup instead of jam.

Short-cook Jam

> Fruit of your choice (see chart)
> Lemon juice (see chart)
> 1   box (1¾ or 2 oz.) dry pectin
> Sugar (see chart)

To prepare jars and fruit, check yield for each fruit to determine how many canning jars you will need. Then follow steps 2 through 4 on page 12.

Rinse fruit; peel, seed, hull, or core as necessary. Cut into cubes. Mash fruit with a potato masher (or whirl briefly in a food processor, but do not purée).

In a heavy-bottomed 8- to 10-quart pan, mix fruit, lemon juice, and pectin. Bring to a full rolling boil over high heat, stirring constantly. Quickly add sugar, still stirring. Return to a full rolling boil; then boil, stirring, for exactly 2 minutes. Remove from heat and skim off any foam.

Ladle hot jam into hot, sterilized half-pint jars, leaving ¼-inch headspace. Wipe rims and threads clean; top with hot lids, then firmly screw on bands. Process in boiling water canner for 5 minutes (see steps 8 through 12 on page 13). Or omit processing and ladle jam into freezer jars or freezer containers, leaving ½-inch headspace; apply lids. Let stand for 12 to 24 hours; then freeze or refrigerate.

Storage time. *Processed:* Up to 1 year. *Unprocessed:* Up to 1 month in refrigerator; up to 1 year in freezer.

Per tablespoon (approximate): 52 calories, 0 g protein, 14 g carbohydrates, 0 g total fat, 0 mg cholesterol, 1 mg sodium

No-cook Freezer Jam

> Fruit of your choice (see chart)
> Sugar (see chart)
> 1   pouch (3 oz.) liquid pectin
> Lemon juice (see chart)

Rinse fruit; peel, seed, hull, or core as necessary. Cut fruit into cubes. Mash fruit with a potato masher (or whirl briefly in a food processor, but do not purée).

In a large bowl, thoroughly mix fruit and sugar; let stand for 10 minutes, stirring occasionally. Meanwhile, mix pectin and lemon juice; add to fruit mixture and stir (don't beat in air) for 3 minutes. Fill freezer jars or freezer containers with jam, leaving ½-inch headspace; apply lids. Let jam stand for 24 hours; then freeze or refrigerate.

Storage time. Up to 1 month in refrigerator; up to 1 year in freezer.

Per tablespoon (approximate): 42 calories, 0 g protein, 11 g carbohydrates, 0 g total fat, 0 mg cholesterol, 0 mg sodium

Short-cook Method (1¾- or 2-oz. box of pectin)					
FRUIT	AMT. OF FRUIT	MASHED FRUIT	LEMON JUICE	SUGAR	YIELD
Fig	3¼ lbs.	5 c. + ½ c. water	½ c.	7 c.	8½ c.
Mango	6 lbs.	4 c.	¼ c.	6 c.	6½ c.
Papaya	5 lbs.	4 c.	¼ c.	6 c.	6½ c.
Peach	3 lbs.	4 c.	¼ c.	6 c.	6¾ c.
Pear	3 lbs.	4 c.	¼ c.	5½ c.	6½ c.

No-cook Freezer Method (3-oz. pouch of pectin)					
FRUIT	AMT. OF FRUIT	MASHED FRUIT	LEMON JUICE	SUGAR	YIELD
Apricot	1 lb.	1½ c.	¼ c.	3 c.	4 c.
Berry	4 c.	2 c.	2 T.	4 c.	4¾ c.
Kiwi	1¼ lbs.	2¼ c.	¼ c.	4 c.	5 c.
Nectarine	1 lb.	1½ c.	¼ c.	3 c.	4 c.
Plum	1¼ lbs.	2¼ c.	2 T.	4 c.	5 c.

Caramel Spice Pear Butter

Caramelized sugar and a trio of sweet spices lend this fragrant pear butter its distinctive flavor. It's perfect for cool-weather breakfasts; try it on hot toast or English muffins.

- 7½ **pounds (about 15 large) firm-ripe Bartlett pears**
- 2 **cups water**
- 6 **cups sugar**
- 1½ **teaspoons ground cinnamon**
- 1 **teaspoon ground cloves**
- ½ **teaspoon ground ginger**
- 2 **tablespoons lemon juice**

Core pears, but do not peel them. Slice pears and place in a heavy-bottomed 8- to 10-quart pan. Add water; bring to a boil over medium-high heat. Then reduce heat to low, cover, and cook until pears are tender when pierced (about 30 minutes). Let cool slightly, then whirl in a food processor, a portion at a time, until finely chopped. Return to pan.

Place 1½ cups of the sugar in a wide frying pan. Cook over medium heat, stirring often, until sugar caramelizes to a medium-brown syrup. Immediately pour syrup into pan with chopped pears (syrup will sizzle and harden, but dissolve again as the mixture cooks). Stir in remaining 4½ cups sugar, cinnamon, cloves, and ginger until well blended.

Bring mixture to a boil over medium-high heat, stirring. Reduce heat and simmer, uncovered, stirring often, until thickened (about 45 minutes); as mixture thickens, reduce heat and stir more often to prevent sticking. Stir in lemon juice just before removing from heat.

Ladle hot pear butter into hot, sterilized half-pint jars, leaving ¼-inch headspace. Wipe rims and threads clean; top with hot lids, then firmly screw on bands. Process in boiling water canner for 5 minutes. Or omit processing and ladle into freezer jars or freezer containers, leaving ½-inch headspace; apply lids. Let stand for 12 to 24 hours at room temperature; freeze or refrigerate. Makes about 9 half-pints.

Storage time. *Processed:* Up to 1 year. *Unprocessed:* Up to 1 month in refrigerator; up to 1 year in freezer.

Per tablespoon: 45 calories, 0 g protein, 12 g carbohydrates, 0 g total fat, 0 mg cholesterol, 0 mg sodium

Spicy Tomato Marmalade

To those of us who think of tomato-based spreads as strictly savory condiments (catsup and chili sauce, for example), the idea of tomato jam is a bit peculiar. But when flavored with citrus and spices, tomatoes make a delicious marmalade.

- 8 **cups peeled, cored, coarsely chopped tomatoes (about 5 lbs. tomatoes)**
- 1 *each* **orange and lemon**
- ¼ **cup cider vinegar (5% acidity)**
- 1½ **teaspoons** *each* **ground cinnamon and ground allspice**
- ¾ **teaspoon ground cloves**
- 3 **cups sugar**

Place tomatoes in a heavy-bottomed 8- to 10-quart non-aluminum pan. Rinse orange and lemon; with a vegetable peeler, carefully remove thin outer peel. Cut peel into slivers and add to tomatoes. Holding fruit over a bowl to catch juice, cut off and discard remaining peel and white membrane from orange and lemon; coarsely chop fruit.

Add chopped orange and lemon (plus any juice) to tomatoes. Stir in vinegar, cinnamon, allspice, cloves, and sugar until well blended. Bring to a boil over high heat, stirring often. Then reduce heat and simmer, uncovered, stirring often, until thickened and reduced to about 4 cups (about 2 hours); as mixture thickens, reduce heat and stir more often to prevent sticking.

Ladle hot marmalade into hot, sterilized half-pint jars, leaving ¼-inch headspace. Wipe rims and threads clean; top with hot lids, then firmly screw on bands. Process in boiling water canner for 5 minutes. Or omit processing and ladle into freezer jars or freezer containers, leaving ½-inch headspace; apply lids. Let stand for 12 to 24 hours at room temperature; freeze or refrigerate. Makes about 4 half-pints.

Storage time. *Processed:* Up to 1 year. *Unprocessed:* Up to 1 month in refrigerator; up to 1 year in freezer.

Per tablespoon: 45 calories, 0 g protein, 11 g carbohydrates, 0 g total fat, 0 mg cholesterol, 3 mg sodium

Safe Seals

Unless you plan to refrigerate or freeze your jams, jellies, and preserves, always process them in canning jars with self-sealing lids and ring bands. Paraffin is no longer recommended for sealing, since air can enter beneath it and encourage molding. (Don't eat jams which have molded, even if only at the surface—the mold may not be as harmless as was once thought.)

Citrus Marmalade

Pictured on page 34

Liven up breakfast breads with the fresh, sweet-tart flavor of this translucent golden spread.

　5　**medium-size oranges**
　2　**small lemons**
　3　**cups water**
　6　**cups sugar**
　½　**cup lemon juice**

Rinse unpeeled oranges and lemons. Halve lengthwise; thinly slice crosswise, discarding seeds. Place slices in a heavy-bottomed 8- to 10-quart pan, add water, and press down fruit to make an even layer. Let stand for 8 to 24 hours at room temperature.

Bring fruit to a boil over high heat, stirring; reduce heat to low and cook, uncovered, stirring occasionally, for 40 minutes. Remove from heat; let stand for 4 hours. Stir in sugar; bring to a boil over high heat, stirring. Continue to boil, uncovered, stirring often, until mixture thickens and reaches the jell point (220°F)—about 20 minutes. As mixture thickens, reduce heat and stir more often to prevent sticking. Remove from heat and stir in lemon juice.

Ladle hot marmalade into hot, sterilized half-pint jars, leaving ¼-inch headspace. Wipe rims and threads clean; top with hot lids, then firmly screw on bands. Process in boiling water canner for 5 minutes. Or omit processing and ladle into freezer jars or freezer containers, leaving ½-inch headspace; apply lids. Let stand for 12 to 24 hours at room temperature; freeze or refrigerate. Makes about 7 half-pints.

Storage time. *Processed:* Up to 1 year. *Unprocessed:* Up to 1 month in refrigerator; up to 1 year in freezer.

Per tablespoon: 45 calories, 0 g protein, 12 g carbohydrates, 0 g total fat, 0 mg cholesterol, 1 mg sodium

Pineapple Marmalade

This exotic rendition of marmalade starts with fresh pineapple; minced ginger adds a zesty accent.

　1　**large orange**
　4½　**cups finely chopped fresh pineapple (chop with a knife, not a food processor)**
　2　**tablespoons minced fresh ginger**
　3　**cups sugar**

Rinse unpeeled orange; finely chop, discarding seeds. In a heavy-bottomed 6- to 8-quart pan, mix orange, pineapple, ginger, and sugar. Bring to a boil over high heat, stirring often; reduce heat to medium-low and cook, uncovered, stirring often, until mixture thickens and reaches the jell point (220°F)—about 40 minutes. As mixture thickens, reduce heat and stir more often to prevent sticking.

Ladle hot marmalade into hot, sterilized half-pint jars, leaving ¼-inch headspace. Wipe rims and threads clean; top with hot lids, then firmly screw on bands. Process in boiling water canner for 5 minutes. Or omit processing and ladle into freezer jars or freezer containers, leaving ½-inch headspace; apply lids. Let stand for 12 to 24 hours at room temperature; freeze or refrigerate. Makes about 5 half-pints.

Storage time. *Processed:* Up to 1 year. *Unprocessed:* Up to 1 month in refrigerator; up to 1 year in freezer.

Per tablespoon: 37 calories, 0 g protein, 10 g carbohydrates, 0 g total fat, 0 mg cholesterol, 0 mg sodium

Lemon Marmalade

Pictured on facing page

Be careful to use *only* the thin, yellow outer layer of peel for this exquisite marmalade.

　　About 12 large lemons
　½　**cup water**
　5　**cups sugar**
　1　**pouch (3 oz.) liquid pectin**

Rinse unpeeled lemons. With a vegetable peeler, remove thin outer peel (colored part only); cut peel into slivers. Then squeeze juice from lemons. You should have 1¾ cups peel and 2 cups juice.

Place water, all the lemon peel, and ½ cup of the lemon juice in a heavy-bottomed 6- to 8-quart pan. Bring to a boil over high heat; then reduce heat, cover, and simmer, stirring occasionally, until peel is tender (about 25 minutes). Stir in sugar and remaining 1½ cups lemon juice. Bring to a full rolling boil over high heat, stirring. Remove from heat, cover, and let stand for 18 to 24 hours at room temperature.

Bring marmalade to a full rolling boil over high heat, stirring constantly. Quickly stir in pectin and return to a full rolling boil; boil, stirring, for 1 minute. Remove from heat and skim off any foam.

Ladle hot marmalade into hot, sterilized half-pint jars, leaving ¼-inch headspace. Wipe rims and threads clean; top with hot lids, then firmly screw on bands. Process in boiling water canner for 5 minutes. Or omit processing and ladle into freezer jars or freezer containers, leaving ½-inch headspace; apply lids. Let stand for 12 to 24 hours at room temperature; freeze or refrigerate. Makes about 5 half-pints.

Storage time. *Processed:* Up to 1 year. *Unprocessed:* Up to 1 month in refrigerator; up to 1 year in freezer.

Per tablespoon: 51 calories, 0 g protein, 13 g carbohydrates, 0 g total fat, 0 mg cholesterol, 0 mg sodium

Sweet-tart, shimmering, and translucent, Lemon Marmalade (facing page) is the perfect accompaniment for tea and crumpets. The marmalade is wonderful on English muffins, biscuits, scones, and toast, too.

Reduced-sugar Spreads

Almost everyone enjoys sparkling, jewel-bright homemade jams and jellies. But if you're like many health-conscious cooks, you may be tempted to reduce the sugar in traditional spreads. Please don't! Cutting down on sugar (or using artificial sweetener) in regular recipes upsets the balance of fruit, pectin, acid, and sugar—and your jelly or jam may turn into syrup. It's better to use the modified pectins (labeled "light" or "less sugar") specially developed for making reduced-sugar jams and jellies. Preserves made with these pectins tend to taste less sweet than regular spreads and may have a firmer consistency.

Another good option is simply to follow tested recipes for low-sugar spreads, such as the two on this page. The first is an all-fruit treat that gets its sweetness from natural fructose; the refrigerator jelly calls for gelatin and artificial sweetener.

To develop your own all-fruit spreads, try boiling fruit pulp or finely chopped fruit (even unsweetened canned fruit) with frozen unsweetened juice concentrates (thawed). Long boiling makes these mixtures thicken to resemble jams, conserves, or fruit butters; if you like, add a little sugar or artificial sweetener. Just keep in mind that it may take you a while to come up with a combination you really like.

Because sugarless and reduced-sugar spreads don't have enough sugar to act as a preservative, you need to process them longer than regular jams and jellies—at least 15 minutes in a boiling water canner. Unprocessed spreads must be frozen; or you can store them in the refrigerator for up to 2 weeks.

Chunky Pear-Pineapple Spread

4   **pounds pears, peeled, cored, and finely chopped**
¼   **cup lemon juice**
1   **large can (about 20 oz.) crushed pineapple packed in its own juice**
1   **can (12 oz.) frozen unsweetened apple juice concentrate, thawed**

In a heavy-bottomed 8- to 10-quart pan, mix pears, lemon juice, undrained pineapple, and apple juice

concentrate. Bring to a boil over medium-high heat, stirring constantly. Continue to boil gently, uncovered, stirring often, until spread is as thick as desired (about 45 minutes); as mixture thickens, reduce heat and stir more often to prevent sticking. If you prefer a smoother spread, whirl mixture, a portion at a time, in a blender or food processor; then return to pan and bring to a boil over medium-high heat, stirring constantly.

Ladle hot spread into prepared, hot half-pint jars, leaving ¼-inch headspace. Wipe rims and threads clean; top with hot lids, then firmly screw on bands. Process in boiling water canner for 15 minutes. Or omit processing and ladle into freezer jars or freezer containers, leaving ½-inch headspace; apply lids. Let the spread cool in jars at room temperature; freeze or refrigerate. Makes about 4 half-pints.

Storage time. *Processed:* Up to 1 year. *Unprocessed:* Up to 2 weeks in refrigerator; up to 1 year in freezer.

Per tablespoon: 32 calories, 0 g protein, 8 g carbohydrates, 0 g total fat, 0 mg cholesterol, 2 mg sodium

Refrigerator Grape Jelly

3   **cups bottled unsweetened grape juice**
2   **tablespoons lemon juice**
2   **envelopes unflavored gelatin**
1   **tablespoon liquid artificial sweetener**

In a heavy-bottomed 8- to 10-quart pan, mix grape juice, lemon juice, and gelatin. Bring to a full rolling boil over medium-high heat, stirring often; then boil, stirring, for 1 minute. Remove from heat; stir in artificial sweetener.

Ladle hot jelly into half-pint jars or refrigerator containers, leaving ¼-inch headspace; apply lids. Refrigerate. Do not freeze or process in a boiling water canner. Makes about 3 half-pints.

Storage time. Up to 2 weeks in refrigerator.

Per tablespoon: 11 calories, 0 g protein, 3 g carbohydrates, 0 g total fat, 0 mg cholesterol, 2 mg sodium

Peach-Pineapple-Orange Conserve

Reminiscent of marmalade, this piquant medley of golden fruits is great with baked ham or poultry. You can use either syrup- or juice-packed pineapple; the latter gives a less sweet preserve.

- 2 **oranges**
- 4 **cups peeled, pitted, finely chopped peaches (about 3 lbs. peaches)**
- 1 **can (about 8 oz.) crushed pineapple**
- 6 **cups sugar**

Rinse unpeeled oranges; then finely chop, discarding any seeds. Place oranges and peaches in a heavy-bottomed 8- to 10-quart pan. Stir in undrained pineapple and sugar until well blended. Bring to a boil over high heat, stirring. Reduce heat to medium-low and cook, uncovered, stirring often, until thickened (about 35 minutes); as mixture thickens, reduce heat and stir more often to prevent sticking.

Ladle hot conserve into hot, sterilized half-pint jars, leaving ¼-inch headspace. Wipe rims and threads clean; top with hot lids, then firmly screw on bands. Process in boiling water canner for 5 minutes. Or omit processing and ladle into freezer jars or freezer containers, leaving ½-inch headspace; apply lids. Let stand for 12 to 24 hours at room temperature; freeze or refrigerate. Makes about 10 half-pints.

Storage time. *Processed:* Up to 1 year. *Unprocessed:* Up to 1 month in refrigerator; up to 1 year in freezer.

Per tablespoon: 34 calories, 0 g protein, 9 g carbohydrates, 0 g total fat, 0 mg cholesterol, 0 mg sodium

Fresh Fig Conserve

The crunch of walnuts, the tang of orange peel, and the sweetness of figs make this richly colored conserve a deliciously memorable spread.

- 2½ **pounds fresh figs**
- 2½ **cups sugar**
- ⅓ **cup lemon juice**
- 1 **tablespoon grated orange peel**
- ¼ **cup chopped walnuts**

Clip off and discard fig stems; then chop figs and place in a heavy-bottomed 8- to 10-quart pan. Stir in sugar until well blended. Let stand for 1 hour.

Bring fig mixture to a boil over medium heat, stirring often. Then boil, uncovered, stirring often, until thickened (about 20 minutes); as mixture thickens, reduce heat and stir more often to prevent

sticking. Stir in lemon juice, orange peel, and walnuts. Return mixture to a boil; then boil, stirring, for 3 minutes.

Ladle hot conserve into hot, sterilized half-pint jars, leaving ¼-inch headspace. Wipe rims and threads clean; top with hot lids, then firmly screw on bands. Process in boiling water canner for 5 minutes. Or omit processing and ladle into freezer jars or freezer containers, leaving ½-inch headspace; apply lids. Let stand for 12 to 24 hours at room temperature; freeze or refrigerate. Makes about 5 half-pints.

Storage time. *Processed:* Up to 1 year. *Unprocessed:* Up to 1 month in refrigerator; up to 1 year in freezer.

Per tablespoon: 37 calories, 0 g protein, 9 g carbohydrates, 0 g total fat, 0 mg cholesterol, 0 mg sodium

Rhubarb Conserve

This chunky conserve, dotted with raisins, dates, and nuts, is good in all ways: as a spread for toast, a relish with meats, or a topping for ice cream.

- 2½ **pounds rhubarb**
- 5½ **cups sugar**
- 2 **oranges**
- 1 **lemon**
- 1½ **cups *each* raisins and snipped pitted dates**
- 1 **cup chopped walnuts**

Dice unpeeled rhubarb stalks; you should have 4 cups. Place rhubarb in a heavy-bottomed 8- to 10-quart pan. Stir in sugar until well blended. Cover and let stand for 8 to 12 hours at room temperature.

Rinse and thinly slice unpeeled oranges and lemon; discard seeds, then cut slices into small pieces. Add orange and lemon pieces, raisins, and dates to rhubarb mixture. Bring to a boil over high heat, stirring. Then reduce heat and simmer, uncovered, stirring often, until thickened (35 to 40 minutes); as mixture thickens, reduce heat and stir more often to prevent sticking. About 5 minutes before removing from heat, stir in walnuts.

Ladle hot conserve into hot, sterilized half-pint jars, leaving ¼-inch headspace. Wipe rims and threads clean; top with hot lids, then firmly screw on bands. Process in boiling water canner for 5 minutes. Or omit processing and ladle into freezer jars or freezer containers, leaving ½-inch headspace; apply lids. Let stand for 12 to 24 hours at room temperature; freeze or refrigerate. Makes about 10 half-pints.

Storage time. *Processed:* Up to 1 year. *Unprocessed:* Up to 1 month in refrigerator; up to 1 year in freezer.

Per tablespoon: 42 calories, 0 g protein, 10 g carbohydrates, 0 g total fat, 0 mg cholesterol, 1 mg sodium

Who wouldn't appreciate a gift basket of home-canned savories? These tangy treats include Giardiniera (left; page 64), a beautiful mixed vegetable pickle, and Garlic Jelly (right; page 54), a savory accompaniment for cold meats. In the center of the basket is Apricot Chutney (page 71), a spicy partner for curries, meats, and cheese.

Apricot-Pear Conserve

The flavors of tangy dried apricots, lemon, and fresh pears blend harmoniously in this colorful conserve.

- **1 lemon**
- **1 cup dried apricots, cut into thin slices**
- **1 cup water**
- **5 cups peeled, cored, chopped firm-ripe Anjou or Bosc pears (about 2½ lbs. pears)**
- **4 cups sugar**

Rinse unpeeled lemon and thinly slice; discard end pieces and any seeds. Place lemon slices in a small pan and stir in apricots and water. Bring mixture to a boil over high heat; reduce heat and simmer, uncovered, for 5 minutes. Remove mixture from heat and set aside.

Place pears in a heavy-bottomed 8- to 10-quart pan. Stir in sugar until well blended. Bring mixture to a boil over medium heat, stirring occasionally. Continue to boil gently, uncovered, stirring often, for 25 minutes; as mixture thickens, reduce heat and stir more often to prevent sticking. Stir in apricot mixture (including liquid); bring to a boil. Then boil, uncovered, stirring often, until reduced to about 5 cups (about 5 more minutes).

Ladle hot conserve into hot, sterilized half-pint jars, leaving ¼-inch headspace. Wipe rims and threads clean; top with hot lids, then firmly screw on bands. Process in boiling water canner for 5 minutes. Or omit processing and ladle into freezer jars or freezer containers, leaving ½-inch headspace; apply lids. Let stand for 12 to 24 hours at room temperature; freeze or refrigerate. Makes about 5 half-pints.

Storage time. *Processed:* Up to 1 year. *Unprocessed:* Up to 1 month in refrigerator; up to 1 year in freezer.

Per tablespoon: 50 calories, 0 g protein, 13 g carbohydrates, 0 g total fat, 0 mg cholesterol, 0 mg sodium

---

Using Commercial Fruits & Juices for Jams & Jellies

You can make excellent jams and jellies from purchased canned and frozen unsweetened fruits and juices. Commercial products may be low in pectin, though—so always add pectin as directed in the recipe (or, for juices, as instructed on page 52).

Quince & Orange Preserves

Bubbling down to glistening goodness, tart quinces are enhanced by orange quarters, cinnamon, and cloves.

- **8 small quinces (about 2 lbs. *total*)**
  About 5½ cups water
- **3 cinnamon sticks (*each* about 2 inches long), broken in half**
- **30 whole cloves**
- **3 medium-size oranges**
- **6 cups sugar**
- **2 cups distilled white vinegar (5% acidity)**

Peel and core quinces; place peels and cores in a 2-quart pan and add 4 cups of the water. Set aside. Pour about 1 inch of water (at least 1½ cups) into a heavy-bottomed 8- to 10-quart pan. Cut quinces into quarters; place in pan.

Bring contents of both the 2-quart pan and the 8- to 10-quart pan to a boil over high heat. Reduce heat, cover, and simmer until quince quarters are tender when pierced (about 30 minutes). Drain quince quarters. Strain cooking liquid from peels and cores; add 1½ cups strained liquid to quince quarters, then discard peels, cores, and remaining liquid.

Tie cinnamon sticks and cloves in a washed square of cheesecloth. Add to quinces. Rinse unpeeled oranges and thinly slice; discard any seeds, then quarter orange slices and add to quinces. Stir in sugar and vinegar until well blended. Bring mixture to a boil over medium heat. Then boil, uncovered, stirring often, until syrup is amber in color and slightly thickened (about 1 hour and 10 minutes); as syrup thickens, reduce heat and stir more often to prevent sticking. Syrup will continue to thicken as it cools. Remove spice packet.

Ladle hot preserves into hot, sterilized half-pint jars, leaving ¼-inch headspace. Wipe rims and threads clean; top with hot lids, then firmly screw on bands. Process in boiling water canner for 5 minutes. Or omit processing and ladle into freezer jars or freezer containers, leaving ½-inch headspace; apply lids. Let stand for 12 to 24 hours at room temperature; freeze or refrigerate. Makes about 8 half-pints.

Storage time. *Processed:* Up to 1 year. *Unprocessed:* Up to 1 month in refrigerator; up to 1 year in freezer.

Per tablespoon: 41 calories, 0 g protein, 11 g carbohydrates, 0 g total fat, 0 mg cholesterol, 0 mg sodium

How to Make Jelly

To make clear and sparkling jelly with a full, sweet flavor, you start by extracting juice from sound, ripe fruit, then strain it and boil it with sugar until it jells. For jellies with the right consistency—tender, yet firm enough to hold a jiggly shape—you'll need to use the right proportions of fruit, sugar, pectin, and acid. If the fruit you're using doesn't contain enough natural pectin and acid for jelly (see below), just add these ingredients to the juice as needed.

Pectin & Acid Contents of Fruits

Consult the lists below to check the pectin and acid content of the fruit you want to use.

Juice from these fruits usually contains enough pectin and acid for jelly: Tart apples, tart blackberries, crabapples, cranberries, red currants, gooseberries, lemons, limes, loganberries, most plums, quinces.

Juice from these fruits usually is low in acid or pectin: Sweet apples, sweet blackberries, sour and sweet cherries, elderberries, grapefruit, eastern Concord grapes, seedless grapes, loquats, oranges.

Juice from these fruits always needs added acid or pectin, or both: Apricots, blueberries, figs, western Concord grapes, guavas, nectarines, peaches, pears, pomegranates, prune plums, raspberries, strawberries.

Testing for Pectin

If the juice you're planning to use is too low in pectin, you'll wind up with runny jelly. To avoid this problem, test the juice—and make any necessary adjustments—before you start making your jelly.

To test the pectin content of fruit juice, combine 1 teaspoon of cooked fruit juice (see steps 2 through 4 on facing page) and 1 tablespoon of rubbing alcohol (70 percent alcohol) in a cup. Stir gently to make sure all the juice comes in contact with the alcohol. *Do not taste* this mixture—it's poisonous. Juices rich in pectin will form a solid, jellylike mass that can be picked up with a fork. Juices low in pectin will form only a few pieces of jellylike material. If more pectin is needed, you can either add commercial liquid pectin or mix the juice with another fruit juice that's higher in pectin. *Discard the alcohol test.*

If pectin is to be added, add 1 tablespoon liquid pectin to 1 cup juice. Test again for jelling. If more pectin is needed, add 1 more tablespoon; test again. Repeat until enough pectin has been added. Measure remaining juice; add pectin in the correct amount.

Testing for Acid

A tart juice is necessary for a good-tasting jelly. Compare the flavor of your cooked juice with that of a mixture of 1 teaspoon bottled lemon juice, 3 tablespoons water, and ½ teaspoon sugar. If your juice does not taste as tart as this lemon mixture, add 1 tablespoon lemon juice per cup of fruit juice.

Choosing Sweeteners

Besides contributing to the flavor of fruit spreads, sugar aids in jelling and acts as a preservative. Light corn syrup and mild-flavored honey may be used to replace part of the sugar in jams and jellies, but they tend to alter the texture and mask the fruit flavor; for best results, use tested recipes that specify honey or corn syrup. Likewise, use artificial sweeteners only when called for in a recipe.

Finding the Jell Point

If you're not using commercial pectin in your jelly, you need to test for doneness. There are three methods you can use. *The first two tests work for jam as well as for jelly; the third is for jelly only.*

Temperature test. The easiest way to tell whether your jelly has reached the jell point is to check its temperature with a jelly or candy thermometer: when it reaches 220°F (at sea level), it's ready. For each 1,000 feet of altitude above sea level, you'll need to subtract 2 degrees; at an elevation of 1,000 feet, for example, jelly is done at 218°F. The thermometer bulb must be completely covered with jelly, but it shouldn't touch the bottom of the pan. Read at eye level, and test your thermometer's accuracy in advance by placing it in boiling water.

Refrigerator test. Remove the pan from the heat; spoon about a tablespoon of boiling jelly onto a small chilled plate. Place in the refrigerator for 3 minutes, then push the jelly from the side; if it wrinkles and seems tender-firm, it's done.

Spoon or sheet test. Dip a cool metal spoon into the boiling fruit juice. Lift the spoon out of the steam and turn it so the juice runs off the side. When the juice begins to boil, it's light and syrupy; when it has almost reached the jell point, it becomes heavy and falls off the spoon two drops at a time. When the two drops form together and slide off the spoon in a sheet, the jelly is ready; remove it from the heat immediately. *This test does not work for jam.*

Remaking Runny Jelly

If your jelly ends up looking like syrup, you can try to remake it; work with just 4 cups at a time.

To remake with dry pectin. For each 4 cups of jelly, mix ¼ cup sugar, ½ cup water, 2 tablespoons bottled lemon juice, and 4 teaspoons dry pectin in a large, heavy-bottomed pan. Bring to a boil over high heat, stirring constantly; add jelly. Bring to a full rolling boil, stirring constantly; then boil, stirring, for 30 seconds. Remove from heat, skim off any foam, and ladle into hot, sterilized jars, leaving ¼-inch headspace. Process in boiling water canner for 5 minutes.

To remake with liquid pectin. For each 4 cups of jelly, mix ¾ cup sugar, 2 tablespoons bottled lemon juice, and 2 tablespoons liquid pectin in a bowl; set aside. In a large, heavy-bottomed pan, bring jelly just to a boil over high heat, stirring constantly. Remove from heat; quickly add pectin mixture. Bring to a full rolling boil over high heat, stirring constantly; then boil, stirring, for 1 minute. Remove from heat, skim off any foam, and ladle into hot, sterilized jars, leaving ¼-inch headspace. Process in boiling water canner for 5 minutes.

Step-by-Step Canning for Jelly

1. Assemble and prepare equipment and sterilize jars, following steps 2 through 4 on page 12.

2. Rinse fruit. Remove stems, hulls, blossom ends, and spoiled parts. Do not core or peel apples or other firm fruits; just cut them into small pieces. If fruit is soft, crush it to start the juice flowing.

3. To extract the juice, put crushed or cut-up fruit into a pan. For firm fruit such as apples, you'll need to add about 1 cup water for each pound of fruit; for semifirm fruit such as plums, add about ½ cup water per pound. Soft fruits usually don't need any additional water. Whatever the type of fruit, add only enough water to prevent scorching, since juice shouldn't be diluted any more than necessary.

4. Bring fruit to a boil over high heat; reduce heat to medium and cook, stirring to prevent scorching, until tender (5 to 10 minutes for grapes and berries, 20 to 25 minutes for apples and other firm fruits). Don't overboil; that reduces jelling strength.

Pour fruit mixture through four thicknesses of wet washed cheesecloth spread over a colander; or pour into a moistened jelly bag made of strong muslin. *Don't squeeze bag;* you'll get a cloudy jelly.

5. You can use one of two methods to make jelly.

The standard or long-cook method uses a little less sugar. Follow the directions on the facing page to test the cooked juice for its natural pectin and acid content; then supply more of either or both, as needed (see facing page).

Cook only 4 to 6 cups juice at a time, using a heavy-bottomed 8- to 10-quart pan. If you like, add ½ teaspoon margarine, butter, or salad oil to the juice to reduce foam (keep in mind that added fat may cause an "off" flavor to develop during long storage).

Bring the juice to a boil, then add the sugar and stir until dissolved. The amount of sugar you use depends upon the pectin and acid content of the juice.

In general, use ¾ to 1 cup sugar per cup of juice if the juice is naturally high in pectin; use ⅔ to ¾ cup sugar per cup of juice if the juice has only a moderate amount of natural pectin (see "Pectin & Acid Contents of Fruits," facing page).

Boil juice rapidly until the jell point is reached (see "Finding the Jell Point," facing page), then immediately remove the pan from the heat. Don't overcook; if you do, the jelly will lose flavor, color, and jelling ability.

The short-cook method, used in all our jelly recipes, depends on commercial pectin and requires a higher proportion of sugar. The boiling time, usually about 1 minute, cannot be varied from recipe or package directions. If the recipe tells you to bring the jelly mixture to a "full rolling boil," you want a hard boil that does not stop when the mixture is stirred. Follow recipe or package directions to cook your jelly, then remove the jelly from the heat at once.

6. Carefully skim off any foam from jelly. Remove a sterilized jar from the hot water. Stand it upright on a cloth towel. Ladle hot jelly into jar, leaving ¼-inch headspace.

7. Seal and process jars as directed in steps 8 through 12 on page 13, using the processing time specified in your recipe. At high altitudes, add an additional minute for each 1,000 feet above sea level.

8. If you choose not to process your jelly, ladle it into clean freezer jars or freezer containers; rinse jars with hot water before filling them to prevent the hot jelly from cracking the glass. Before storing filled jars or containers, let them stand for 12 to 24 hours at room temperature; this gives the jelly time to jell completely.

Ruby Wine Jelly

The wine lovers among your friends will enjoy this full-flavored jelly, superb with beef or lamb.

- 1¾ **cups ruby port**
- ¾ **cup dry red wine, such as Cabernet Sauvignon**
- 3 **cups sugar**
- 1 **pouch (3 oz.) liquid pectin**

In a heavy-bottomed 8- to 10-quart pan, mix port, dry red wine, and sugar. Stir over low heat until sugar is completely dissolved (about 5 minutes). Stir in pectin all at once; skim off any foam.

Ladle hot jelly into hot, sterilized half-pint jars, leaving ¼-inch headspace. Wipe rims and threads clean; top with hot lids, then firmly screw on bands. Process in boiling water canner for 5 minutes. Or omit processing and ladle jelly into freezer jars or freezer containers, leaving ½-inch headspace; apply lids. Let stand for 12 to 24 hours at room temperature; freeze or refrigerate. Makes about 5 half-pints.

Storage time. *Processed:* Up to 1 year. *Unprocessed:* Up to 1 month in refrigerator; up to 1 year in freezer.

Per tablespoon: 39 calories, 0 g protein, 8 g carbohydrates, 0 g total fat, 0 mg cholesterol, 1 mg sodium

Garlic or Shallot Jelly

Pictured on page 50

This bold-flavored jelly is a wonderful relish for meats; it's also good with cream cheese and crackers.

- ½ **cup finely chopped garlic or shallots**
  About 3 cups white wine vinegar (5% acidity)
- 1½ **cups water**
- 6 **cups sugar**
- 2 **pouches (3 oz. *each*) liquid pectin**

Combine garlic or shallots and 3 cups of the vinegar in a 2- to 2½-quart pan. Bring to a simmer over medium heat; simmer gently, uncovered, for 15 minutes. Remove from heat; pour into a glass jar. Cover and let stand for 24 to 36 hours at room temperature; then pour through a fine strainer into a bowl, pressing garlic or shallots with the back of a spoon to squeeze out as much liquid as possible. Discard residue. Measure liquid; if necessary, add vinegar to make 2 cups or boil liquid to reduce to 2 cups.

In a heavy-bottomed 8- to 10-quart pan, mix flavored vinegar, water, and sugar. Bring to a full rolling boil over medium-high heat, stirring. Stir in pectin all at once, return to a full rolling boil, and boil for 1 minute, stirring constantly. Remove from heat and skim off any foam.

Ladle hot jelly into hot, sterilized half-pint jars, leaving ¼-inch headspace. Wipe rims and threads clean; top with hot lids, then firmly screw on bands. Process in boiling water canner for 5 minutes. Or omit processing and ladle jelly into freezer jars or freezer containers, leaving ½-inch headspace; apply lids. Let stand for 12 to 24 hours at room temperature; freeze or refrigerate. Makes about 7 half-pints.

Storage time. *Processed:* Up to 1 year. *Unprocessed:* Up to 1 month in refrigerator; up to 1 year in freezer.

Per tablespoon: 43 calories, 0 g protein, 11 g carbohydrates, 0 g total fat, 0 mg cholesterol, 0 mg sodium

Apricot–Red Pepper Jelly

Pictured on facing page

You'll enjoy the combination of tangy-sweet dried apricots, red bell pepper, and feisty hot chiles in this jelly. It's fabulous with meat and poultry; or try it with cream cheese, as a spread for crackers.

- 1 **package (about 6 oz.) dried apricots (about 1¼ cups), chopped**
- ¾ **cup chopped red bell pepper**
- ¼ **cup seeded, chopped fresh red Fresno chiles or red (or green) jalapeño chiles (4 to 6 medium-size chiles)**
- 2½ **cups cider vinegar (5% acidity)**
- 1½ **cups water**
- 1 **box (1¾ or 2 oz.) dry pectin**
- 6 **cups sugar**

In a blender or food processor, whirl apricots, bell pepper, chiles, and 1¾ cups of the vinegar until fruit and vegetables are finely ground. Pour into a heavy-bottomed 8- to 10-quart pan. Rinse blender with the 1½ cups water and remaining ¾ cup vinegar; pour into pan. Stir in pectin; bring to a full rolling boil over high heat, stirring constantly. Quickly add sugar, still stirring. Return to a full rolling boil; then boil, stirring, for 1 minute. (If using a 2-oz. box of pectin, boil for 2 minutes.) Remove from heat and skim off any foam.

Ladle hot jelly into hot, sterilized half-pint jars, leaving ¼-inch headspace. Wipe rims and threads clean; top with hot lids, then firmly screw on bands. Process in boiling water canner for 5 minutes. Or omit processing and ladle jelly into freezer jars or freezer containers, leaving ½-inch headspace; apply lids. Let stand for 12 to 24 hours at room temperature; freeze or refrigerate. Makes about 6 half-pints.

Storage time. *Processed:* Up to 1 year. *Unprocessed:* Up to 1 month in refrigerator; up to 1 year in freezer.

Per tablespoon: 55 calories, 0 g protein, 14 g carbohydrates, 0 g total fat, 0 mg cholesterol, 0 mg sodium

*Two savory pepper jellies add verve and flavor to a bountiful cold platter of
sliced meats, goat cheese, vegetables, and lavosh (Armenian cracker bread).
Apricot–Red Pepper Jelly (at left; recipe on facing page) and Jalapeño Jelly
(page 56) are also good with cream cheese and crackers.*

Jalapeño Jelly

Pictured on page 34 and page 55

Hot, spicy jalapeño jelly is a delightful Southwest-style condiment to serve with chicken, pork, or beef.

- ¼ **cup chopped green jalapeño chiles (4 to 6 medium-size chiles; remove half the seeds before chopping)**
- ¾ **cup chopped green bell pepper**
- 6 **cups sugar**
- 2½ **cups cider vinegar (5% acidity)**
- 2 **pouches (3 oz. *each*) liquid pectin**

In a blender or food processor, whirl chiles and bell pepper until finely ground. Place ground vegetables and any juice in a heavy-bottomed 8- to 10-quart pan. Stir in sugar and vinegar until well blended.

Bring to a full rolling boil over high heat, stirring constantly. Stir in pectin all at once. Return to a full rolling boil; then boil, stirring, for 1 minute. Remove from heat and skim off any foam.

Ladle hot jelly into hot, sterilized half-pint jars, leaving ¼-inch headspace. Wipe rims and threads clean; top with hot lids, then firmly screw on bands. Process in boiling water canner for 5 minutes. Or omit processing and ladle jelly into freezer jars or freezer containers, leaving ½-inch headspace; apply lids. Let stand for 12 to 24 hours at room temperature; freeze or refrigerate. Makes about 7 half-pints.

Storage time. *Processed:* Up to 1 year. *Unprocessed:* Up to 1 month in refrigerator; up to 1 year in freezer.

Per tablespoon: 42 calories, 0 g protein, 11 g carbohydrates, 0 g total fat, 0 mg cholesterol, 0 mg sodium

Lime-Mint Jelly

Pictured on page 34

Fresh lime juice and finely chopped mint combine in a jelly with an outstanding, delicately sweet flavor.

- 8 **to 10 limes**
- 4 **cups sugar**
- 1¾ **cups water**
  Green food coloring (optional)
- 1 **pouch (3 oz.) liquid pectin**
- 3 **tablespoons finely chopped fresh mint**

Rinse unpeeled limes. Grate thin outer peel (colored part only) from 5 limes; set aside. Squeeze enough limes (use remaining limes as needed) to make ¾ cup juice. Pour lime juice, sugar, and water into a heavy-bottomed 8- to 10-quart pan and stir until well blended. Bring to a boil over medium-high heat,

stirring occasionally. (At this point, stir in enough food coloring, if desired, to get the desired tint.)

Stir in pectin all at once. Add grated lime peel and mint. Bring to a full rolling boil; boil, stirring, for 1 minute. Remove from heat and skim off any foam.

Ladle hot jelly into hot, sterilized half-pint jars, leaving ¼-inch headspace. Wipe rims and threads clean; top with hot lids, then firmly screw on bands. Process in boiling water canner for 5 minutes. Or omit processing and ladle jelly into freezer jars or freezer containers, leaving ½-inch headspace; apply lids. Let stand for 12 to 24 hours at room temperature; then freeze or refrigerate. Makes about 5 half-pints.

Storage time. *Processed:* Up to 1 year. *Unprocessed:* Up to 1 month in refrigerator; up to 1 year in freezer.

Per tablespoon: 40 calories, 0 g protein, 10 g carbohydrates, 0 g total fat, 0 mg cholesterol, 0 mg sodium

Apple-Herb Jelly

Apple jelly with a whisper of herb flavor is a much-appreciated gift. To make plain apple jelly, don't boil the juice, add herbs, or strain the mixture; just begin by stirring in the lemon juice and sugar.

- 2 **cups bottled filtered unsweetened apple juice**
- ¼ **cup dry thyme, ⅓ cup dry basil, 2 tablespoons dry rosemary, or ¼ cup dry mint**
- 3 **tablespoons lemon juice**
- 3½ **cups sugar**
- 1 **pouch (3 oz.) liquid pectin**

In a heavy-bottomed 6- to 8-quart pan, bring apple juice to a boil. Remove from heat, stir in thyme, and cover. Let stand for 30 minutes (or 2 hours for basil; 15 minutes for rosemary; 10 minutes for mint).

Pour mixture through a jelly bag or a cheesecloth-lined colander. Squeeze out and reserve all liquid; discard herbs. Rinse pan; return liquid to pan. Stir in lemon juice and sugar. Bring to a boil over high heat, stirring constantly. Pour in pectin all at once, bring to a full rolling boil, and boil, stirring, for 1 minute. Remove from heat and skim off any foam.

Ladle hot jelly into hot, sterilized half-pint jars, leaving ¼-inch headspace. Wipe rims and threads clean; top with hot lids, then firmly screw on bands. Process in boiling water canner for 5 minutes. Or omit processing and ladle jelly into freezer jars or freezer containers, leaving ½-inch headspace; apply lids. Let stand for 12 to 24 hours at room temperature; freeze or refrigerate. Makes about 4 half-pints.

Storage time. *Processed:* Up to 1 year. *Unprocessed:* Up to 1 month in refrigerator; up to 1 year in freezer.

Per tablespoon: 46 calories, 0 g protein, 12 g carbohydrates, 0 g total fat, 0 mg cholesterol, 1 mg sodium

Cranberry-Apple Jelly

Pictured on page 34

This shimmering, rosy jelly, subtly flavored with cranberry and apple juices, looks lovely on a holiday table.

- 2 cups bottled cranberry juice cocktail
- 2 cups bottled unsweetened apple juice
- 1 tablespoon lemon juice
- 1 box (1¾ or 2 oz.) dry pectin
- 4½ cups sugar

In a heavy-bottomed 8- to 10-quart pan, mix cranberry juice cocktail, apple juice, lemon juice, and pectin. Bring to a full rolling boil over high heat, stirring constantly. Quickly add sugar, still stirring. Return to a full rolling boil; then boil, stirring, for 1 minute. (If using a 2-oz. box of pectin, boil for 2 minutes.) Remove from heat and skim off any foam.

Ladle hot jelly into hot, sterilized half-pint jars, leaving ¼-inch headspace. Wipe rims and threads clean; top with hot lids, then firmly screw on bands. Process in boiling water canner for 5 minutes. Or omit processing and ladle jelly into freezer jars or freezer containers, leaving ½-inch headspace; apply lids. Let stand for 12 to 24 hours at room temperature; freeze or refrigerate. Makes about 5 half-pints.

Storage time. *Processed:* Up to 1 year. *Unprocessed:* Up to 1 month in refrigerator; up to 1 year in freezer.

Per tablespoon: 52 calories, 0 g protein, 13 g carbohydrates, 0 g total fat, 0 mg cholesterol, 1 mg sodium

Quick Grape Jelly

Here's a bright grape jelly you can "put up" in a jiffy, at any time of year.

- 3 cups bottled unsweetened grape juice
- ½ cup water
- 1 tablespoon lemon juice
- 1 package (1¾ or 2 oz.) dry pectin
- 3½ cups sugar

In a heavy-bottomed 8- to 10-quart pan, mix grape juice, water, lemon juice, and pectin. Bring to a full rolling boil over high heat, stirring constantly. Quickly add sugar, still stirring. Return to a full rolling boil; then boil, stirring, for 1 minute. (If using a 2-oz. box of pectin, boil for 2 minutes.) Remove from heat and skim off any foam.

Ladle hot jelly into hot, sterilized half-pint jars, leaving ¼-inch headspace. Wipe rims and threads clean; top with hot lids, then firmly screw on bands. Process in boiling water canner for 5 minutes. Or omit

processing and ladle jelly into freezer jars or freezer containers, leaving ½-inch headspace; apply lids. Let stand for 12 to 24 hours at room temperature; then freeze or refrigerate. Makes about 4 half-pints.

Storage time. *Processed:* Up to 1 year. *Unprocessed:* Up to 1 month in refrigerator; up to 1 year in freezer.

Per tablespoon: 51 calories, 0 g protein, 13 g carbohydrates, 0 g total fat, 0 mg cholesterol, 1 mg sodium

Pomegranate Jelly

Pomegranate seeds provide the juice for this sweet-tart red jelly. Submerging the fruit in water makes it quite easy to separate seeds from peel and pulp, but it's still wise to allow extra time for preparation.

- About 10 large pomegranates
- 2 tablespoons lemon juice
- 6 cups sugar
- 1 pouch (3 oz.) liquid pectin

Cut blossom end off each pomegranate and lightly score peel lengthwise, dividing fruit into quarters. Immerse fruit in a bowl of cool water; soak for 5 minutes. Holding fruit under water, break sections apart with your fingers and separate seeds from pulp; seeds will sink, and pulp and peel will float. Skim off pulp and peel; discard. Scoop up seeds, drain in a colander, and let dry on paper towels.

Whirl seeds, 1½ to 2 cups at a time, in a blender or food processor until liquefied. Set a colander in a bowl; line colander with moistened cheesecloth. Pour in purée and let juice drip through cloth. To speed the process, gather edges of cloth with rubber-gloved hands and twist *slowly* (juice tends to squirt) to extract liquid. You need 3½ cups juice *total*.

In a heavy-bottomed 8- to 10-quart pan, mix pomegranate juice, lemon juice, and sugar. Bring to a full rolling boil over medium-high heat, stirring constantly. Stir in pectin all at once. Return to a full rolling boil; then boil, stirring, for 1 minute. Remove from heat and skim off any foam.

Ladle hot jelly into hot, sterilized half-pint jars, leaving ¼-inch headspace. Wipe rims and threads clean; top with hot lids, then firmly screw on bands. Process in boiling water canner for 5 minutes. Or omit processing and ladle jelly into freezer jars or freezer containers, leaving ½-inch headspace; apply lids. Let stand for 12 to 24 hours at room temperature; freeze or refrigerate. Makes about 7 half-pints.

Storage time. *Processed:* Up to 1 year. *Unprocessed:* Up to 1 month in refrigerator; up to 1 year in freezer.

Per tablespoon: 53 calories, 0 g protein, 14 g carbohydrates, 0 g total fat, 0 mg cholesterol, 1 mg sodium

Brighten up your mealtimes with homemade pickles, relishes, and chutneys like these. The bottom shelf of the cupboard holds Quick Dill Pickles (page 61). On countertop are (clockwise from left) Sweet Pickle Sticks (page 64), Bread & Butter Pickles (page 61), Mango-Peach Chutney (page 70), Papaya-Plum Chutney (page 71), and Refrigerator Corn Relish (page 68).

Pickles, Relishes & Chutneys

Piquant pickles, tangy relishes, enticing chutneys

For streamlined pickle making, turn to these easy relishes, chutneys, and pickled vegetables. You'll find that your pickles taste best if left to stand for several weeks after processing—but if you want to sample the results of your efforts a bit sooner, try the quick refrigerator pickles on page 66. They're ready to eat within a day or two after you prepare them. ● *Pickles* are most often made from cucumbers, but other vegetables and fruits are also delicious pickled. We've included a wide variety. ● *Relishes* are piquant blends of vegetables, fruits, spices, and vinegar. They're always welcome at casual meals—as embellishments for hot dogs, hamburgers, or grilled meats—and they're equally appropriate for more formal occasions. Cranberry-Pear Relish and Plum Relish, for example, are just right at your holiday table. ● *Chutneys,* made from fruit, vinegar, and spices, are a type of relish too; the flavor ranges from hot and spicy to mild and tangy. Chutneys are ideal accompaniments for Middle Eastern and Indian entrées, but you'll enjoy them with many other foods as well.

Pickling Fruits & Vegetables

Delicious pickles start with fresh produce. Choose the best fruits and vegetables you can find; then refrigerate them until you're ready to start pickling—preferably within 24 hours after you purchase (or pick) your produce.

Important Ingredients

Cucumbers should be firm, fresh, and unblemished. Use unwaxed young pickling cucumbers: they're smaller and spinier than ordinary garden cucumbers, and make crunchier pickles. Rinse any dirt from cucumbers, then pull off any blossoms that weren't removed by rinsing (the blossoms may contain an enzyme that causes pickles to soften).

Vinegar. To ensure safe pickles, the vinegar you use should always have an acidity of 5 percent; check the label. *Never* use homemade vinegars or those of unknown acidity. And don't boil vinegar solutions longer than necessary; if you do, their preserving properties, and thus the safety of your pickles, may be reduced. Cider and distilled white vinegars are both popular for pickling; cider vinegar is mellower in flavor but gives a darker product.

Water. Use soft water for pickling, since minerals in hard water adversely affect pickle quality. If your tap water isn't soft, buy bottled distilled water.

Salt. If possible, use canning or pickling salt; supermarkets carry canning salt seasonally, alongside the canning supplies. Table salt is an acceptable substitute, though it contains an anticaking additive (sodium silicoaluminate) that may make pickle brine slightly cloudy or leave a harmless precipitate. (Use only *noniodized* table salt, since the iodized type tends to darken pickles.) On the whole, though, most pickles made with table salt are indistinguishable from those put up with canning salt—and some canning salts also contain sodium silicoaluminate (check the label).

Salt is not necessary for the safety of the fresh-pack pickles in this chapter, and you'll even find several reduced-sodium recipes. Keep in mind, though, that cutting down on salt can affect texture and flavor slightly, with softer pickles the most frequent result. *Do not use salt substitutes in pickles.*

Sugar. Use granulated white sugar unless your recipe calls for another sweetener. Brown sugar tends to darken pickles.

Equipment You'll Need

Unless you intend to refrigerate and use your pickles within a short period of time, they must be processed in standard canning jars in a boiling water canner.

To prepare pickled products, use only stainless steel, unchipped enamel, or glass utensils. Copper may turn pickles an unappetizing off-green; iron turns them black. *Never* use galvanized containers; the interaction of acid or salt with zinc may cause the metal to dissolve partially, contaminating your pickles and rendering them inedible.

Step-by-Step Canning for Pickles

1. Read the preceding information on pickling. Check recipe instructions and gather the necessary ingredients. Assemble and prepare equipment and jars, following steps 2 through 4 on page 12.

2. Pickle vegetables and fruits as soon as possible after selecting them. Prepare just one canner load at a time; rinse produce well (don't use detergent). Follow recipe instructions carefully. *For safety's sake, do not alter the proportions of vinegar, vegetables and fruits, or water.*

3. In a large, heavy-bottomed stainless steel or unchipped enamel pan, bring the food to a boil and cook according to recipe instructions. Then remove a jar from the hot water. Stand it upright on a cloth towel; fill with hot food and liquid, leaving recommended headspace. *Avoid overpacking cucumbers and other vegetables;* you must leave space for the packing liquid, since it contains the acid that will make your pickles safe to eat. Gently run a narrow nonmetallic spatula between food and jar sides to release air bubbles; add more liquid, if necessary.

4. Seal and process jars as directed in steps 8 through 12 on page 13, processing jars for the time specified in your recipe. At high altitudes, add an additional minute for each 1,000 feet above sea level.

5. If you choose not to process condiments such as relishes and chutneys, you can ladle them into clean jars or refrigerator containers; rinse jars with hot water before filling them to prevent the hot food from cracking the glass. Before refrigerating filled jars or containers, let them cool completely.

Quick Dill Pickles

Pictured on page 58

Choose the freshest pickling cucumbers you can find: the fresher the cucumbers, the crisper the pickles. If you're watching the salt in your diet, you may want to try our reduced-sodium dills; the pickles may be somewhat softer, with a slightly different flavor.

- 6 **cups cider vinegar (5% acidity)**
- 6 **cups soft tap water or bottled distilled water**
- ½ **cup canning salt or noniodized table salt**
- ½ **cup sugar**
- 9 **small cloves garlic, peeled and halved**
- 6 **fresh dill seed heads (***each* **about 4 inches in diameter), separated into thirds (8 to 12 flowerets** *each***)**
- 2 **tablespoons mustard seeds**
- 6 **pounds pickling cucumbers (***each* **3 to 4 inches long)**

In a 5- to 6-quart stainless steel or unchipped enamel pan, combine vinegar, water, salt, and sugar; bring to a boil over medium-high heat.

Meanwhile, put 3 garlic-clove halves, 2 pieces of dill, and 1 teaspoon mustard seeds into each of 6 prepared, hot wide-mouth quart jars. Pack cucumbers firmly into hot jars, leaving ½-inch headspace. Top each jar with an additional piece of dill. Pour hot vinegar solution over cucumbers, leaving ½-inch headspace. Gently run a narrow nonmetallic spatula between cucumbers and jar sides to release air bubbles. Wipe rims and threads clean; top with hot lids, then firmly screw on bands. Process in boiling water canner for 15 minutes. Or omit processing; let stand for 12 to 24 hours at room temperature, then refrigerate. Makes 6 quarts.

Note: For firmer pickles, process pickles in boiling water canner for 30 minutes in water at 180° to 185°F (rather than in boiling water at 212°F). This process also prevents spoilage, but the water *must* remain within the specified temperature range for the entire 30 minutes. Use a candy or jelly thermometer to make sure the temperature is always at least 180°F; don't let it rise above 185°F, or your pickles may not have the desired firmness. (Do not use this method for other recipes in this book.)

Storage time. *Processed:* Up to 1 year. *Unprocessed:* Up to 1 month in refrigerator.

Per ¼ cup: 11 calories, 0 g protein, 3 g carbohydrates, 0 g total fat, 0 mg cholesterol, 550 mg sodium

Reduced-sodium Quick Dill Pickles

Follow directions for **Quick Dill Pickles**, but reduce salt to 2 tablespoons. Makes 6 quarts.

Per ¼ cup: 11 calories, 0 g protein, 3 g carbohydrates, 0 g total fat, 0 mg cholesterol, 138 mg sodium

Bread & Butter Pickles

Pictured on page 58

A forkful or two of this crisp, sweet-tart cucumber-onion mixture demonstrates why bread and butter pickles are so popular. Our version gets extra color and flavor from red bell pepper strips.

- 4 **pounds pickling cucumbers (***each* **4 to 6 inches long)**
- 1½ **pounds onions, thinly sliced**
- 2 **medium-size red bell peppers, seeded and cut into ¼-inch-wide strips**
- ¼ **cup canning salt or noniodized table salt**
  Ice cubes or crushed ice
- 3 **cups cider vinegar (5% acidity)**
- 3 **cups sugar**
- 2 **tablespoons mustard seeds**
- 1½ **teaspoons celery seeds**
- 1 **teaspoon ground turmeric**

Cut ends from cucumbers; then cut cucumbers into ¼-inch-thick slices. Place in a deep stainless steel, glass, or unchipped enamel bowl; mix in onions, bell peppers, and salt. Top with a 2- to 3-inch layer of ice cubes or crushed ice. Let stand for 3 hours, replenishing ice as needed.

In a heavy-bottomed 8- to 10-quart stainless steel or unchipped enamel pan, mix vinegar, sugar, mustard seeds, celery seeds, and turmeric. Bring to a boil over high heat. Drain and rinse vegetable mixture; add to hot vinegar solution and return to a boil. Pack hot into prepared, hot wide-mouth pint jars, leaving ½-inch headspace. Gently run a narrow nonmetallic spatula between pickles and jar sides to release air bubbles. Wipe rims and threads clean; top with hot lids, then firmly screw on bands. Process in boiling water canner for 10 minutes. Or omit processing; let stand for 12 to 24 hours at room temperature, then refrigerate. Makes about 7 pints.

Storage time. *Processed:* Up to 1 year. *Unprocessed:* Up to 1 month in refrigerator.

Per ¼ cup: 54 calories, 0 g protein, 14 g carbohydrates, 0 g total fat, 0 mg cholesterol, 472 mg sodium

Flavored Vinegars

Pictured on facing page

*I*t's easy to make your own flavored vinegars. Simply put fresh herbs and spices (or petals of edible flowers) in a decorative bottle or jar, then fill with wine vinegar and cork or cover tightly.

After the vinegar has mellowed in a cool, dark place for a time (usually about 3 weeks), it's ready to use or to give as a gift. Try it as a flavorful pick-me-up for salads, soups, or vegetables; or sprinkle it on cooked meat or seafood. Rose Petal Vinegar, infused with the fragrance of roses, is a lovely addition to fresh fruit salads.

Whether you keep the vinegar yourself or give it away, identify the flavor with a tag or label. Once opened, any of these vinegars should be stored in a cool, dark place and used within 4 months.

Herb Vinegar

- 2 to 4 rosemary sprigs (*each* about 5 inches long)
- 2 thyme sprigs (optional)
- 1 teaspoon whole black peppercorns
  White wine vinegar

Poke rosemary and, if desired, thyme sprigs into a 3½-cup bottle. Add peppercorns, then fill bottle with vinegar. Cork bottle and let stand in a cool, dark place for 3 weeks to develop flavor. Makes about 3½ cups.

Storage time. Up to 4 months.

Per tablespoon: 2 calories, 0 g protein, 1 g carbohydrates, 0 g total fat, 0 mg cholesterol, 0 mg sodium

Garlic–Green Onion Vinegar

Follow directions for **Herb Vinegar,** but substitute 4 cloves **garlic** (impale on a thin bamboo skewer, if desired) and 2 **green onions** (root ends and tops trimmed) for rosemary, thyme, and peppercorns. Makes about 3½ cups.

Per tablespoon: 3 calories, 0 g protein, 1 g carbohydrates, 0 g total fat, 0 mg cholesterol, 0 mg sodium

Basil-Oregano-Peppercorn Vinegar

Follow directions for **Herb Vinegar,** but substitute 2 **basil sprigs** and 4 **oregano sprigs** (*each* about 5 inches long) for rosemary and thyme. Substitute **red wine vinegar** for white wine vinegar, if desired. Makes about 3½ cups.

Per tablespoon: 2 calories, 0 g protein, 1 g carbohydrates, 0 g total fat, 0 mg cholesterol, 0 mg sodium

Spicy Chile Vinegar

Follow directions for **Herb Vinegar,** but substitute 4 **dry bay leaves,** 6 **small dried hot red chiles,** and 4 large cloves **garlic** (impale on a thin bamboo skewer, if desired) for rosemary, thyme, and peppercorns. Makes about 3½ cups.

Per tablespoon: 3 calories, 0 g protein, 1 g carbohydrates, 0 g total fat, 0 mg cholesterol, 0 mg sodium

Rose Petal Vinegar

- 2 cups lightly packed fresh rose petals, rinsed and drained (make sure the blossoms you use have never been sprayed with a pesticide)
- 3 cups white wine vinegar

Place rose petals in a wide-mouth quart jar with a tight-fitting lid. Add vinegar. Cover and let stand at room temperature until next day. Uncover and push petals down into vinegar; cover and let stand until petals are bleached and vinegar tastes of roses (about 3 more days). Strain, discarding petals; pour vinegar into a clean bottle. Cork bottle and store in a cool, dark place. Makes about 3 cups.

Storage time. Up to 4 months.

Per tablespoon: 2 calories, 0 g protein, 1 g carbohydrates, 0 g total fat, 0 mg cholesterol, 0 mg sodium

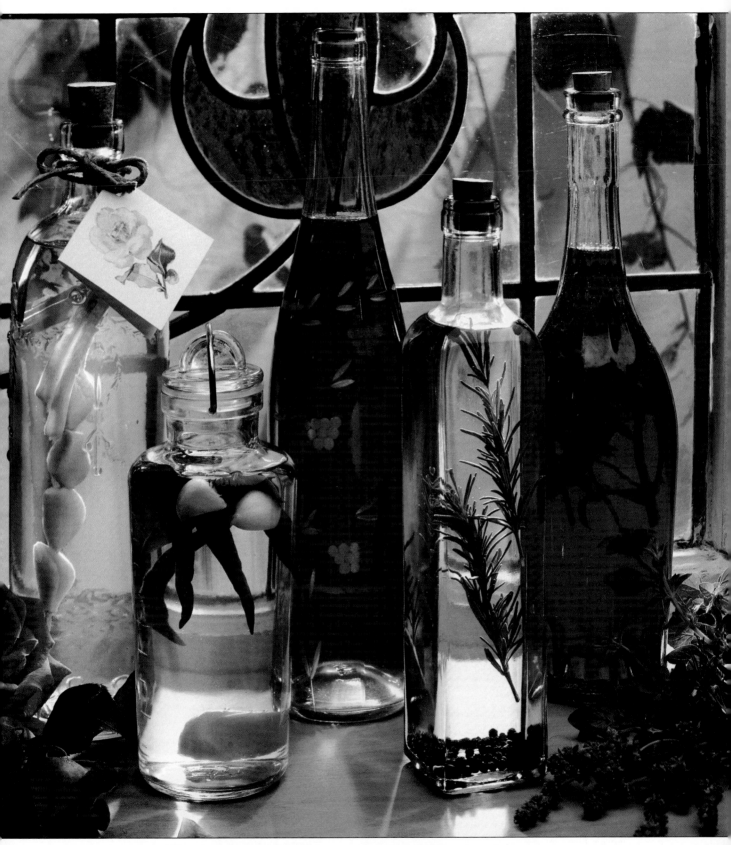

The gourmets on your gift list are sure to enjoy a bottle or two of flavored vinegar. Shown here are (left to right) Garlic-Green Onion Vinegar, Spicy Chile Vinegar, Rose Petal Vinegar, Herb Vinegar, and Basil-Oregano-Peppercorn Vinegar. The recipes are on the facing page.

Sweet Pickle Sticks

Pictured on page 58

Crisp, with a sweet-tart flavor, these pickle sticks perk up sandwich plates and give lunchboxes a lift.

- 4 **pounds pickling cucumbers** (*each* 3 to 4 inches long)
- 4 **cups cider vinegar (5% acidity)**
- 3 **cups sugar**
- 2 **tablespoons canning salt or noniodized table salt**
- 2 **teaspoons ground turmeric**
- 1 **teaspoon mustard seeds**

Cut ends from cucumbers; cut cucumbers lengthwise into quarters. Place cucumbers in a large stainless steel, glass, or unchipped enamel bowl; pour boiling water over them to cover. Let stand for 2 hours.

In a medium-size stainless steel or unchipped enamel pan, mix vinegar, sugar, salt, turmeric, and mustard seeds. Bring to a boil over high heat. Drain cucumber quarters and firmly pack them vertically into prepared, hot wide-mouth pint jars, leaving ½-inch headspace. Pour hot vinegar solution over cucumbers, leaving ½-inch headspace. Gently run a narrow nonmetallic spatula between cucumbers and jar sides to release air bubbles. Wipe rims and threads clean; top with hot lids, then firmly screw on bands. Process in boiling water canner for 10 minutes. Or omit processing; let stand for 12 to 24 hours at room temperature, then refrigerate. Makes about 5 pints.

Storage time. *Processed:* Up to 1 year. *Unprocessed:* Up to 1 month in refrigerator.

Per ¼ cup: 62 calories, 0 g protein, 17 g carbohydrates, 0 g total fat, 0 mg cholesterol, 330 mg sodium

Reduced-sodium Sweet Pickle Chips

Pictured on page 58

Whether or not you're cutting down on sodium, you'll enjoy these good-tasting pickles.

- 4 **pounds pickling cucumbers** (*each* 3 to 5 inches long)
- 4 **cups cider vinegar (5% acidity)**
- ½ **cup sugar**
- 1 **tablespoon canning salt or noniodized table salt**
- 1 **tablespoon mustard seeds**
  Canning Syrup (recipe follows)

Cut ends from cucumbers; then cut cucumbers into ¼-inch-thick slices. In a heavy-bottomed 8- to 10-quart stainless steel or unchipped enamel pan, mix vinegar, sugar, salt, and mustard seeds. Stir in cucumbers; cover and bring to a boil over medium-high heat. Reduce heat and simmer, covered, stirring occasionally, until cucumbers change from bright to dull green in color (about 5 minutes). Drain well.

While cucumbers are simmering, prepare Canning Syrup. When cucumbers are done, pack into prepared, hot wide-mouth pint jars, leaving ½-inch headspace. Pour hot syrup over cucumbers, leaving ½-inch headspace. Gently run a narrow nonmetallic spatula between cucumbers and jar sides to release air bubbles. Wipe rims and threads clean; top with hot lids, then firmly screw on bands. Process in boiling water canner for 10 minutes. Or omit processing; let stand for 12 to 24 hours at room temperature, then refrigerate. Makes about 5 pints.

Canning Syrup. In a medium-size pan, combine 3¼ cups **sugar**, 2 cups **cider vinegar (5% acidity)**, 1 tablespoon **whole allspice**, 2 teaspoons **celery seeds**, and 1 teaspoon **ground turmeric**. Bring to a boil over high heat.

Storage time. *Processed:* Up to 1 year. *Unprocessed:* Up to 1 month in refrigerator.

Per ¼ cup: 73 calories, 0 g protein, 19 g carbohydrates, 0 g total fat, 0 mg cholesterol, 23 mg sodium

Giardiniera

Pictured on pages 50 and 58

Great for the appetizer tray, these brightly colored mixed vegetable pickles are much like those you'll find in supermarkets and fancy food stores. If you enjoy spicy flavors, be sure to include the jalapeños (you can even use up to half a pound, if you like).

- 1 **pound baby carrots (or regular carrots)**
- 1 **pound celery**
- 1 **pound cauliflower flowerets**
- 1 **pound white boiling onions** (*each* ½ to 1 inch in diameter)
- 1 **pound** *each* **red and green bell peppers**
- ¼ **pound fresh jalapeño chiles (optional)**
- 6 **cloves garlic**
- 5 **cups distilled white vinegar (5% acidity)**
- 1½ **cups soft tap water or bottled distilled water**
- 1½ **cups sugar**
- ¼ **cup mustard seeds**
- 1 **tablespoon canning salt or noniodized table salt**

If using baby carrots, peel and cut in half lengthwise; then cut crosswise into 1½-inch-long pieces. If using regular carrots, peel and cut into 1½-inch-long julienne strips. Remove strings from celery; cut stalks in half lengthwise, then cut crosswise into 1½-inch-long pieces. Break cauliflower flowerets into 1½-inch pieces. Peel onions. Stem and seed bell peppers; then cut into ½- by 2-inch strips. If using chiles, leave whole; make 2 small slits in each one. Peel garlic and cut each clove in half.

In a heavy-bottomed 8- to 10-quart stainless steel or unchipped enamel pan, mix vinegar, water, sugar, mustard seeds, and salt. Bring to a boil, over high heat; then boil for 3 minutes. Add all vegetables except garlic. Bring to a boil (this will take about 10 minutes) stirring occasionally. Reduce heat to medium and cook, uncovered, pushing vegetables down into liquid occasionally, until vegetables are almost tender when pierced (about 10 minutes). Remove from heat.

Place 2 pieces of garlic in each prepared, hot wide-mouth pint jar. With a slotted spoon, remove vegetables from hot vinegar solution and distribute among jars, leaving ½-inch headspace. Pour remaining vinegar solution over vegetables in jars, leaving ½-inch headspace. Gently run a narrow nonmetallic spatula between vegetables and jar sides to release air bubbles. Wipe rims and threads clean; top with hot lids, then firmly screw on bands. Process in boiling water canner for 15 minutes. Or omit processing; let stand for 12 to 24 hours at room temperature, then refrigerate. Makes 6 pints.

Storage time. *Processed:* Up to 1 year. *Unprocessed:* Up to 1 month in refrigerator.

Per ¼ cup: 48 calories, 1 g protein, 11 g carbohydrates, 0 g total fat, 0 mg cholesterol, 152 mg sodium

Pickled Peppers

Pictured on page 58

Make your pickled peppers with sweet bells, hot or mild chiles, or some of each. Choose the color you like best, too: red, yellow, green, or a combination. If you use hot chiles, wear rubber gloves during preparation, since the oils can burn your skin.

- 6 **pounds bell peppers and/or fresh chiles**
- 4 **cups distilled white vinegar (5% acidity)**
- 4 **cups soft tap water or bottled distilled water**
- 1 **tablespoon canning salt or noniodized table salt**

Stem and seed bell peppers or large chiles; cut into 1-inch-wide strips. Leave smaller chiles whole; cut 2 small slits in each. In a heavy-bottomed 8- to 10-quart stainless steel or unchipped enamel pan, mix vinegar, water, and salt. Bring to a boil over high heat; add peppers, return to a boil, and remove from heat.

Pack hot peppers firmly into prepared, hot wide-mouth pint jars, leaving ½-inch headspace. Cover with hot vinegar solution, leaving ½-inch headspace. Gently run a narrow nonmetallic spatula between

peppers and jar sides to release air bubbles. Wipe rims and threads clean; top with hot lids, then firmly screw on bands. Process in boiling water canner for 10 minutes. Or omit processing; let stand for 12 to 24 hours at room temperature, then refrigerate. Makes about 7 pints.

Storage time. *Processed:* Up to 1 year. *Unprocessed:* Up to 1 month in refrigerator.

Per ¼ cup: 13 calories, 0 g protein, 3 g carbohydrates, 0 g total fat, 0 mg cholesterol, 119 mg sodium

Zucchini Pickles

What do you do with excess zucchini? There's zucchini bread, zucchini quiche, stuffed zucchini—and these easy pickles. They taste much like bread and butter pickles, and they're every bit as good with sandwiches, alongside salads, and as a snack.

- 5 **pounds medium-size zucchini, cut into ¼-inch-thick slices**
- 2 **pounds mild white onions, thinly sliced**
- ¼ **cup canning salt or noniodized table salt**
  Ice water
- 4 **cups cider vinegar (5% acidity)**
- 2 **cups sugar**
- 2 **tablespoons mustard seeds**
- 1 **tablespoon *each* celery seeds and ground turmeric**
- 2 **teaspoons ground ginger**
- 3 **cloves garlic, minced or pressed**

Place zucchini, onions, and salt in a large stainless steel, glass, or unchipped enamel bowl; cover with ice water and let stand for 1 to 2 hours. Drain, rinse well, and drain again.

In a heavy-bottomed 10- to 12-quart stainless steel or unchipped enamel pan, mix vinegar, sugar, mustard seeds, celery seeds, turmeric, ginger, and garlic. Bring to a boil over high heat, stirring to dissolve sugar; boil for 2 to 3 minutes. Stir in zucchini mixture, return to a boil, and boil for 2 more minutes.

Pack hot zucchini mixture into prepared, hot wide-mouth pint jars, leaving ½-inch headspace. Gently run a narrow nonmetallic spatula between pickles and jar sides to release air bubbles. Wipe rims and threads clean; top with hot lids, then firmly screw on bands. Process in boiling water canner for 10 minutes. Or omit processing; let stand for 12 to 24 hours at room temperature, then refrigerate. Makes about 8 pints.

Storage time. *Processed:* Up to 1 year. *Unprocessed:* Up to 1 month in refrigerator.

Per ¼ cup: 38 calories, 1 g protein, 9 g carbohydrates, 0 g total fat, 0 mg cholesterol, 414 mg sodium

No-fuss Pickling

When you're craving homemade pickles but don't have time for canning, try one of these recipes. The first is for freezer pickles; the other two can be quickly put together and stored in the refrigerator.

Sweet Freezer Chips

2½	pounds pickling or regular cucumbers
1	medium-size mild white onion, thinly sliced
2	tablespoons salt
8	cups ice cubes
4	cups sugar
2	cups cider vinegar (5% acidity)

Cut ends from cucumbers; then cut cucumbers into ⅛-inch-thick slices. Mix cucumbers, onion, and salt in a large bowl; cover mixture with ice cubes and refrigerate for 2 to 3 hours.

Drain off water and discard unmelted ice cubes; do not rinse vegetables. Pack cucumber and onion slices into 3 pint freezer jars or freezer containers, leaving ½-inch headspace.

In a 2-quart pan, mix sugar and vinegar; bring to a boil, stirring until sugar is dissolved. Pour just enough hot syrup over cucumbers to cover. Apply lids; let cool. To allow flavor to develop, freeze pickles for at least 1 week before serving. To thaw, let stand in refrigerator for at least 8 hours. Makes 3 pints.

Storage time: Up to 6 months in freezer.

Per ¼ cup: 138 calories, 0 g protein, 36 g carbohydrates, 0 g total fat, 0 mg cholesterol, 551 mg sodium

Pickled Maui Onions

2	medium-size Maui or other mild white onions
1½	cups water
¾	cup distilled white vinegar (5% acidity)
⅓	cup sugar
3	cloves garlic, pressed or minced
2	small dried hot red chiles
1	tablespoon salt

Cut onions into 1-inch chunks; separate chunks into layers. Place onions in a wide-mouth quart (or slightly larger) jar. In a 1- to 2-quart pan, mix water, vinegar, sugar, garlic, chiles, and salt; bring to a boil. Pour over onions; apply a leakproof lid to jar. Let onions cool. To allow flavor to develop, refrigerate onions for at least 3 days before serving, turning jar over occasionally. To serve, pour into a bowl; provide wooden picks for spearing onion pieces. Makes about 4 cups.

Storage time. Up to 1 month in refrigerator.

Per ¼ cup: 32 calories, 1 g protein, 8 g carbohydrates, 0 g total fat, 0 mg cholesterol, 415 mg sodium

Quick Refrigerator Cucumber Pickles

8	or 9 pickling cucumbers (*each* 3 to 4 inches long), 3 large regular cucumbers, or 2 long thin-skinned (English or Armenian) cucumbers
1	large red bell pepper, seeded and cut into ½-inch-wide strips
1	medium-size onion, thinly sliced
1	tablespoon salt
2	teaspoons dill seeds
¾	cup sugar
½	cup white wine vinegar (5% acidity)

Cut ends from cucumbers, then cut cucumbers into 1/16-inch-thick slices; you should have about 6 cups. In a large bowl, combine cucumbers, bell pepper, and onion. Sprinkle with salt and dill seeds; then stir well. Let stand for 1 to 2 hours, stirring occasionally.

In a small bowl, mix sugar and vinegar, stirring until sugar is dissolved; pour vinegar mixture over vegetables and mix gently. Ladle vegetable mixture into 4 pint canning jars; apply lids. To allow flavor to develop, refrigerate for at least 24 hours before serving. Makes 4 pints.

Storage time. Up to 3 weeks in refrigerator.

Per ¼ cup: 24 calories, 0 g protein, 6 g carbohydrates, 0 g total fat, 0 mg cholesterol, 207 mg sodium

Pickle-packed Beets

Delicious in salads or on their own as a side dish, these beet and onion pickles make a festive gift.

- **6 to 8 medium-size beets (about 2 lbs. *total*)**
- **1 medium-size mild white onion, thinly sliced**
- **1 cup distilled white vinegar (5% acidity)**
- **⅔ cup sugar**
- **1 clove garlic, minced or pressed (optional)**

Scrub beets well, but do not peel; leave roots, 1 inch of stems, and skins intact to prevent "bleeding" during cooking. Place beets in a 5-quart pan; add water to cover. Bring to a boil over high heat; cover and boil until beets are tender throughout when pierced (20 to 45 minutes). Drain; let cool. Holding beets under running water, trim off roots and stems and slip off skins. Cut beets into ¼-inch-thick slices.

Firmly pack beet and onion slices in alternating layers into wide-mouth pint canning jars. In a small bowl, mix vinegar, sugar, and garlic (if used); stir until sugar is dissolved, then pour over beets and onion to fill jars. Cover jars tightly and shake well. To allow flavor to develop, refrigerate pickles for at least 1 day before serving. Makes about 2 pints.

Storage time. Up to 3 weeks in refrigerator.

Per ¼ cup: 54 calories, 1 g protein, 14 g carbohydrates, 0 g total fat, 0 mg cholesterol, 29 mg sodium

Spiced Apple Rings

A jar of sweet, spicy apple rings is a wonderful, inexpensive gift. You'll find that the cheery red color brightens up meals at any time of year.

- **6 cups sugar**
- **1⅔ cups cider vinegar (5% acidity)**
- **1 teaspoon red food coloring (optional)**
- **4 cinnamon sticks (*each* about 3 inches long)**
- **2 teaspoons whole cloves**
- **4 pounds (about 12 medium-size) firm-ripe Golden Delicious apples, peeled and cored**

In a heavy-bottomed 8- to 10-quart stainless steel or unchipped enamel pan, mix sugar, vinegar, food coloring (if used), cinnamon sticks, and cloves. Bring to a boil over medium-high heat; then reduce heat and simmer, uncovered, stirring often, for 10 minutes.

Cut apples crosswise into ⅓-inch-thick rings. Add to simmering syrup and cook, uncovered, turning occasionally, until apples are barely tender when pierced and are just turning translucent around edges (6 to 8 minutes).

With a fork, lift apples from syrup; evenly fill prepared, hot wide-mouth pint jars, leaving ½-inch headspace. Leaving spices in pan, ladle hot syrup into jars, leaving ½-inch headspace. Gently run a narrow nonmetallic spatula between apples and jar sides to release air bubbles. Wipe rims and threads clean; top with hot lids, then firmly screw on bands. Process in boiling water canner for 10 minutes. Or omit processing; let stand for 12 to 24 hours at room temperature, then refrigerate. Makes about 4 pints.

Storage time. *Processed:* Up to 1 year. *Unprocessed:* Up to 1 month in refrigerator.

Per ¼ cup: 175 calories, 0 g protein, 45 g carbohydrates, 0 g total fat, 0 mg cholesterol, 1 mg sodium

Spiced Pineapple Spears

If you're looking for new ways to enjoy fresh pineapple, try these unusual, spicy spears.

- **3 medium-size pineapples (3 to 3½ lbs. *each*)**
- **1½ cups distilled white vinegar (5% acidity)**
- **2 cups sugar**
- **2 tablespoons whole cloves**
- **1 tablespoon whole cardamom, lightly crushed**
- **1 teaspoon whole allspice**
- **3 cinnamon sticks (*each* about 3 inches long)**
- **1 small dried hot red chile, seeded**

Peel and core pineapples, reserving as much juice as possible. Cut pineapples into 3-inch-long, ½-inch-thick spears. Set aside. Measure reserved juice; add enough water to make 1½ cups liquid. Pour liquid into a heavy-bottomed 8- to 10-quart stainless steel or unchipped enamel pan; stir in vinegar, sugar, cloves, cardamom, allspice, cinnamon sticks, and chile. Bring to a boil over high heat; reduce heat, cover, and simmer for 15 minutes. Add half the pineapple spears; cover and simmer for 5 more minutes.

With a fork, lift spears from syrup and fill 2 prepared, hot wide-mouth pint jars, leaving ½-inch headspace. Leaving spices in pan, ladle hot syrup into jars, leaving ½-inch headspace. Gently run a narrow nonmetallic spatula between pineapple and jar sides to release air bubbles. Wipe rims and threads clean; top with hot lids, then firmly screw on bands.

Add remaining spears to syrup. Cover; simmer for 5 minutes. Fill 2 more jars as directed above.

Process in boiling water canner for 10 minutes. Or omit processing; let stand for 12 to 24 hours at room temperature, then refrigerate. Makes 4 pints.

Storage time. *Processed:* Up to 1 year. *Unprocessed:* Up to 1 month in refrigerator.

Per ¼ cup: 88 calories, 0 g protein, 23 g carbohydrates, 0 g total fat, 0 mg cholesterol, 2 mg sodium

Refrigerator Corn Relish

Pictured on page 58

A quick refrigerator version of an old-fashioned favorite, this colorful relish is a popular appetizer at picnics and barbecues—and a favorite accompaniment for frankfurters, hamburgers, and other meats.

- 1¼ **cups distilled white vinegar (5% acidity)**
- ¾ **cup sugar**
- 2½ **teaspoons salt**
- 1¼ **teaspoons celery seeds**
- ¾ **teaspoon mustard seeds**
- ½ **teaspoon liquid hot pepper seasoning**
- 8 **cups fresh corn kernels (cut from about 10 large ears of corn)**
- 1 *each* **small green and red bell pepper, seeded and chopped**
- 3 **green onions, thinly sliced**

In a heavy-bottomed 8- to 10-quart stainless steel or unchipped enamel pan, mix vinegar, sugar, salt, celery seeds, mustard seeds, hot pepper seasoning, and corn. Bring to a simmer over medium heat; simmer, uncovered, for 5 minutes. Remove from heat and let cool.

Stir bell peppers and onions into corn mixture. Pack into pint jars; cover tightly and refrigerate. Makes about 4 pints.

Storage time. Up to 1 month in refrigerator.

Per ¼ cup: 54 calories, 1 g protein, 13 g carbohydrates, 0 g total fat, 0 mg cholesterol, 180 mg sodium

Pickled Jicama

Enjoy crisp jicama in a piquant refrigerator pickle accented with cilantro, red pepper, dill, and mustard seeds.

- 2 **pounds jicama, peeled and cut into 5-inch-long, ½-inch-thick sticks**
- 4 **teaspoons canning salt or noniodized table salt**
- 1½ **cups distilled white vinegar (5% acidity)**
- ½ **cup finely chopped onion**
- ⅓ **cup sugar**
- 1 **teaspoon** *each* **mustard seeds and dry dill weed**
- ½ **teaspoon crushed red pepper flakes**
- 6 **cilantro sprigs**

Place jicama in a stainless steel, glass, or unchipped enamel bowl. Sprinkle with 1 tablespoon of the salt, then add enough water to cover. Stir until salt is dissolved, then let stand for 1 to 2 hours. Drain.

In a 2- to 3-quart stainless steel or unchipped enamel pan, mix vinegar, remaining 1 teaspoon salt, onion, and sugar. Bring to a boil over high heat; then boil for 1 minute.

Meanwhile, pack jicama sticks vertically into 2 hot wide-mouth pint jars. Place half *each* of the mustard seeds, dill weed, red pepper flakes, and cilantro in each jar. Pour hot vinegar solution into jars to cover jicama. Let cool, then cover jars tightly. To allow flavor to develop, refrigerate pickles for at least 1 day before serving. Makes 2 pints.

Storage time. Up to 1 month in refrigerator.

Per ¼ cup: 44 calories, 1 g protein, 10 g carbohydrates, 0 g total fat, 0 mg cholesterol, 554 mg sodium

Cranberry-Pear Relish

Add sparkle to your holidays with a zesty cranberry-pear relish that goes beautifully with turkey, baked ham, or roast pork (it's good in sandwiches, too). You'll want to make another batch as gifts for special friends.

- 3 **pounds pears, peeled, cored, and cut into about 1-inch chunks**
- 6 **cups (about 1½ lbs.) fresh or frozen cranberries**
- 2½ **cups firmly packed brown sugar**
- 1 **cup orange juice**
- ½ **cup cider vinegar (5% acidity)**
- 2 **teaspoons minced fresh ginger**

Coarsely chop pear chunks and cranberries by hand or in a food processor (do not purée). In a heavy-bottomed 8- to 10-quart pan, mix pears, cranberries, sugar, orange juice, vinegar, and ginger. Bring to a boil over medium-high heat, stirring constantly; then reduce heat and simmer, uncovered, stirring often to prevent sticking, until pears are tender to bite and relish is thickened (about 20 minutes).

Ladle hot relish into prepared, hot pint jars, leaving ½-inch headspace. Gently run a narrow nonmetallic spatula between relish and jar sides to release air bubbles. Wipe rims and threads clean; top with hot lids, then firmly screw on bands. Process in boiling water canner for 10 minutes. Or omit processing and ladle into jars or refrigerator containers, leaving ½-inch headspace; apply lids. Let cool, then refrigerate. Makes about 4 pints.

Storage time. *Processed:* Up to 1 year. *Unprocessed:* Up to 3 weeks in refrigerator.

Per ¼ cup: 101 calories, 0 g protein, 26 g carbohydrates, 0 g total fat, 0 mg cholesterol, 5 mg sodium

Plum Relish

Luscious flavor and attractive color make this sweet fruit relish a real standout. Serve it with baked ham, pork chops, grilled or roasted poultry, or curries.

- 2 **medium-size oranges**
- 5 **pounds plums, pitted and finely chopped**
- 3 **cups sugar**
- 1 **cup cider vinegar (5% acidity)**
- 1 **teaspoon ground cinnamon**

Rinse unpeeled oranges and grate off peel (colored part only); set peel aside. Holding fruit over a bowl to catch juice, cut off and discard remaining peel and all white membrane from oranges; coarsely chop fruit, discarding seeds.

In a heavy-bottomed 8- to 10-quart pan, mix grated orange peel, chopped oranges (plus any juice), plums, sugar, vinegar, and cinnamon. Bring to a boil over medium-high heat, stirring constantly; reduce heat and simmer, uncovered, stirring often to prevent sticking, until thickened (about 40 minutes).

Ladle hot relish into prepared, hot pint jars, leaving ½-inch headspace. Gently run a narrow nonmetallic spatula between relish and jar sides to release air bubbles. Wipe rims and threads clean; top with hot lids, then firmly screw on bands. Process in boiling water canner for 10 minutes. Or omit processing and ladle into jars or refrigerator containers, leaving ½-inch headspace; apply lids. Let cool, then refrigerate. Makes about 4 pints.

Storage time. *Processed:* Up to 1 year. *Unprocessed:* Up to 1 month in refrigerator.

Per ¼ cup: 116 calories, 1 g protein, 29 g carbohydrates, 0 g total fat, 0 mg cholesterol, 0 mg sodium

Red Pepper Relish

Pictured on page 58

This delicious blend of sweet red peppers and onions is a delightful gift—and a fantastic accompaniment to any grilled meat or poultry.

- 6 **pounds red bell peppers, seeded and cut into 1-inch squares**
- 3 **pounds onions, cut into 1-inch chunks**
- 4 **cups distilled white vinegar (5% acidity)**
- 3 **cups sugar**
- 2 **tablespoons canning salt or noniodized table salt**
- 1 **tablespoon mustard seeds**

Coarsely chop bell peppers and onions, a portion at a time, in a food processor; or put through a food chopper with a medium blade. Pour chopped vegetables into a heavy-bottomed 8- to 10-quart stainless steel or unchipped enamel pan. Mix in vinegar, sugar, salt, and mustard seeds. Bring to a boil over medium-high heat, stirring occasionally. Reduce heat to medium-low; boil gently, uncovered, stirring often to prevent sticking, until relish is thickened but still juicy (about 50 minutes).

Ladle hot relish into prepared, hot pint jars, leaving ½-inch headspace. Gently run a narrow nonmetallic spatula between relish and jar sides to release air bubbles. Wipe rims and threads clean; top with hot lids, then firmly screw on bands. Process in boiling water canner for 15 minutes. Or omit processing and ladle into jars or refrigerator containers, leaving ½-inch headspace; apply lids. Let cool, then refrigerate. Makes about 7 pints.

Storage time. *Processed:* Up to 1 year. *Unprocessed:* Up to 1 month in refrigerator.

Per ¼ cup: 63 calories, 1 g protein, 16 g carbohydrates, 0 g total fat, 0 mg cholesterol, 237 mg sodium

Papaya-Tomatillo Relish

Sweet papayas and tart tomatillos combine in this unique fruit relish. Try it hot or cold, with grilled lamb, pork chops, hamburgers, stews, or curries.

- 1 **tablespoon salad oil**
- ½ **small onion, thinly sliced**
- ¼ **teaspoon ground cinnamon**
- ⅛ **teaspoon ground red pepper (cayenne)**
- 1 **pound fresh tomatillos, husked, cored, and finely chopped**
- 1 **small ripe papaya (about ¾ lb.), peeled, seeded, and cut into ¼-inch chunks**
- ⅓ **cup cider vinegar (5% acidity)**
- ¼ **cup *each* firmly packed brown sugar and dried currants**

Heat oil in a wide frying pan over medium heat. Add onion, cinnamon, and red pepper; cook, stirring often, until onion is soft (about 7 minutes). Add tomatillos, papaya, vinegar, sugar, and currants. Bring to a boil over high heat; then boil, uncovered, stirring occasionally, until liquid has evaporated. Pack into hot half-pint jars or into a refrigerator container; cover tightly and refrigerate. Makes about 2 half-pints.

Storage time. Up to 3 weeks in refrigerator.

Per ¼ cup: 81 calories, 1 g protein, 16 g carbohydrates, 2 g total fat, 0 mg cholesterol, 3 mg sodium

Whole Cranberry–Orange Sauce

Traditional, tart, and luscious, this whole-berry cranberry sauce is accented with orange juice and sweetened with brown sugar.

- **4 cups (about 1 lb.) fresh or frozen cranberries**
- **2 cups firmly packed brown sugar**
- **3 tablespoons frozen orange juice concentrate, thawed**
- **1¼ cups water**

In a heavy-bottomed 6- to 8-quart pan, mix cranberries, sugar, orange juice concentrate, and water. Bring to a boil over high heat, stirring occasionally; then boil, uncovered, stirring occasionally, until almost all berries have split open (about 5 minutes).

Ladle hot sauce into prepared, hot half-pint or pint jars, leaving ½-inch headspace. Gently run a narrow nonmetallic spatula between sauce and jar sides to release air bubbles. Wipe rims and threads clean; top with hot lids, then firmly screw on bands. Process in boiling water canner for 10 minutes. Or omit processing and ladle into jars or refrigerator containers, leaving ½-inch headspace; apply lids. Let cool, then refrigerate. Makes about 4 half-pints or 2 pints.

Storage time. *Processed:* Up to 1 year. *Unprocessed:* Up to 3 weeks in refrigerator.

Per ¼ cup: 122 calories, 0 g protein, 31 g carbohydrates, 0 g total fat, 0 mg cholesterol, 9 mg sodium

Pear-Ginger Chutney

You'll enjoy this easy-to-make chutney with roast chicken or pork—and with curry, of course.

- **1 small lemon**
- **1½ cups *each* sugar and cider vinegar (5% acidity)**
- **½ cup *each* chopped onion and dried currants**
- **1 clove garlic, minced or pressed**
- **3 tablespoons minced fresh ginger**
- **½ teaspoon ground allspice**
- **5 pounds (about 10 large) firm-ripe Bartlett pears, peeled, cored, and cut into ¾-inch chunks**

Rinse unpeeled lemon, then thinly slice; discard seeds. Place lemon slices in a heavy-bottomed 8- to 10-quart stainless steel or unchipped enamel pan and mix in sugar, vinegar, onion, currants, garlic, ginger, and allspice. Bring to a boil over medium-high heat, stirring occasionally. Reduce heat to medium-low and simmer, uncovered, stirring often, until a thin

syrup forms (about 15 minutes). Add pears; continue to cook, uncovered, stirring occasionally, until chutney is thickened (about 1¼ hours).

Ladle hot chutney into prepared, hot pint jars, leaving ½-inch headspace. Gently run a narrow nonmetallic spatula between chutney and jar sides to release air bubbles. Wipe rims and threads clean; top with hot lids, then firmly screw on bands. Process in boiling water canner for 15 minutes. Or omit processing and ladle into jars or refrigerator containers, leaving ½-inch headspace; apply lids. Let cool, then refrigerate. Makes about 3 pints.

Storage time. *Processed:* Up to 1 year. *Unprocessed:* Up to 3 weeks in refrigerator.

Per ¼ cup: 113 calories, 1 g protein, 30 g carbohydrates, 1 g total fat, 0 mg cholesterol, 1 mg sodium

Mango-Peach Chutney

Pictured on page 58

Mangoes make a delicious chutney. To reduce the cost, just extend the mangoes with fresh peaches in season.

- **1 lime**
- **1½ cups *each* sugar and distilled white vinegar (5% acidity)**
- **½ cup chopped onion**
- **1 clove garlic, minced or pressed**
- **1½ teaspoons ground cinnamon**
- **1 teaspoon salt**
- **½ teaspoon *each* ground cloves and allspice**
- **⅛ to ¼ teaspoon ground red pepper (cayenne)**
- **½ cup raisins**
- **3 large ripe mangoes (about 2½ lbs. *total*)**
- **2 pounds peaches**

Rinse unpeeled lime, then thinly slice; discard seeds. Place lime slices in a heavy-bottomed 8- to 10-quart pan; mix in sugar, vinegar, onion, garlic, cinnamon, salt, cloves, allspice, red pepper, and raisins. Bring to a boil over high heat; then reduce heat to medium-low and simmer, uncovered, stirring occasionally to prevent sticking, until onion is limp and syrup is slightly thickened (about 15 minutes).

Meanwhile, peel mangoes; slice fruit off pits and cut into 1½-inch pieces (you should have about 3½ cups). Peel, pit, and slice peaches. Add mangoes and peaches to syrup and simmer, uncovered, stirring often to prevent sticking, until peaches are tender when pierced and chutney is thickened (about 30 minutes).

Ladle hot chutney into prepared, hot pint jars, leaving ½-inch headspace. Gently run a narrow nonmetallic spatula between chutney and jar sides to release air bubbles. Wipe rims and threads clean; top with hot lids, then firmly screw on bands. Process in boiling water canner for 15 minutes. Or omit processing and ladle into jars or refrigerator containers, leaving ½-inch headspace; apply lids. Let cool, then refrigerate. Makes about 3 pints.

Storage time. *Processed:* Up to 1 year. *Unprocessed:* Up to 3 weeks in refrigerator.

Per ¼ cup: 96 calories, 0 g protein, 25 g carbohydrates, 0 g total fat, 0 mg cholesterol, 93 mg sodium

Apricot Chutney

Pictured on page 50

This medium-hot chutney is superb with curries, lamb, and cheese. For a milder version, remove the seeds from the chiles before crushing them (or use fewer chiles than the recipe specifies).

- 1 **small lime**
- 1 **cup** *each* **granulated sugar, firmly packed brown sugar, dried currants, and cider vinegar (5% acidity)**
- 1 **tablespoon minced fresh ginger or ¾ teaspoon ground ginger**
- 1 **teaspoon** *each* **dry mustard and ground allspice**
- ¼ **teaspoon salt**
  Dash of ground cloves
- 3 **small dried hot red chiles, crushed**
- ½ **cup chopped onion**
- 1 **small clove garlic, minced or pressed**
- 4 **pounds apricots, pitted and quartered**

Rinse unpeeled lime; then chop, discarding seeds. Place chopped lime in a heavy-bottomed 8- to 10-quart pan; mix in granulated sugar, brown sugar, currants, vinegar, ginger, mustard, allspice, salt, cloves, chiles, onion, and garlic. Bring to a boil over medium-high heat. Stir in apricots; return to a boil, stirring constantly. Reduce heat and simmer, uncovered, stirring often to prevent sticking, until slightly thickened (about 45 minutes).

Ladle hot chutney into prepared, hot pint jars, leaving ½-inch headspace. Gently run a narrow nonmetallic spatula between chutney and jar sides to release air bubbles. Wipe rims and threads clean; top with hot lids, then firmly screw on bands. Process in boiling water canner for 15 minutes. Or omit processing and ladle into jars or refrigerator containers, leaving ½-inch headspace; apply lids. Let cool, then refrigerate. Makes about 4 pints.

Storage time. *Processed:* Up to 1 year. *Unprocessed:* Up to 1 month in refrigerator.

Per ¼ cup: 93 calories, 1 g protein, 23 g carbohydrates, 0 g total fat, 0 mg cholesterol, 3 mg sodium

Papaya-Plum Chutney

Pictured on page 58

Colorful papayas and red plums combine with raisins and sweet spices in an exotic-tasting chutney you'll enjoy all year round with curries, game, and poultry.

- 1¼ **cups cider vinegar (5% acidity)**
- 1¾ **cups sugar**
- ½ **cup golden raisins**
- 2 **cloves garlic, minced or pressed**
- 3 **tablespoons chopped crystallized ginger**
- 1 **cinnamon stick (about 3 inches long)**
- 1 **teaspoon salt**
- ⅛ **to ¼ teaspoon ground red pepper (cayenne)**
- 2 **medium-size ripe papayas (about 1 lb.** *each***)**
- 2 **pounds red plums**

In a heavy-bottomed 8- to 10-quart pan, mix vinegar, sugar, raisins, garlic, ginger, cinnamon stick, salt, and red pepper. Bring to a boil over high heat, stirring often. Reduce heat to medium-low and simmer, uncovered, stirring occasionally to prevent sticking, until syrup is slightly thickened (about 15 minutes).

Peel and halve papayas; scoop out seeds. Cut fruit into ½-inch chunks. Pit and quarter plums. Add papayas and plums to syrup and continue to simmer, uncovered, stirring occasionally, until papaya is tender when pierced and chutney is thickened (about 35 minutes). Discard cinnamon stick.

Ladle hot chutney into prepared, hot pint jars, leaving ½-inch headspace. Gently run a narrow nonmetallic spatula between chutney and jar sides to release air bubbles. Wipe rims and threads clean; top with hot lids, then firmly screw on bands. Process in boiling water canner for 15 minutes. Or omit processing and ladle into jars or refrigerator containers, leaving ½-inch headspace; apply lids. Let cool, then refrigerate. Makes about 3 pints.

Storage time. *Processed:* Up to 1 year. *Unprocessed:* Up to 1 month in refrigerator.

Per ¼ cup: 104 calories, 1 g protein, 27 g carbohydrates, 0 g total fat, 0 mg cholesterol, 94 mg sodium

Questions & Answers

About canning...

Q. Why do jars break during canning?

A. Several explanations are possible. Jars with hairline cracks are likely to break during processing, as are commercial food jars (as opposed to those manufactured expressly for home canning). Breakage may also occur if hot food is placed in a cold jar, or when jars of unheated food are placed directly in boiling water in the canner.

Q. What foods may be safely canned in a boiling water canner?

A. All acid foods, such as fruits, acidified tomatoes, pickles, relishes, jams, and jellies.

Q. What foods must always be canned in a pressure canner?

A. All vegetables (except acidified tomatoes and pickled vegetables), meat, poultry, and seafood.

Q. Is it normal for lids to make a popping sound after jars are removed from the canning kettle?

A. Yes. The "pop" indicates that the sealing process is complete.

Q. Is it all right to reuse canning lids?

A. No. Because the sealing compound is damaged by the first use, lids may not seal again. Ring bands, however, may be used repeatedly if they're in good shape.

Q. Can foods be processed in an oven or micro-wave oven?

A. No. Jars may explode in conventional ovens; and in both conventional and microwave ovens, the bottled food may not heat evenly, possibly leading to spoilage.

Q. Can food be reprocessed if the lid does not seal?

A. Yes—as long as you reprocess within 24 hours. To reprocess, remove the lid and check the jar sealing surface for tiny nicks. If the jar is not flawed, just add a new lid; if it is flawed, reheat the food and pack it into a prepared, hot new jar, then apply a new lid. Reprocess, using the same processing time. (You may notice changes in the food's color and texture.)

Q. What makes the undersides of metal canning lids turn dark?

A. The natural acids and salts in some foods may corrode the metal, causing harmless brown or black deposits to form under the lid.

Q. Is it all right to let jars cool in the boiling water canner in which they were processed?

A. No. The food will keep right on cooking in the water—and will end up overcooked.

Q. When foods are canned in half-pint jars, can processing time be reduced?

A. No. You must process half-pints for the same amount of time as pints.

Q. What causes sealed jars to come open during storage?

A. Such failures may result from gas produced by microbes still alive in the food; in low-acid foods, it may indicate the growth of botulism bacteria. *Never* eat food from such jars.

About fruit...

Q. Do fruits have to be canned in syrups made with white sugar?

A. No. Fruit juice, water, or syrups made with honey may be used instead. Sugar improves flavor, stabilizes color, and helps fruit retain its shape. But fruit juice, particularly juice from the fruit being canned, is an excellent choice. (Commercial unsweetened juices are also good.) Honey often masks fruit flavor, so it's best not to substitute honey for more than half the sugar called for in a syrup. Water-packed fruit tends to be inferior in flavor, texture, and color.

Q. When is ascorbic acid required during prepara-tion for canning?

A. When you're preparing any fruit that darkens when cut—apples, pears, peaches, and apricots, for example. Ascorbic acid (vitamin C), an antidarkening agent, retards the oxidation that browns these fruits.

Q. What causes fruits to float?

A. The syrup used may have been too heavy; or the fruit may have been overripe or packed too loosely into the jar. Hot-packed fruit is less likely to float.

Q. Why does fruit sometimes darken at the top of the jar?

A. Prepared cut fruit may have been exposed to the air too long, or it may not have been covered by liquid in the jar. This kind of darkening may also result if headspace is too great or if air bubbles are left in the jar.

About jams and jellies...

Q. Is it all right to double a favorite jam recipe?

A. No—you're inviting trouble. The larger quantity of fruit and juice requires too long a boiling period, destroying pectin and resulting in a product that will not jell.

Q. Should jelly be boiled slowly or rapidly?

A. Boil it rapidly. Slow boiling destroys the pectin in fruit juice.

Q. Why is my jelly too soft?

A. The mixture may have had too much juice, too much acid, or too little sugar; or it may have been heated too slowly for too long.

Q. Why is my jelly syrupy?

A. The mixture may have too little pectin or acid, or too much or too little sugar. Or you may have doubled the batch.

Q. Why is my jelly too stiff?

A. You may have used too much pectin or fruit that wasn't ripe enough; overcooking is another possible cause. Reduced-sugar jellies and jams made with modified ("light") pectins also tend to be stiff.

Q. Why is my jelly cloudy?

A. Jelly that stands too long before being poured into the jars may turn out cloudy. Cloudy jelly can also result if you didn't strain the juice well enough or if you squeezed the jelly bag; if you used underripe fruit; if

you cooked your jelly too long; or if you used a pectin containing an artificial sweetener.

About pickles...

Q. Why are my pickles hollow?

A. You may have used regular slicing cucumbers rather than pickling cucumbers; or the cucumbers may have been overmature or simply have had faulty growth. Or you may have waited too long between harvesting and pickling.

Q. What causes pickles to turn dark?

A. Minerals such as iron may have been present in the water or vinegar; or iron, zinc, copper, or brass utensils may have been used. Iodized table salt and ground spices will also cause darkening.

Q. Why did the garlic cloves in my pickles turn bluish green?

A. If metals such as iron, tin, or aluminum are present in your pans, water, or water pipes, they may react with pigments in the garlic to cause a color change. Some garlic has a naturally bluish tinge that becomes more evident after pickling. In any case, don't worry. Your pickles are safe to eat.

About vegetables...

Q. Are the vegetables safe to eat if the liquid in the jars has turned cloudy?

A. No. Spoilage may have occurred, and the food should not be eaten. See "Guarding against Botulism" (page 25) for information on how to dispose of spoiled food.

Q. Must I sterilize glass jars before canning vegetables and fruits?

A. No, not if you plan to process them in a pressure canner, or for 10 minutes or more in a boiling water canner. Just make sure they're clean—and to prevent breakage, rinse them with hot water before filling with hot food. But yes, you must sterilize jars by boiling them in water for 10 minutes if they will be processed for less than 10 minutes in a boiling water canner.

Q. Which vegetables should be packed loosely?

A. Corn, peas, and lima beans, all of which expand.

Freezing

Fresh-tasting foods for quick, convenient meals

*I*f you're like many busy cooks today, you've probably wondered how you'd ever manage without your freezer. ● Freezing is a great way to stock up on wholesome, delicious foods for your family. It lets you preserve fruit from your own trees, vegetables from your own garden, and made-from-scratch soups, sauces, main dishes, and desserts from your own kitchen. We offer a few recipes that freeze beautifully on pages 86 and 88, and you'll find many other superb choices—jams, preserves, chutneys, relishes, freezer pickles, and more—in earlier chapters. ● Of course, you'll want to keep some commercially frozen items on hand—but for most cooks, home-frozen foods have pride of place in the freezer. ● When you consider what to freeze, keep in mind what you like and how much food you really need. For help in choosing the best local fruit and vegetable varieties for freezing, consult your local Cooperative Extension office. ● Whatever you freeze, always start with top-quality foods and handle them under the most sanitary conditions. And to ensure that the quality stays high after thawing, use all frozen foods within the recommended storage time.

What Happens in Freezing?

When food is frozen quickly, its natural color and flavor are preserved. And as long as it's kept solidly frozen throughout the storage period, it won't spoil: bacteria, yeasts, and molds can't grow, and oxidation and enzyme activity slow down. Once food begins to thaw, however, enzyme action and growth of microorganisms resume.

Freezing Basics

For successful home freezing, you'll need to follow a few simple rules.

Begin with quality. Freezing maintains quality, but can't improve it—so start with the best, freshest food you can find. Then prepare it under sanitary conditions and store it at 0°F or below.

Freeze it fast. During the freezing process, the water in food forms ice crystals that can puncture cell walls. If such puncturing occurs, the food's natural juices run out during thawing, resulting in a mushy texture. The faster food freezes, the smaller the ice crystals—and the better the texture upon thawing. To ensure quick freezing, turn the freezer to its coldest setting a day before freezing a significant amount of food; then place foods in a single layer in the coldest part of the freezer until frozen. To determine which shelves or positions are coldest, check the manufacturer's instructions. You'll usually use the nonremovable shelves in upright freezers; in chest freezers, a small compartment at one end is typically the coldest area. Once the foods are frozen solid, return the freezer setting to 0°F.

Changes in texture after thawing are most noticeable in fruits and vegetables with a high water content. Tomatoes, for example, always turn to mush if frozen raw, so it's best to cook them before freezing. If you're absolutely swamped with tomatoes, you can package and freeze some of them raw for cooking or seasoning, but you'll need to use them within 2 to 3 weeks; they deteriorate rapidly. To peel frozen tomatoes, hold them under cold water for a second or two; then slip off the skins.

Control enzyme activity. Though the freezing process naturally slows enzyme action, it doesn't work rapidly enough to preserve top quality. Thus, if vegetables and fruits are to maintain good flavor and color during storage, most of the enzymes they contain must be inactivated *before* freezing. In the case of vegetables, inactivation can be achieved by heat treatment (blanching). Blanching typically involves immersing the vegetable in boiling water for a short time, but you can also blanch vegetables in steam or in a microwave oven. To control enzyme activity in fruits, add an antioxidant (see "Protecting Fruit Colors," page 83) and sugar.

Prevent freezer burn. When frozen foods aren't packaged correctly, evaporation from the surface produces *freezer burn:* brownish or whitish areas that are dry, tough, and grainy. Foods damaged in this way are still safe to eat, but their texture is unappealing and they're less flavorful than properly stored foods. To prevent freezer burn, seal foods airtight in moisture- and vaporproof materials specifically designed for use in the freezer (see "Choosing the Right Packaging," page 76).

Avoid overload. Overloading your freezer slows down the freezing process, resulting in poor quality after thawing. Consult the manufacturer's guidelines for the maximum amount you can freeze at one time; typical freezers can handle no more than 2 pounds of food per cubic foot of space per 24 hours.

Avoid partial thawing and refreezing. Fluctuating temperatures cause the ice crystals in frozen foods to begin melting, then refreeze. With each such cycle, the crystals grow larger, damaging cell walls further and resulting in mushy thawed food. (Manual-defrost freezers maintain a more uniform temperature than frostless types do.)

About Your Freezer

A freezer is a long-term investment, so make your choice carefully. Consider the size of your family, how much (and what) you produce in your garden, and your available floor space.

Which Size to Buy?

Freezers come in many sizes, usually stated in cubic feet. Larger models are more energy efficient—*if* you use the space (obviously, you're wasting electricity if you're simply cooling empty shelves). You'll also save energy if you fill and empty your freezer several times a year; doing so just once annually raises your energy cost per package of food.

Which Type to Buy?

The three freezer types most commonly available are upright, chest, and freezer-refrigerator combinations. Units to be used for long-term storage must maintain a temperature of 0°F; some models (both newer and older types) do not, so check carefully with the salesperson before you buy.

Upright freezers are easy to load and unpack, and they take little floor space. However, a fair amount of cold air escapes each time you open the door.

Chest freezers are less expensive to buy and operate than are upright models, and they lose less cold air when opened. They do have drawbacks, though; they require more space than upright freezers, and they're difficult to load and unload unless equipped with lift-out or sliding baskets.

Freezer-refrigerator combinations, commonly found in most kitchens, vary in freezing reliability and efficiency. To maintain the ideal temperature of 0°F required for long-term food storage, the freezer component must be a true freezer, not merely a freezing compartment in the refrigerator.

Choosing the Right Packaging

The way a food is packaged directly affects its quality when thawed. The packaging you use should always be:

■ moisture- and vaporproof, odorless, and tasteless;

■ capable of protecting foods against absorption of "off" flavors and odors;

■ easy to seal;

■ easy to mark;

■ suitable in size;

■ in the case of wrappings, durable and pliable at low temperatures.

Two basic types of freezer packaging materials meet these criteria: first, rigid containers; and second, flexible bags and wraps.

Rigid plastic or glass containers are appropriate for freezing many foods, and most are reusable. In general, you need not leave headspace if you're filling the containers with dry foods or individually frozen pieces of food—but in all other cases, leave ½-inch headspace for pints, 1 inch for quarts. Always make sure the container lid fits tightly; if necessary, use freezer tape—designed to remain sticky at low temperatures—to reinforce the seal.

If you use plastic containers, you can usually transfer them directly from the freezer to a microwave oven to thaw the contents; just be sure to remove any tape from the container before microwaving.

Among glass containers, wide-mouth dual-purpose freezer/canning jars are the best choice. The sides are sloped, so the jar contents slide upward as they expand during freezing, and the wide openings make it easy to remove partially frozen food. Regular glass canning jars are another possibility, but don't use them for foods packed in water; water expands so much that it may crack or break the glass. Do not thaw foods stored in glass in a microwave oven, since microwaving can break jars.

Avoid freezing foods in cardboard cartons used for ice cream and milk. Unless you line them with a freezer bag or wrap, most of these aren't sufficiently moisture- and vaporproof for long-term storage.

Flexible freezer bags & wraps are good for packaging irregularly shaped foods.

Plastic freezer bags, designed especially for freezing, come in various sizes. *Never* use garbage or trash bags, since these contain chemicals not approved for use with foods. Once a bag has been filled, press out any air, beginning from the bottom of the bag and moving toward the top to prevent air from reentering. Then close the bags tightly, leaving ½-inch headspace. To make stacking easier, place the filled bags flat on the freezer shelves until they're solidly frozen; then stack.

Freezer wraps include plastic wrap, various types of coated or laminated freezer papers, and heavy-duty foil. If you use foil, keep in mind that it's relatively expensive, tears and punctures easily, and may pit if used with acid foods. Shape the wrap around the food to exclude as much air as possible; seal packages with freezer tape.

Thawing & Refreezing

Though some foods to be cooked can go straight from freezer to oven, most must be partially or completely thawed before use. When you thaw any food, leave it in its sealed package (unless otherwise instructed) to preserve nutrients and prevent darkening.

Thaw all poultry, meat, fish, and dairy products in the refrigerator; or thaw them in a microwave oven just prior to preparation. *Do not* defrost these foods at room temperature. Vegetables may be steamed or boiled still frozen; you may also thaw them in the refrigerator (but *not* at room temperature). Fruits are best thawed in the refrigerator, though you may thaw them at room temperature if they'll thaw in 2 hours or less. Baked goods such as bread and cookies may safely be thawed at room temperature.

Thaw only enough food for one meal, and once it's thawed, use it immediately. Don't hesitate to discard any food that smells or tastes odd: it could contain harmful microorganisms.

Food that has been partially thawed—whether intentionally or simply due to a freezer failure—may be refrozen as long as it still feels cold and contains ice crystals. Remember, though, that refrozen food will lose some quality and should be used as quickly as possible.

What about Power Failures?

If you have advance warning of a brownout or blackout, immediately turn your freezer to the coldest setting: the lower the temperature, the longer the food will stay frozen. A fully packed freezer will usually keep food frozen for 48 hours after a power failure, provided you avoid opening and closing the freezer door. Half-full freezers may not remain cold for over 24 hours.

Adding dry ice to your freezer helps food stay frozen longer. If added as soon as possible after the power goes off, a 50-pound quantity should keep the food temperature in a 20-cubic-foot freezer below freezing for 3 to 4 days in a full freezer, 2 to 3 days in a half-full (or emptier) one. Have the vendor prepare the ice for you in 2- to 3-inch pieces, and don't place these directly on packaged food. Instead, cover the food with heavy cardboard and arrange the ice on that. Don't touch dry ice with your bare hands; wear heavy gloves. Open the freezer door only to take food out or to add more dry ice. And to avoid any risk of carbon dioxide accumulation, make sure the room is well ventilated.

Tips for the Best Frozen Foods

As noted in "Freezing Basics" (page 75), it's crucial to start with fresh, top-quality products and to work under sanitary conditions. Also keep these hints in mind:

■ For each food, follow the relevant directions in the guides for freezing prepared foods, fruits, and vegetables. The instructions will tell you if the food should be packed dry or with added liquid; if it requires blanching or precooking; and if you need to add an antidarkening agent.

■ Pack foods tightly, leaving as little air in the package as possible. Leave the appropriate headspace, then seal securely; you may need to reinforce lids of rigid containers with freezer tape.

■ Label packages with the name of the product, the date, and the amount or number of servings.

■ Freeze packaged food immediately, placing food in single layers in the coldest part of your freezer (see "Freeze it fast," page 75). Leave a little space for air circulation between and around packages. Once the packages are frozen, you can set them closer together or stack them.

■ Maintain a freezer temperature of 0°F or lower at all times. A freezer thermometer is invaluable in checking for the proper temperature.

■ Keep an inventory of the foods stored in your freezer; use them within the recommended storage period.

Foods That Don't Freeze Well	

Certain foods do not freeze successfully and should not be stored in the freezer. Some of these are listed below.

FOOD	UNDESIRABLE CHARACTERISTICS WHEN THAWED
Cabbage, celery, cucumbers, radishes, salad greens	Waterlogged, limp, poor color and flavor
Cheese or crumb toppings for casseroles	Cheese turns tough, stringy; crumbs are soggy
Cream & custard fillings	Separated, lumpy, watery
Egg whites, cooked	Rubbery, tough
Fried foods	Less crisp or soggy
Gelatin	Tough; tends to weep
Icing containing egg whites	Tends to weep
Jam, jelly in sandwiches	Bread may be soaked
Mayonnaise, salad dressing	Separated
Meringue (in desserts)	Tough
Pasta, cooked	Rubbery, mushy, altered flavor
Potatoes, cooked	Waterlogged, soft, mealy
Rice, cooked	Mushy, altered flavor
Sauces made with milk	Separated or curdled
Sour cream, yogurt	Separated, watery

Guide for Freezing Prepared Foods

When you freeze foods such as soups, stews, or any other saucy or liquid mixture (creamed fish, for example), always leave headspace in the bag or container. In general, leave ½-inch headspace for pint containers, 1-inch headspace for quarts. If packing foods in plastic freezer bags, leave ½-inch headspace.

Dry foods and individually frozen food pieces do not require headspace.

When reheating foods in a microwave oven, *do not* heat them in freezer jars—the glass may break. You may, however, safely microwave foods frozen in most rigid plastic freezer containers.

Food	How to prepare & package	Freezer storage time at 0°F*	How to serve
Appetizers Cream puff shells; cheese rolls; cheese balls; open-faced sandwiches and canapés; dips, spreads, and fillings that contain cooked ham, seafood, cooked egg yolk mixtures, cheese, and avocado	Do not freeze appetizers that include mayonnaise, sour cream, yogurt, cooked egg whites, crisp vegetables, or tomatoes. Prepare other appetizers as usual, but do not combine cream puff shells or crisp toast bases with fillings before freezing. Freeze dips, spreads, and fillings in rigid freezer containers; freeze other appetizers in single layers on trays until solid, then tightly pack individually or in small quantities in moisture- and vaporproof plastic wrap, plastic freezer bags, heavy-duty foil, or shallow rigid freezer containers. Pack cream puff shells and crisp-base appetizers separately from other appetizers.	2 to 4 weeks	Thaw cream puff shells and crisp toast bases, still wrapped, for 2 to 3 hours at room temperature. You may need to recrisp them in the oven before serving. Thaw dips, spreads, and fillings in their containers in the refrigerator. Thaw appetizers containing meat, seafood, or vegetables, still wrapped, in the refrigerator. Unwrap other appetizers, arrange on serving trays, and thaw for about 1 hour at room temperature.
Biscuits	Prepare as usual and bake until light brown; let cool. Freeze unwrapped on trays until solid. Then pack in plastic freezer bags or heavy-duty foil, separating biscuits with wax paper or plastic wrap.	3 to 6 months	Thaw, still wrapped, for 30 to 45 minutes at room temperature. Or unwrap and heat in microwave oven, following manufacturer's instructions; or heat in foil wrapping in a 350° oven for 15 to 20 minutes.
Breads & rolls, yeast	Prepare and bake as usual; let cool. Pack in plastic freezer bags, moisture- and vaporproof plastic wrap, or heavy-duty foil.	3 months	Thaw, still wrapped, for about 1 hour at room temperature. Or unwrap and thaw in microwave oven, following manufacturer's instructions; or heat in foil wrapping in a 300° oven for about 20 minutes for bread, 5 to 10 minutes for rolls.
Breads, quick Coffeecake, gingerbread, nut and fruit breads	Prepare and bake as usual; let cool. Freeze unwrapped on a tray until solid; then pack in plastic freezer bags or heavy-duty foil.	3 to 4 months	Thaw, still wrapped, for about 1 hour at room temperature. Or unwrap and thaw in microwave oven, following manufacturer's instructions; or heat in foil wrapping in a 400° oven until heated through. (Slice nut and fruit breads while still partially frozen to prevent crumbling.)
Cakes & cupcakes Angel food, chiffon, and sponge cakes; shortening cakes (including chocolate, yellow, spice and pound)	Do not freeze cakes with cream or custard fillings, or with frostings containing egg white. Prepare as usual, but do not use synthetic vanilla; cut down on spices, especially cloves, in spice cakes. Bake as usual; remove from pans and let cool. Freeze unwrapped on a tray until solid. Then pack in moisture- and vaporproof plastic wrap or in plastic freezer bags. Store large whole cakes in a light box (if a tube pan has been used, fill hole in cake with crumpled plastic wrap). Store sliced cake with a double layer of plastic wrap between slices.	***Angel food, chiffon, and sponge cakes:*** 2 months ***Shortening cakes:*** 4 to 6 months	Unwrap. Thaw large cakes for 2 hours at room temperature, cupcakes for 30 to 45 minutes. To prevent beads of moisture from forming on frosted cakes, cover them with a large cake cover or pan that doesn't touch sides of cake.

* Food will be safe to eat after this time, but will lose quality

Food	How to prepare & package	Freezer storage time at 0°F*	How to serve
Casseroles, unbaked Fish, poultry, or meat with vegetables and/ or pasta	Prepare casserole mixture with less pepper, cloves, onion, and garlic than usual; flavors of these ingredients grow stronger during storage. Let cool. Spoon mixture into freezer-to-oven casserole dishes, leaving 1-inch headspace; seal lids with freezer tape. Or freeze in shallow foil containers until firm, then cover tightly with heavy-duty foil. Or freeze in foil-lined casserole dishes, then remove food from dish; wrap tightly in moisture- and vaporproof plastic wrap or heavy-duty foil or place in a plastic freezer bag.	2 to 4 weeks	*If stored in freezer-to-oven casserole dishes or shallow foil containers,* remove any tape from lids. Bake, still frozen, in a 400° oven for about 1¾ hours per quart. (Do not preheat oven.) Keep covered for first half of baking time, then uncover. *If not stored in ovenproof containers,* remove wrapping and slip frozen mixture into casserole dish in which it was originally frozen. Bake as directed above.
Cheesecake	Prepare and bake as usual. Freeze unwrapped on a tray until solid, then wrap in moisture- and vaporproof plastic wrap or in a large plastic freezer bag. Store in a light box or carton to prevent crushing.	2 to 4 months	Unwrap and thaw in refrigerator for 4 to 6 hours.
Cookies, baked or unbaked	**Baked cookies** Prepare and bake as usual; let cool. To prevent crushing, pack cookies in rigid freezer containers or in plastic freezer bags, with plastic wrap between layers and crumpled to fill spaces.	6 months	Thaw **crisp cookies,** still packaged, for 15 to 20 minutes at room temperature. (They will be less crisp than cookies baked from frozen dough.) Thaw **soft cookies** on a serving plate for about 15 minutes.
	Unbaked cookies (except meringue) **Refrigerator cookies.** Form dough into a roll. Slice, if desired. Wrap in moisture- and vaporproof plastic wrap or pack in plastic freezer bags.	3 to 6 months	Bake slices without thawing.
	Drop cookies. Drop onto a tray and freeze unwrapped until solid. Then pack in rigid freezer containers or plastic freezer bags, with plastic wrap between layers. Or simply pack bulk dough in rigid freezer containers or plastic freezer bags.	3 to 6 months	Bake formed cookies, still frozen, in a 400° oven. Thaw bulk dough, still packaged, at room temperature until soft enough to drop by teaspoonfuls onto a greased baking sheet.
Fish, flaked In cheese or tomato sauces	Prepare as usual, but keep fat to a minimum and slightly undercook any vegetables. Cool quickly by placing pan in ice water. Pack in rigid wide-mouth freezer containers, making sure that sauce covers fish.	2 to 4 months	Heat in microwave oven, following manufacturer's instructions. Or partially thaw in refrigerator; then remove from containers and heat over boiling water.
Fish, fried Pieces or sticks	Fry as usual, just until done. Let cool. Freeze unwrapped on trays until solid; then pack in plastic freezer bags or in moisture- and vaporproof plastic wrap.	1 to 2 months	Unwrap frozen pieces or sticks and place in a single layer in a well-greased baking pan. Bake, uncovered, in a 400° oven until fish is crisp and heated through (20 to 25 minutes; frozen fried fish may lose some crispness).
Fish cakes & balls, cooked	Let cool. Freeze unwrapped on a tray until solid. Then pack in rigid freezer containers, in moisture- and vaporproof plastic wrap, or in plastic freezer bags.	2 to 4 weeks	Unwrap and heat on a microwave-safe serving plate in microwave oven, following manufacturer's instructions.
Fish loaf, unbaked	Prepare as usual. Pack in loaf pan, but do not bake. Wrap in moisture- and vaporproof plastic wrap or place in a plastic freezer bag.	1 to 2 months	Thaw, still wrapped, for 1 to 2 hours in refrigerator. Unwrap and bake in a 450° oven for 15 minutes; reduce heat to 350° for remainder of baking time.

* Food will be safe to eat after this time, but will lose quality

Food	How to prepare & package	Freezer storage time at 0°F*	How to serve
Frostings & fillings	Do not freeze fillings containing cream or eggs. Uncooked frostings based on powdered sugar freeze best. Cooked frostings may crack; those made with large amounts of granulated sugar may become grainy. Pack in rigid freezer containers.	1 to 2 months	Thaw in container in refrigerator.
Gravy	Because gravy tends to separate and curdle when thawed, it's best simply to freeze broth, then prepare gravy just before serving. If you do freeze gravy, add ¼ teaspoon unflavored gelatin to each quart of gravy to reduce curdling. Pour into rigid freezer containers.	2 to 3 months	Heat in microwave oven, following manufacturer's instructions. Or remove from containers and heat over boiling water, breaking up frozen blocks as gravy begins to thaw.
Meat & poultry, fried	Fry as usual, just until done. Let cool. Freeze unwrapped on trays until solid. Package pieces in plastic freezer bags or in moisture- and vaporproof plastic wrap.	1 to 3 months	Thaw, still wrapped, in refrigerator. Then unwrap, place in a shallow baking pan, and bake, uncovered, in a 350° oven until crisp and heated through (30 to 45 minutes; frozen fried meat and poultry may lose some crispness).
Meat & poultry, roasted	Roast as usual. Remove as much fat as possible. Turkey and other large birds should be cut off the bone to save space; smaller birds may be boned if you wish, but keep pieces large. Cured meats such as ham lose their color and become rancid more quickly than other meats. Sauce or broth helps keep meat from drying out and losing color. Pack **dry meat** (for short storage) in moisture- and vaporproof plastic wrap or heavy-duty foil. Pack **meat with sauce or broth** in rigid freezer containers, making sure that sauce or broth covers meat.	2 to 3 months	Thaw **dry meat,** still wrapped, in refrigerator. Or thaw or heat in microwave oven, following manufacturer's instructions. Or heat in foil wrapping in a 325° oven until heated through. Thaw **meat with sauce or broth** in refrigerator for 5 to 6 hours. Or heat in microwave oven, following manufacturer's instructions; or heat slowly on top of range or in oven until heated through.
Meat, fish, & poultry, creamed	Prepare as usual, using recipes fairly low in fat. Cool quickly by placing pan in ice water. Pack in rigid wide-mouth freezer containers.	2 to 3 months	Thaw in refrigerator. Then remove from containers and heat over boiling water or in microwave oven, following manufacturer's instructions.
Meat dishes, combination Stews; pasta sauce with meat, meatballs, or ravioli; meat with gravy	Prepare as usual, but keep fat to a minimum and omit potatoes; slightly undercook other vegetables. Cool combination dishes quickly by placing pan in ice water. Pack in freezer jars or in rigid freezer containers, making sure that sauce, broth, or gravy covers meat.	2 to 3 months	Partially thaw in refrigerator to prevent overcooking. Then remove from containers and heat over boiling water; or transfer to a baking dish and heat in a 400° oven until hot through. Or heat (if in rigid plastic containers) in microwave oven, following manufacturer's instructions.
Meat loaf	Prepare as usual. Bake or leave unbaked. Wrap in moisture- and vaporproof plastic wrap or place in a plastic freezer bag.	3 to 4 months	For **frozen unbaked loaf,** unwrap; if not frozen in pan, place in pan. Bake in a 350° oven for about 1½ hours. For **baked loaf:** to serve cold, thaw, still wrapped, in refrigerator. To reheat, unwrap frozen baked loaf, place in pan, and bake, uncovered, in a 350° oven for about 1 hour.
Muffins	Prepare and bake as usual; remove from pans and let cool. Freeze on trays until solid; then pack in plastic freezer bags or in heavy-duty foil.	3 to 4 months	Thaw, still wrapped, for about 1 hour at room temperature. Or unwrap and heat in microwave oven, following manufacturer's instructions; or heat in foil wrapping in a 300° oven for about 20 minutes.
		* Food will be safe to eat after this time, but will lose quality	

Food	How to prepare & package	Freezer storage time at 0°F*	How to serve
Pastry (Pie shells)	**Baked pastry** Prepare and bake as usual; let cool. Leave in pie pan; place in a plastic freezer bag or wrap in moisture- and vaporproof plastic wrap. Or freeze, unwrapped, on a tray until solid; remove from pan and freeze as above, storing in a light carton to prevent breakage.	2 to 3 months	Thaw, still wrapped, for 10 to 20 minutes at room temperature. Add filling.
	Unbaked pastry Prepare pastry or crumb crust as usual. Fit into pie pans. Prick pastry if you don't intend to bake it with a filling. Stack pans, separating them with double layers of plastic wrap. Cover top pie shell with an inverted paper plate for protection; tape edges to pan. Place stack in a large plastic freezer bag; or wrap in moisture- and vapor-proof plastic wrap. Or omit fitting into pans; instead, store rounds of pastry on lined cardboard, with a double layer of plastic wrap between each round and the next.	1½ to 2 months	Bake, still frozen, in a 475° oven until lightly browned. Or fill and bake as usual.
Pies	**Chiffon pie** Make with gelatin base. Freeze unwrapped on a tray until solid. Place in a plastic freezer bag or wrap in moisture- and vaporproof plastic wrap. Store in a light box or carton to prevent crushing.	2 to 4 weeks	Thaw, still wrapped, for 1 hour at room temperature.
	Fruit, mince, and nut pies, unbaked Do not freeze unbaked pecan pie. If desired, treat sliced light-colored fruits for pies with a commercial anti-darkening agent, following package directions. Prepare as usual, but add 1 extra tablespoon flour or tapioca or 1½ teaspoons cornstarch to very juicy fillings to prevent boil-over during baking. Do not cut slits in top crust. Freeze fruit pies in pans, using metal or other freezer-to-oven pie pans. Cover with an inverted paper plate for protection; tape edges to pan. Place in a plastic freezer bag; or wrap in moisture- and vaporproof plastic wrap.	2 to 4 months	Unwrap. Cut slits in top of frozen pie; cover edges with foil. Bake in a 450° oven for 15 minutes; reduce temperature to 375° and bake for 15 more minutes. Remove foil; bake until done (about 30 more minutes).
	Pumpkin pie, unbaked Prepare pie shell and filling as usual. Chill filling before adding it to unbaked pie shell. Package as for fruit pies.	1 month	Unwrap. Bake, still frozen, in a 400° oven for 10 minutes; then reduce oven temperature to 325° for remainder of baking time.
Pizza	Prepare as usual; do not bake. If topping is warm, let cool. Freeze unwrapped until solid. Pack in a plastic freezer bag or in moisture- and vaporproof plastic wrap.	1 month	Unwrap. Bake, still frozen, in a 450° oven for 10 to 20 minutes, depending on size.
Sandwiches	Use day-old bread; spread bread to edges with softened butter or margarine. Use cheese, meat, poultry, tuna, salmon, or peanut butter filling. Omit hard-cooked egg white, jellies, jams, mayonnaise, tomatoes, and crisp vegetables such as lettuce and celery. Wrap individually or in groups of the same type in moisture- and vapor-proof plastic wrap, then place in plastic freezer bags.	2 months	Thaw meat, poultry, or fish sand-wiches, still wrapped, for 1 to 2 hours in refrigerator. Thaw other sandwiches at room temperature. Frozen sandwiches in a lunchbox thaw in 3 to 4 hours and help keep other food cold.
Soups & purées	Omit potatoes. Use vegetables that freeze well, and undercook them slightly. (For cream soups, vegetables may be cooked and puréed.) Omit salt and thickening if soup is to be kept longer than 2 months. If possible, make a concentrate by using less liquid when cooking. Cool quickly by placing pan in ice water. Pour into rigid freezer containers. Or freeze in ice cube trays, then store cubes in plastic freezer bags.	1 to 3 months	Heat without thawing. Heat cream soups over boiling water; stir to keep smooth. If concentrated, add hot liquid. Add potatoes or other vegetables, if necessary. Heat vegetable purée over boiling water; then add milk or cream.
Waffles	Prepare as usual. Let cool. Wrap individually in moisture- and vaporproof plastic wrap; then pack in plastic freezer bags.	2 to 3 months	Unwrap; heat, still frozen, in a toaster or microwave oven, following manufacturer's instruc-tions. Or heat on a baking sheet in a 400° oven for 2 to 3 minutes.

* Food will be safe to eat after this time, but will lose quality

On a sweltering summer day, treat yourself to the cooling fruit flavors of raspberry, papaya, and pineapple ices. All three recipes are on page 86.

Freezing Fresh Fruits

Most fruits can be frozen; the chart on pages 84 and 85 lists the types that freeze best. Always select un-blemished firm-ripe fruits, and remember to treat them with an antidarkening agent if needed. Work carefully but quickly, preparing just enough fruit to fill a few containers at a time.

Basic Fruit Packs

When you freeze fruit, you can pack it in syrup, with sugar, or with no sweetener at all. Syrup-packed fruits are usually best for uncooked desserts and sauces, while those frozen with sugar or packed entirely unsweetened are a better choice for cooking. Be aware that color, flavor, and texture change more rapidly when fruit is frozen unsweetened than when it's packed with sugar or syrup.

Packing fruit unsweetened. While many fruits are best frozen sweetened, others maintain high quality without sugar or syrup. Cranberries, raspberries, blueberries, and rhubarb are all good choices for freezing unsweetened. The technique is simple: just pack the fruit in rigid freezer containers, seal, and freeze. Or spread it on a tray, freeze uncovered until solid, and transfer to rigid containers or plastic freezer bags. This second method—freezing fruits or fruit pieces individually *before* packaging—makes it easy to remove just the amount you want at one time.

Unsweetened fruit can also be frozen in water or unsweetened fruit juice. The fruits usually aren't as plump as those frozen without liquid, and they'll take longer to thaw.

Packing fruit in pectin syrup. This lightly sweetened pack may help certain fruits—strawberries, cherries, and peaches, for example—retain better texture. To prepare the pectin syrup, combine one package (1¾ oz.) dry pectin with 1 cup water in a small pan. Bring to a boil; boil for 1 minute, stirring constantly. Add ½ cup sugar and stir until dissolved. Remove from heat, add enough cold water to make 2 cups liquid, and refrigerate. To use the syrup, pour it into a large bowl; add the fruit and stir until it's lightly coated with syrup, then pack.

Packing fruit in sugar. To freeze fruit in a *sugar pack* or *dry pack*—with sugar, but no liquid—spread it in a shallow pan and sprinkle with sugar (see chart, pages 84 and 85, for amounts). Gently mix until the fruit releases its juice and the sugar is dissolved.

Packing fruit in syrup. The syrups used to pack fruit for freezing can be made in different concentrations; to prepare them, simply mix the ingredients until well blended, then chill before using. (You may substitute honey for a fourth of the sugar.) When you pack the fruit, add enough cold syrup to cover it—usually ½ to ⅔ cup per pint.

Syrups for Freezing Fruits			
% Sugar	Water (in cups)	Sugar (in cups)	Yield (in cups)
20%	4	1	4¾
30%	4	1¾	5
40%	4	2¾	5⅓
50%	4	4	6

Protecting Fruit Colors

Some light-colored fruits have a tendency to darken after cutting. The chart on pages 84 and 85 specifies the treatment needed to preserve their color.

Ascorbic acid, sold in drugstores and health food stores, is one common antidarkening agent. Commercial antidarkening products containing ascorbic and/or citric acids (and often sugar) are also available; look for them in your supermarket. Lemon juice prevents darkening, too, but the quantity needed often makes the fruit too tart in flavor.

Antidarkening agents can be added to fruit in two ways. You can mix them into the packing syrup; or you can dissolve them in water, then sprinkle the solution over the fruit before packing. For syrup packs, you'll generally need ½ to ¾ teaspoon pure ascorbic acid per quart of 20 to 40 percent syrup. If you can't find pure ascorbic acid, you can substitute vitamin C tablets, keeping in mind that 1 teaspoon of ascorbic acid equals 3,000 milligrams of vitamin C. Crush the tablets thoroughly before using them.

Packaging & Headspace

Rigid plastic freezer containers and wide-mouth freezer/canning jars are good choices for any fruit pack. Freezer bags are also suitable for sugar-packed fruits and those packed unsweetened without liquid, but not convenient for fruits packed in syrup.

When packing unsweetened fruit frozen in individual pieces, you don't need to leave headspace. If you're using a sugar, juice, water, or syrup pack, leave ½-inch headspace for plastic freezer bags or pint containers, 1 inch for quarts. Do not freeze fruits with liquid in standard glass canning jars. Seal all containers tightly; label with the type of fruit and the date, then freeze. For easier stacking, freeze filled bags flat on freezer shelves until solid; then stack.

Guide for Freezing Fruits

The chart below indicates possible packs for a number of fruits. When packing, leave headspace as directed in "Packaging & Headspace" (page 83).

Unless otherwise noted, fruits of all kinds will keep for up to a year if solidly frozen.

Fruit & varieties	Quantity to yield 1 pint	How to prepare
Apples Golden Delicious, Granny Smith, Gravenstein, Jonathan, Newtown Pippin, Rome Beauty	1¼ to 1½ lbs.	For pies, use a sugar or dry pack. For uncooked desserts, use a syrup pack. For a firmer texture, steam sliced apples (1 lb. at a time) for 2 minutes. Cool in cold water; drain. Then pack in sugar or syrup. **To pack in sugar,** rinse, peel, core, and slice apples. As you work, coat them with a solution of ½ teaspoon ascorbic acid to 3 tablespoons cold water (about the amount you'll need per quart of fruit). Mix ½ cup sugar with each quart of fruit. Pack slices in plastic freezer bags or rigid freezer containers; press fruit down, leaving headspace. **To pack in syrup,** use a 20% to 40% syrup; add ½ teaspoon ascorbic acid per quart. Pour ½ cup cold syrup into each rigid pint freezer container. Rinse, peel, and core apples; slice directly into syrup. Press slices down; add syrup to cover, leaving headspace.
Apricots Royal-Blenheim, Tilton	1 to 1¼ lbs.	Rinse, halve, and pit. Dip fruit in boiling water for 30 seconds (this keeps skins from toughening). Cool in cold water; drain. Peel and slice, if desired. **To pack in syrup,** use a 20% to 40% syrup; add ¾ teaspoon ascorbic acid per quart. Pack apricots in rigid freezer containers; add cold syrup to cover, leaving headspace. **To pack in sugar,** dissolve ¼ teaspoon ascorbic acid in 3 tablespoons cold water. Mix this ascorbic acid solution and ½ cup sugar with each quart of fruit; stir until sugar is dissolved. Pack apricots and liquid in plastic freezer bags or rigid freezer containers; press down, leaving headspace.
Avocados Fuerte, Haas	4 medium-size	Pit, peel, and mash; as you mash, add 1 tablespoon lemon juice for every 2 avocados. Pack in plastic freezer bags or rigid freezer containers, leaving headspace. Store for up to 4 months.
Berries Raspberries, blackberries, boysenberries, loganberries, blueberries, huckleberries, elderberries; cranberries (unsweetened only)	¾ to 1½ lbs.	Rinse berries gently; drain. **To pack unsweetened,** spread berries on trays and freeze until solid, then transfer to plastic freezer bags or rigid freezer containers. **To pack in sugar,** use ¼ cup sugar per quart of raspberries; ½ cup sugar per quart of blueberries, elderberries, or huckleberries; and ¾ cup sugar per quart of blackberries, boysenberries, or loganberries. Mix gently until sugar is dissolved; fill plastic freezer bags or rigid freezer containers, leaving headspace. (To pack crushed berries, see "Fruit purées & sauces," below.) **To pack in syrup** (for berries to be served uncooked), place berries in rigid freezer containers and cover with cold 20% to 40% syrup, leaving headspace.
Cherries, sour Early Richmond, English Morello, Montmorency	1¼ to 1½ lbs.	Rinse, stem, and pit, working quickly to prevent color and flavor changes. **To pack in syrup,** use a 50% syrup; add ½ teaspoon ascorbic acid per quart. Pack cherries in rigid freezer containers; cover with cold syrup, leaving headspace. **To pack in sugar,** use ¾ cup sugar per quart of cherries; mix until sugar is dissolved. Pack in plastic freezer bags or rigid freezer containers, leaving headspace.
Cherries, sweet Bing, Black Tartarian, Lambert, Rainier, Royal Ann	1¼ to 1½ lbs.	Rinse, stem, and pit, working quickly to prevent color and flavor changes. **To pack in syrup,** use a 30% or 40% syrup; add ½ teaspoon ascorbic acid per quart. Pack cherries in rigid freezer containers; cover with cold syrup, leaving headspace. **To pack in sugar,** use ⅔ cup sugar per quart of cherries; mix until sugar is dissolved. Pack in plastic freezer bags or rigid freezer containers, leaving headspace. **To pack in pectin syrup,** cover fruit with cold pectin syrup (see page 83). Pack in rigid freezer containers, leaving headspace.
Figs Black Mission, Kadota	¾ to 1¼ lbs.	**To pack unsweetened,** rinse fully ripe fruit; remove stems. Pack in rigid freezer containers; cover with water (to which you have added ¾ teaspoon ascorbic acid per quart), leaving headspace. **To pack in syrup,** use a 20% to 40% syrup; add ¾ teaspoon ascorbic acid per quart. Pack figs in rigid freezer containers; cover with cold syrup, leaving headspace. Store unsweetened and syrup-packed figs for up to 6 months.
Fruit purées & sauces		Steam or simmer fruit until soft; then mash it, purée it in a blender, or press it through a strainer. Add sugar and/or lemon juice to taste. Heat mixture to 180°F; remove from heat and refrigerate until cold. Pack in rigid freezer containers, leaving headspace.

Fruit & varieties	Quantity to yield 1 pint	How to prepare
Grapefruit & oranges *Grapefruit:* Marsh *Oranges:* Any except navel	1½ to 2 lbs.	Rinse and peel, cutting deep enough to remove white membrane under rind. Holding fruit over a bowl to catch juice, cut between membranes to release segments. Remove and discard membranes and seeds from segments; reserve juice. **To pack in syrup,** use a 30% syrup made with reserved juice (and water, if needed). Pack in rigid freezer containers; cover with cold syrup, leaving headspace.
Mangoes Philippine, Hayden	2 or 3 medium-size	**To pack in syrup,** put ½ cup cold 20% or 30% syrup in each rigid pint freezer container. Rinse and peel mangoes; cut a slice off stem end. Then slice fruit (avoiding flesh near pit) directly into syrup. Press slices down; add more syrup to cover, leaving headspace. **To pack in sugar,** rinse and peel mangoes; cut a slice off stem end. Then slice fruit, avoiding flesh near pit. Place 5 to 6 cups mango slices in a shallow bowl; sprinkle with ½ cup sugar. Let stand for a few minutes, or until sugar is dissolved; mix gently. Pack in plastic freezer bags or rigid freezer containers, leaving headspace.
Melons Cantaloupe, casaba, Crenshaw, honeydew, Persian, watermelon	1 to 1¼ lbs.	Cut in half; cut off rind and scoop out seeds. **To pack in syrup,** use a 20% or 30% syrup, adding 1 teaspoon lemon juice per cup of syrup for flavor. Pour ½ cup cold syrup into each rigid pint freezer container. Cut melon into slices, cubes, or balls, dropping directly into syrup; add more syrup to cover, leaving headspace. Store for up to 6 months.
Oranges *See* Grapefruit & Oranges		
Peaches & nectarines *Peaches:* Elberta, J.H. Hale, O'Henry, Redglobe, Redhaven, Rio Oso Gem *Nectarines:* Flavortop, Gold Mine, Panamint, Stanwick	1 to 1½ lbs.	Do not peel nectarines. To peel peaches, dip in boiling water for 1 to 1½ minutes, then plunge into cold water; slip off skins. (For less "ragged" fruit, peel without boiling water dip.) **To pack in syrup,** use a 20% to 40% syrup; add ½ teaspoon ascorbic acid per quart of syrup. Pour ½ cup cold syrup into each rigid pint freezer container. Cut fruit into halves or slices directly into cold syrup; discard pits. Press fruit down; add more syrup to cover, leaving headspace. **To pack in sugar,** coat cut fruit with a solution of ¼ teaspoon ascorbic acid to 3 tablespoons cold water (about the amount you'll need per quart of fruit). Add ½ to ⅔ cup sugar to each quart of prepared fruit; stir gently until sugar is dissolved. Pack in plastic freezer bags or rigid freezer containers, leaving headspace. **To pack in pectin syrup or water,** cover cut fruit with cold pectin syrup (see page 83) or with cold water to which you've added 1 teaspoon ascorbic acid per quart. Leave headspace. Store water-packed peaches or nectarines for up to 6 months.
Pears		Not recommended for freezing.
Pineapple	1 to 1¼ lbs.	Peel; remove eyes and cores. Cut into wedges, cubes, sticks, or thin slices; or crush. **To pack unsweetened,** pack fruit tightly in rigid freezer containers (enough juice will squeeze out to fill spaces), leaving headspace. **To pack in syrup,** pack fruit in rigid freezer containers. Cover with cold 20% or 30% syrup, leaving headspace.
Plums & fresh prunes Casselman, El Dorado, French Prune, Italian Prune, Queen Ann, Satsuma	1 to 1½ lbs.	**To pack in syrup,** rinse and cut into halves or quarters; discard pits. Use a 20% to 40% syrup; add ½ teaspoon ascorbic acid per quart. Pack plums in rigid freezer containers and cover with cold syrup, leaving headspace. **To pack unsweetened,** leave whole. Rinse; dry well. Spread on a tray; freeze until solid. Pack in freezer bags or rigid freezer containers. Use cooked or in pies within 3 months.
Rhubarb	⅔ to 1 lb.	Rinse unpeeled rhubarb stalks and cut into pieces of the desired length. Immerse in boiling water; return to a boil and cook for 1 minute. Drain; cool quickly in ice water, then drain well. **To pack unsweetened,** pack tightly in rigid freezer containers, leaving headspace. Store for up to 6 months. **To pack in syrup,** pack rhubarb tightly in rigid freezer containers. Cover with cold 40% syrup, leaving headspace.
Strawberries Tioga, Tufts, Sequoia, Pajaro, Douglas, Aiko	¾ to 1½ lbs.	Rinse gently in cold water; drain and hull. **To pack in sugar,** leave berries whole (if small); or slice lengthwise. Add ⅔ cup sugar per quart of berries; mix gently until sugar is dissolved. Pack in freezer bags or rigid freezer containers, leaving headspace. (To pack crushed, see "Fruit purées & sauces," facing page.) **To pack in syrup,** pack whole berries in rigid freezer containers; cover with cold 30% or 40% syrup, leaving headspace. **To pack in pectin syrup or water,** cover fruit with cold pectin syrup (page 83) or with cold water to which you've added 1 teaspoon ascorbic acid per quart. Leave headspace.

Raspberry Ice

Pictured on page 82

You'll appreciate the fresh, sparkling flavor of this easy make-ahead dessert and its variations.

- 4 cups raspberries
- ¾ cup sugar
- ½ cup water
- 1 tablespoon lemon juice

In a food processor, purée berries. Press through a sieve; discard seeds. Return purée to food processor. Add sugar, water, and lemon juice; whirl to blend. Pour purée into divided ice cube trays, cover, and freeze until solid (at least 3 hours). Remove cubes from trays; use at once or transfer to plastic freezer bags and freeze for up to 3 weeks.

To prepare ice, whirl cubes, a portion at a time, in a food processor; use on-off pulses at first to break up cubes, then whirl continuously until mixture is smooth and slushy. (Or place all cubes in large bowl of an electric mixer; beat until smooth and slushy, increasing mixer speed from low to high as ice softens.) Spoon mixture into a 9-inch-square metal pan, cover airtight, and freeze until solid (at least 4 hours) or for up to 3 weeks.

To serve, let ice stand at room temperature until you can break it up with a spoon. Whirl in a food processor until smooth and free of ice crystals. Serve at once. Makes 6 servings (about 2¾ cups *total*).

Storage time. Up to 6 weeks in freezer (3 weeks as cubes, plus 3 weeks in pan after beating).

Per serving: 137 calories, 1 g protein, 24 g carbohydrates, 0 g total fat, 0 mg cholesterol, 0 mg sodium

Strawberry Ice

In a food processor, purée 4 cups hulled **strawberries**. Add ½ cup each **sugar** and **water** and 2 tablespoons **lemon juice;** whirl to blend. Freeze, beat, and serve as directed for **Raspberry Ice**. Makes 6 servings (about 3 cups *total*).

Per serving: 96 calories, 1 g protein, 24 g carbohydrates, 0 g total fat, 0 mg cholesterol, 2 mg sodium

Pineapple Ice

Peel and core 1 large **pineapple** (about 5 lbs.); cut into chunks. Purée fruit in a food processor, a portion at a time (you should have 4 cups). Add 1 cup **water**, 2 tablespoons **sugar**, and 2 tablespoons **lemon juice;** whirl to blend. Freeze, beat, and serve as directed for **Raspberry Ice**. Makes 10 servings (about 5 cups *total*).

Per serving: 41 calories, 0 g protein, 10 g carbohydrates, 0 g total fat, 0 mg cholesterol, 1 mg sodium

Papaya Ice

Peel, halve, and seed 1 large **papaya** (about 1¼ lbs.); cut into chunks. Purée in a food processor (you should have 1½ cups). Add 2 tablespoons **lime juice**, 3 tablespoons **sugar,** and ⅓ cup **water;** whirl to blend. Freeze, beat, and serve as directed for **Raspberry Ice**. Makes 3 servings (about 1⅔ cups *total*).

Per serving: 78 calories, 1 g protein, 20 g carbohydrates, 0 g total fat, 0 mg cholesterol, 4 mg sodium

Peach Pie Filling

Pictured on facing page

To vary this filling's flavor, omit the orange peel and orange juice; then increase the lemon juice in the filling to ¼ cup and add 1 teaspoon grated lemon peel.

- 2 quarts water
- ¼ cup lemon juice
- 6 pounds (about 18 medium-size) peaches
- 2¼ cups sugar
- ½ cup all-purpose flour
- 1 teaspoon ground cinnamon
- ¼ teaspoon ground nutmeg
- 1 tablespoon grated orange peel
- ¼ cup orange juice

In a large bowl, mix water with 2 tablespoons of the lemon juice. Peel and pit peaches; slice directly into lemon water.

In a 6- to 8-quart pan, combine sugar, flour, cinnamon, nutmeg, orange peel, orange juice, and remaining 2 tablespoons lemon juice. Drain peaches; add to sugar mixture and stir gently. Let stand for 20 minutes. Then cook, uncovered, over medium heat, stirring often, until mixture begins to thicken (about 10 minutes). Let cool. Pack in rigid pint freezer containers or freezer jars, leaving ½-inch headspace; apply lids and freeze. Makes about 6 pints.

Storage time. Up to 6 months in freezer.

Per ½ cup (unbaked): 121 calories, 1 g protein, 31 g carbohydrates, 0 g total fat, 0 mg cholesterol, 1 mg sodium

Apple Pie Filling

Follow directions for **Peach Pie Filling,** but substitute 6 pounds **tart apples** (peeled, cored, and sliced) for peaches. Omit orange juice and peel, reduce sugar to 1¾ cups, reduce flour to ¼ cup, and increase cinnamon to 1½ teaspoons. Makes about 8 pints.

Per ½ cup (unbaked): 88 calories, 0 g protein, 23 g carbohydrates, 0 g total fat, 0 mg cholesterol, 1 mg sodium

With Peach Pie Filling (facing page) on hand in the freezer, it's easy to enjoy homemade peach pie all year long. Just thaw the filling in the refrigerator until it's spreadable, spoon it into a pastry shell, and bake.

Garden Marinara Sauce

Pictured on page 90

This made-from-scratch marinara sauce is great with pasta, but it also goes into two classic Italian appetizer relishes—Caponata and Peperonata (below).

- ¼ cup olive oil
- 3 large onions, coarsely chopped
- 3 or 4 cloves garlic, minced or pressed
- 6 pounds (15 to 18 medium-size) ripe tomatoes, peeled, cored, and chopped
- 1 cup lightly packed fresh basil leaves, chopped
- ½ to 1 tablespoon sugar
  Salt and pepper

Heat oil in a wide frying pan over medium heat; add onions and garlic and cook, stirring often, until onions are soft (about 15 minutes). Add tomatoes and basil. Cook, uncovered, stirring occasionally, until sauce is reduced to 2 quarts (45 to 60 minutes); as sauce thickens, reduce heat and stir more often to prevent sticking. Add sugar; season to taste with salt and pepper.

Let sauce cool, then ladle into pint freezer jars or freezer containers, leaving ½-inch headspace; apply lids. Freeze or refrigerate. Makes about 4 pints.

Storage time. Up to 2 weeks in refrigerator; up to 6 months in freezer.

Per ½ cup: 80 calories, 2 g protein, 11 g carbohydrates, 4 g total fat, 0 mg cholesterol, 15 mg sodium

Caponata

Pictured on page 90

Peppers, olives, and creamy-textured eggplant combine with homemade marinara sauce in this Italian relish. Include it in an antipasto assortment; or serve it on its own, as a dip for pocket bread or butter lettuce leaves.

- ½ cup olive oil
- 1½ pounds eggplant (unpeeled), cut into ½-inch cubes
- 2 large red or green bell peppers, seeded and diced
- 1 large onion, chopped
- 1 clove garlic, minced or pressed
- 2½ cups Garden Marinara Sauce (this page)
- 1 cup sliced pimento-stuffed green olives or sliced ripe olives
  Salt and pepper

Heat oil in a wide frying pan over medium heat. Add eggplant; cover and cook, stirring occasionally, until slightly softened (about 5 minutes). Uncover and cook, stirring often, until eggplant is browned (10 to 15 more minutes). Add bell peppers, onion, and garlic; cook, stirring, until onion is soft (about 10 minutes). Add Garden Marinara Sauce; cook, uncovered, until mixture is thick (about 10 more minutes). Stir in olives; season to taste with salt and pepper. Let caponata cool, then pack in pint freezer jars or freezer containers, leaving ½-inch headspace; apply lids. Freeze or refrigerate. Makes about 4 pints.

Storage time. Up to 2 weeks in refrigerator; up to 6 months in freezer.

Per ¼ cup: 57 calories, 1 g protein, 4 g carbohydrates, 5 g total fat, 0 mg cholesterol, 106 mg sodium

Peperonata

Pictured on page 90

This colorful blend of sweet red, green, and yellow peppers is a good meat relish and a tasty dip for crackers.

- ¼ cup olive oil
- 2 large onions, cut into 1-inch pieces, layers separated
- 2 cloves garlic, minced or pressed
  About 10 medium-size bell peppers (use an assortment of red, yellow, and green peppers), seeded and thinly sliced (you should have 8 cups)
- 2½ cups Garden Marinara Sauce (this page)
  Salt and pepper

Heat oil in a wide frying pan over medium heat. Add onions and cook, stirring, for 3 minutes. Add garlic, bell peppers, and Garden Marinara Sauce; cover and cook until peppers are tender when pierced (8 to 10 minutes). Season to taste with salt and pepper.

Let cool, then pack in pint freezer jars or freezer containers, leaving ½-inch headspace; apply lids. Freeze or refrigerate. Makes about 4 pints.

Storage time. Up to 2 weeks in refrigerator; up to 6 months in freezer.

Per ¼ cup: 38 calories, 1 g protein, 4 g carbohydrates, 2 g total fat, 0 mg cholesterol, 3 mg sodium

Freezing Vegetables

If you're a gardener with more fresh vegetables than you can use at home or give away, consider yourself lucky—those surplus peas, squash, and carrots can be frozen to enjoy later in the year.

For consistently excellent results, be careful to pick your vegetables at peak maturity and freeze them without delay. It's also important that your freezer maintain a temperature of 0°F or lower, without much fluctuation. The freezer compartments of many refrigerators do not meet this requirement, nor do some models of freezers, including both old and newer appliances.

About Blanching

Blanching—quick heating to inactivate enzymes and retard spoilage—helps preserve color, flavor, texture, and nutritive value. You'll need to blanch most vegetables before freezing them. The most common method involves a dip in boiling water, but you may also blanch in steam or in a microwave oven. Steam- and microwave-blanched vegetables often have a fresher flavor and retain more water-soluble vitamins than do those treated in boiling water, but water blanching is generally more effective in removing surface residues and microorganisms.

Regardless of the method you select, always adhere to the times recommended in the chart on pages 91 to 93. Blanching too briefly may allow continued enzyme activity, giving you a poor-quality product. Overblanching results in diminished nutritive value and loss of color and flavor.

To blanch vegetables in boiling water, you'll need an 8-quart or larger pan filled with about 1 gallon of rapidly boiling water (for greens, use 2 gallons of water). A blanching pot with a perforated basket and lid is ideal. Place about 1 pound of prepared raw vegetables at a time in a wire basket or metal colander (or in blanching pot basket); then immerse in the boiling water. Let the water return to a boil; then cover the pot and begin timing as directed in the chart on pages 91 to 93.

To blanch vegetables in steam, use a steam blanching pot or an 8-quart or larger pan with a tight-fitting lid and a wire or perforated basket that will hold food at least 3 inches off the pan bottom. Pour 2 inches of water into the pan, cover, and bring to a boil over high heat. Place 1 to 2 pounds of prepared raw vegetables in a single layer in the basket; cover.

When steam begins to flow from the pan, begin timing as directed in the chart on pages 91 to 93.

To blanch vegetables in a microwave oven, you'll need an oven at least 1 cubic foot in size. Use a 1-quart round microwave-safe glass casserole or other microwave-safe container of similar size. Add ¼ cup water and no more than 2 cups prepared raw vegetables (or no more than 4 cups leafy greens). Larger amounts of vegetables and water (or large vegetable pieces) increase blanching times. Cover the container with microwave-safe plastic wrap; don't use glass lids, since they, too, may increase blanching times unpredictably.

To determine the appropriate blanching time, you'll need to consider both the vegetable you're blanching and the characteristics of your microwave, since ovens differ in size, power levels, heating rates, and uniformity of heating. If you have a relatively new 650- to 700-watt, medium-size to large oven with a built-in microwave mixer or revolving turntable, use the times given for high-wattage ovens (see the chart on pages 91 to 93). Otherwise, use the times stated for low-wattage ovens. Always blanch on **HIGH (100%)** power.

To cool blanched vegetables, immediately plunge them into a large quantity of cold (60°F or lower) water; change the water frequently. Or place the vegetables in a colander under cold running water. As a rule of thumb, cool vegetables for about the same amount of time you blanched them. Drain vegetables thoroughly after cooling.

Packaging & Headspace

Loose vegetables are usually packed in plastic freezer bags, then often placed in cardboard freezer cartons to protect the bags and make stacking easier. Rigid freezer containers may also be used; they're especially convenient for purées.

Unless otherwise noted in the chart (pages 91 to 93), leave headspace in bags or containers. For plastic freezer bags, leave ½-inch headspace. After filling the bags, press out as much air as possible, beginning from the bottom of each bag and moving toward the top to prevent air from reentering. Seal the bags tightly.

If you're packing vegetables in plastic containers or freezer jars, leave ½-inch headspace for pints, 1 inch for quarts.

Label all containers with the type of vegetable and the date; then freeze at once.

The unbeatable flavors of sweet, red-ripe tomatoes and fresh basil guarantee that made-from-scratch Garden Marinara Sauce will win raves. Serve it over pasta—or use it in our Caponata or Peperonata. You'll find all three recipes on page 88.

Guide for Freezing Vegetables

For details on blanching methods and cooling techniques, see "About Blanching" (page 89). Consult "Packaging & Headspace" (page 89) for instructions on how much headspace to leave.

Mushrooms and eggplant will keep well in the freezer for up to 3 months; all other vegetables keep for up to a year.

Vegetable	Quantity to yield 1 pint	How to prepare
Artichokes	20 to 25 (1- to 1¼-inch) trimmed whole small artichokes	Cut off thorny tops and stem ends. Remove coarse outer leaves, leaving only tender inner leaves. Rinse well. Blanch for 3 minutes in boiling lemon water (½ cup lemon juice per 2 quarts water). Cool; then drain and pack in plastic freezer bags or rigid freezer containers, leaving headspace.
Asparagus	1 to 1½ lbs.	Remove tough ends and scales; sort spears according to size. Rinse and drain. **For small spears,** blanch for 2 minutes in boiling water, 3 minutes in steam, 3 minutes in a high-wattage microwave oven, or 4 minutes in a low-wattage microwave oven. **For large spears,** blanch for 4 minutes in boiling water, 6 minutes in steam, 3 minutes in a high-wattage microwave oven, or 5 minutes in a low-wattage microwave oven. Cool; then drain and pack in plastic freezer bags or rigid freezer containers, leaving headspace.
Beans, fresh butter & lima	2 to 2½ lbs. (unshelled)	Shell and rinse beans; sort according to size. **For small beans,** blanch for 2 minutes in boiling water or for 3 minutes in steam. **For large beans,** blanch for 4 minutes in boiling water or for 6 minutes in steam. Cool; then drain and pack in plastic freezer bags or rigid freezer containers, leaving headspace.
Beans, snap Green, wax, Italian	⅔ to 1 lb.	Rinse beans and trim ends; remove strings, if necessary. Leave whole or cut into pieces of desired length. **For small beans (and thin cut pieces),** blanch for 2 minutes in boiling water, 3 minutes in steam, 3 minutes in a high-wattage microwave oven, or 4 minutes in a low-wattage microwave oven. **For large beans (and thick cut pieces),** blanch for 3 minutes in boiling water, 5 minutes in steam, 3 minutes in a high-wattage microwave oven, or 5 minutes in a low-wattage microwave oven. Cool; then drain and pack in plastic freezer bags or rigid freezer containers, leaving headspace.
Beets	1¼ to 1½ lbs.	To keep color from bleeding, leave root ends and 1 inch of tops on beets. Scrub well; don't peel. Cover with boiling water and boil gently until tender when pierced (20 to 45 minutes). Cool. Remove skins; trim off stems and roots. Leave small beets whole; slice or dice larger ones. Pack in plastic freezer bags or rigid freezer containers, leaving headspace.
Broccoli	1 lb.	Trim off outer leaves and tough stalk bases. Rinse broccoli. Trim flowerets from stalks; cut into pieces 1 to 2 inches in diameter. Cut tender stalks into ½-inch-thick pieces. Sort pieces according to size. If desired, soak for 30 minutes in salt water (¼ cup salt per gallon of cold water) to help remove insects; drain. **For small pieces,** blanch for 3 minutes in boiling water, 5 minutes in steam, 5 minutes in a high-wattage microwave oven, or 8 minutes in a low-wattage microwave oven. **For large pieces,** blanch for 4 minutes in boiling water, 6 minutes in steam, 5 minutes in a high-wattage microwave oven, or 8 minutes in a low-wattage microwave oven. Cool; drain and pack in plastic freezer bags or rigid freezer containers, leaving headspace.
Brussels sprouts	1 lb.	Trim off stalk bases and remove outer leaves. Rinse sprouts. Sort according to size. **For small sprouts,** blanch for 3 minutes in boiling water, 5 minutes in steam, 5 minutes in a high-wattage microwave oven, or 8 minutes in a low-wattage microwave oven. **For large sprouts,** blanch for 5 minutes in boiling water, 7 minutes in steam, 5 minutes in a high-wattage microwave oven, or 8 minutes in a low-wattage microwave oven. Cool; then drain and pack in plastic freezer bags or rigid freezer containers, leaving headspace.
Cabbage	1 to 1½ lbs.	Remove outer leaves. Rinse cabbage; cut into quarters or smaller wedges. **For quarters,** blanch for 4 minutes in boiling water or for 6 minutes in steam. **For smaller wedges,** blanch for 2 minutes in boiling water or for 3 minutes in steam. Cool; then drain and pack in plastic freezer bags or rigid freezer containers, leaving headspace.
Carrots	1¼ to 1½ lbs.	Rinse and peel. Leave small, tender carrots whole; cut others into ½-inch cubes or slices. **For diced or sliced carrots,** blanch for 2 minutes in boiling water, 3 minutes in steam, 5 minutes in a high-wattage microwave oven, or 7 minutes in a low-wattage microwave oven. **For whole carrots,** blanch for 5 minutes in boiling water, 8 minutes in steam, 5 minutes in a high-wattage microwave oven, or 7 minutes in a low-wattage oven. Cool; then drain and pack in plastic freezer bags or rigid freezer containers, leaving headspace.

Vegetable	Quantity to yield 1 pint	How to prepare
Cauliflower	1¼ lbs.	Break into 1- to 2-inch flowerets. Sort pieces according to size. If desired, soak for 30 minutes in salt water (¼ cup salt per gallon of cold water) to help remove insects; drain. **For small pieces,** blanch for 3 minutes in boiling water, 5 minutes in steam, 5 minutes in a high-wattage microwave oven, or 7 minutes in a low-wattage microwave oven. **For large pieces,** blanch for 5 minutes in boiling water, 7 minutes in steam, 5 minutes in a high-wattage microwave oven, or 7 minutes in a low-wattage microwave oven. Cool; then drain and pack in plastic freezer bags or rigid freezer containers, leaving headspace.
Corn	2 to 3 lbs. (in husks)	Discard husks and silk; rinse corn. **For whole-kernel corn,** blanch whole ears for 4 minutes in boiling water, 6 minutes in steam, 4 minutes in a high-wattage microwave oven, or 6 minutes in a low-wattage microwave oven. Drain; cool. Cut kernels from cobs with a sharp knife. Pack in plastic freezer bags, leaving headspace. **For cream-style corn,** blanch whole ears as for whole-kernel corn (above). Drain; cool. Cut kernels from cob with a sharp knife, then scrape remaining kernel tips and juice from cobs. Combine kernels, juice, and tips. Pack in plastic freezer bags, leaving headspace. **For corn on cob,** blanch **small ears** (less than 1¼-inch diameter) for 7 minutes in boiling water or for 10 minutes in steam. Blanch **medium-size ears** (1¼- to 1½-inch diameter) for 9 minutes in boiling water or for 13 minutes in steam. Blanch **large ears** (over 1½-inch diameter) for 11 minutes in boiling water or for 16 minutes in steam. Cool; then drain and pack in plastic freezer bags, leaving headspace.
Eggplant	1 to 1½ lbs.	Rinse, peel, and cut into ⅓-inch-thick slices. Blanch in boiling lemon water (½ cup lemon juice per gallon of water) for 4 minutes. Cool; then drain and pack in plastic freezer bags or rigid freezer containers, leaving headspace.
Ginger root	1 whole piece	Rinse and pat dry. No blanching required. Freeze whole in moisture- and vaporproof plastic wrap or in a small freezer bag. To use, grate or slice frozen root. Return unused portion to freezer.
Greens (including spinach) Beet, collard, kale, mustard, spinach, turnip	1 to 1½ lbs.	Rinse carefully, working with 2 to 3 pounds of greens at a time. Drain; continue to rinse until water is clear and free of grit. Cut tough stems from leaves; then tear or cut leaves into 2- to 4-inch pieces. Blanch for 2 minutes in boiling water, 3 minutes in steam, 4 minutes in a high-wattage microwave oven, or 6 minutes in a low-wattage microwave oven. Cool; then drain and pack in plastic freezer bags or rigid freezer containers, leaving headspace.
Mushrooms Commercial mushrooms only	1 to 1½ lbs.	Rinse well. Trim off stems and cut out discolored parts. Leave whole or slice. **For sliced mushrooms,** blanch for 3 minutes in boiling lemon water (½ cup lemon juice per gallon of water). **For whole mushrooms,** blanch for 6 minutes in boiling lemon water (½ cup lemon juice per gallon of water). Cool; then drain and pack in plastic freezer bags or rigid freezer containers, leaving headspace.
Okra	1 to 1½ lbs.	Rinse; trim ends, but don't open seed cells. Sort according to size. **For small pods,** blanch for 3 minutes in boiling water or for 5 minutes in steam. **For large pods,** blanch for 5 minutes in boiling water or for 8 minutes in steam. Cool; then drain and pack in plastic freezer bags or rigid freezer containers, leaving headspace.
Onions, yellow or white	1 lb.	Peel; remove outer layers until bulb is free of blemishes. Rinse. Chop; or leave small onions whole. No blanching required. Spread chopped or whole onions on trays and freeze for 4 to 6 hours. Pack in plastic freezer bags or rigid freezer containers. No headspace is needed.
Parsnips *See* Turnips, parsnips & rutabagas		
Peas, green or black-eyed	2 to 3 lbs. (unshelled)	Shell and rinse. Sort according to size. **For small peas,** blanch for 1½ minutes in boiling water, 3 minutes in steam, 4 minutes in a high-wattage microwave oven, or 6 minutes in a low-wattage microwave oven. **For large peas,** blanch for 2½ minutes in boiling water, 5 minutes in steam, 4 minutes in a high-wattage microwave oven, or 6 minutes in a low-wattage microwave oven. Cool; drain and pack in plastic freezer bags or rigid freezer containers, leaving headspace.
Peas, snow or sugar snap	⅔ to 1 lb.	Rinse. Remove ends and any strings from pods. Sort according to size. **For small pods,** blanch for 2 minutes in boiling water, 4 minutes in steam, 4 minutes in a high-wattage microwave oven, or 6 minutes in a low-wattage microwave oven. **For large pods,** blanch for 3 minutes in boiling water, 5 minutes in steam, 4 minutes in a high-wattage microwave oven, or 6 minutes in a low-wattage microwave oven. Cool; then drain and pack in plastic freezer bags or rigid freezer containers, leaving headspace.

Vegetable	Quantity to yield 1 pint	How to prepare
Peppers, bell, all colors	1 to 2 lbs.	Rinse. Remove stems and seeds. Cut into rings or strips. Blanch for 2 minutes in boiling water or for 3 minutes in steam. Spread on trays and freeze until solid. Pack in plastic freezer bags or rigid freezer containers. No headspace is needed.
Peppers, hot chile	1 to 2 lbs.	Wear rubber gloves when preparing. Rinse and remove stems. No blanching required. Pack in plastic freezer bags or rigid freezer containers, leaving headspace.
Peppers, mild chile	1 to 2 lbs.	Wear rubber gloves when preparing. Rinse chiles; make two ¼-inch slits in each one. Place in a shallow pan and broil, turning as needed, until skins blister. To make peeling easier, cover tightly with foil or place in a plastic bag and close bag. Let stand for about 10 minutes, then peel. Discard stems and seeds. Flatten; or slice or dice. Spread on trays and freeze until solid. Pack in plastic freezer bags or rigid freezer containers. No headspace is needed.
Potatoes, sweet	1 to 1½ lbs.	Rinse well. No blanching required. Boil or steam until tender. Peel, halve, slice, or mash. Dip slices and halves in lemon water (½ cup lemon juice per quart of water); or add 1 tablespoon lemon juice to each pint of mashed sweet potatoes. Pack in rigid freezer containers, leaving headspace.
Potatoes, white French fries	1 to 2 lbs.	Cut peeled potatoes into ⅜-inch-thick strips. No blanching required. Soak for 1 minute in cold water. Drain, rinse, and pat dry with towels. Fry for about 5 minutes in hot oil (360°F) to cover. Drain on paper towels, let cool, and pack in plastic freezer bags, leaving headspace. To reheat, spread potatoes, still frozen, on baking sheets. Heat in a 475° oven for 5 to 6 minutes.
Rutabagas *See* Turnips, parsnips & rutabagas		
Spinach *See* Greens (including spinach)		
Squash, spaghetti	1 to 1½ lbs.	Rinse. No blanching required. Boil or bake until tender when pierced (about 45 minutes in boiling water, about 1 hour in a 350° oven). Let cool; then cut into halves, scoop out strands, and pack in rigid freezer containers, leaving headspace.
Squash, summer Crookneck, pattypan, zucchini	1 to 1¼ lbs.	Rinse squash and trim ends. Cut into ¼- to ½-inch-thick slices. Blanch for 3 minutes in boiling water or for 5 minutes in steam. Cool; then drain and pack in plastic freezer bags or rigid freezer containers, leaving headspace.
Squash, winter (including pumpkin) Banana, butternut, Hubbard, pumpkin	1 to 1½ lbs.	Rinse. Scrape out all seeds and fibrous material; cut into chunks or slices. No blanching required. Steam, boil, or bake until tender. Let cool; remove and discard skin. Purée flesh; pack in rigid freezer containers, leaving headspace.
Tomatoes		Rinse; dip for 30 to 60 seconds in boiling water. Cool and slip off skins. Quarter and simmer until tender (5 to 10 minutes). Press through a sieve, if desired. Let cool. Pack in rigid freezer containers, leaving headspace. Or freeze raw whole unpeeled tomatoes in rigid freezer containers for no longer than 2 to 3 weeks to use for cooking or seasoning. To peel, hold frozen tomatoes under cold water for a second or two; then slip off skins.
Turnips, parsnips & rutabagas	1¼ to 1½ lbs.	Rinse. Peel; cut into ½-inch pieces. Blanch for 3 minutes in boiling water, 5 minutes in steam, 4 minutes in a high-wattage microwave oven, or 6 minutes in a low-wattage microwave oven. Cool; then drain and pack in plastic freezer bags or rigid freezer containers, leaving headspace.
Vegetable mixes (for use in soups and stews)	1 to 1½ lbs.	Prepare each vegetable as specified above. Mix prepared vegetables and pack in plastic freezer bags or rigid freezer containers, leaving headspace.

Freezing Meat, Poultry & Seafood

What's for dinner? If you keep plenty of meat, poultry, and seafood in the freezer, you'll always have an answer to that question. The freezer can help with the food budget, too, when you take advantage of specials to stock up on favorite meats.

Buying Meat for Freezing

Select only fresh, high-quality meats. Remember that cured meats such as bologna and ham are best if used within a short period of time—1 to 3 months. Sliced bacon should be used within a month; if frozen longer, it tends to dry out and taste very salty after cooking.

How much to buy? The amount of meat you buy for freezing—not only the total poundage, but also the types of cuts and their size and weight—will depend on several factors. You'll need to consider your available freezer space, your family's needs, your budget, and the quantity your freezer can handle at one time (see the manufacturer's instructions). If you've purchased or plan to freeze a large amount of meat, it's best to have the market or a butcher cut, wrap, and freeze it. Slower home freezing can cause large ice crystals to form in the meat; these damage cell membranes, so that juices are lost during thawing.

Preparing Meat for the Freezer

Common notions notwithstanding, freezing neither tenderizes nor sterilizes meat. What it does do is reduce enzyme activity and stop the growth of bacteria and molds.

When you're cutting up meat to freeze yourself, make sure all utensils and cutting boards are spotlessly clean. Begin by chilling the meat; then cut it into pieces. To save freezer space, trim off excess fat before wrapping; remove bones from relatively bony pieces. Freeze meat in portions that suit your family's needs, remembering that smaller packages freeze and thaw more rapidly.

To package meat for freezing, use moisture- and vaporproof materials. Wrap all cuts closely, eliminating all air if possible; place a double thickness of freezer wrap or wax paper between chops, steaks, or ground meat patties so they won't stick together. Then pack the wrapped meat in plastic freezer bags or moisture- and vaporproof wrap. Be aware that packaged meat from the supermarket should be overwrapped at home before freezing, since typical see-through packaging is not moisture- and vaporproof.

You can use two wrapping techniques: the drugstore wrap and the butcher wrap. Both are illustrated below.

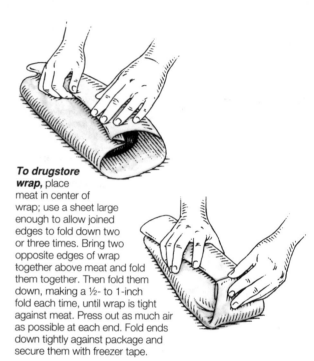

To drugstore wrap, place meat in center of wrap; use a sheet large enough to allow joined edges to fold down two or three times. Bring two opposite edges of wrap together above meat and fold them together. Then fold them down, making a ½- to 1-inch fold each time, until wrap is tight against meat. Press out as much air as possible at each end. Fold ends down tightly against package and secure them with freezer tape.

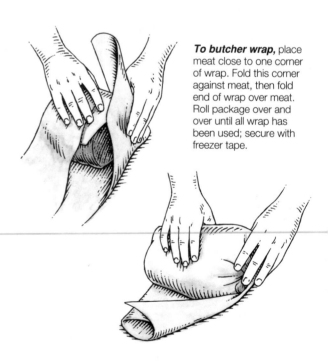

To butcher wrap, place meat close to one corner of wrap. Fold this corner against meat, then fold end of wrap over meat. Roll package over and over until all wrap has been used; secure with freezer tape.

For convenient storage and easier preparation at mealtime, cut large fish into steaks or fillets and freeze in meal-size portions. Separate the pieces with a double thickness of freezer wrap or wax paper; then freeze in plastic freezer bags or wrap. For more on preparing seafood for freezing, see page 96.

Label all packages with the cut of meat, the weight or number of servings, and the date. Then freeze at 0°F or below, making sure to leave space for air circulation between packages.

For recommended storage times at 0°F for different meats, check the chart below. Meat that has been partially thawed in the refrigerator can safely be refrozen, but you can expect some loss of quality.

Beef	
Ground & stew meat	3 to 4 months
Roasts & steaks	8 to 12 months

Lamb	
Ground & stew meat	3 to 4 months
Roasts & chops	6 to 9 months

Pork	
Ground sausage (patties or chunks) or link sausage	1 to 2 months
Roasts & chops	4 to 6 months
Pork & ham, smoked	1 to 3 months
Ham, fully cooked	1 to 2 months
Bacon, sliced	Up to 1 month

Preparing Poultry for the Freezer

Poultry can be frozen whole, halved, quartered, or in pieces. *Never* stuff whole poultry before freezing; the stuffing takes so long to cool during freezing—and to thaw and reheat during roasting—that spoilage and bacterial growth can occur.

Before freezing any poultry, rinse it well in cold water; pat dry with paper towels.

To freeze whole birds, start by freezing the giblets separately in a small plastic freezer bag or in moisture- and vaporproof plastic wrap; use them within 3 months, since they develop an "off" flavor if stored longer. (If you plan to use the poultry within 3 months, you can simply tuck the wrapped giblets into the body cavity; remember to remove them after thawing the bird.) Tie the drumsticks together at the tips; press the wings close to the body or tuck them behind the bird, akimbo-style. Then place each bird in a plastic freezer bag. To remove as much air as possible before sealing, submerge the bag in water up to the opening, then press it against the poultry.

Or simply press out as much air as you can with your hands.

You can also package each bird by placing it in the center of a sheet of moisture- and vaporproof wrap. Bring the long edges together over the bird and fold them down about 1 inch; continue to fold until the wrap is tight and flat over the bird. Force out air by pressing the wrap against the bird; then fold the corners of the wrap toward each other at each end of the bird, making a tight package. Secure with freezer tape.

To freeze poultry halves or quarters, separate the pieces with a double thickness of freezer wrap or wax paper, then place in plastic freezer bags. Or wrap and freeze pieces individually.

To freeze poultry pieces, separate the meaty pieces from the bony ones (bony parts can be used in soup). Spread the pieces in a single layer on a tray and freeze until solid, then place in plastic freezer bags. Or separate unfrozen pieces with a double layer of freezer wrap or wax paper, then pack the pieces close together in plastic freezer bags or moisture- and vaporproof plastic wrap. (The meat near the leg bones may darken, but its quality isn't affected.)

Store all poultry at 0°F for 6 to 12 months.

Preparing Seafood for the Freezer

To freeze fish and shellfish successfully, you must keep them cold after you purchase (or catch) them, then clean and freeze them as quickly as possible.

Freeze *small fish* whole, packaged in moisture- and vaporproof plastic wrap or plastic freezer bags. You may also pack them in rigid freezer containers, adding water to cover. Or place in plastic freezer bags in a large carton; fill the bags with water, leaving ¼-inch headspace, and seal.

Dress *medium-size fish* and package (individually or in meal-size quantities) in moisture- and vapor-proof plastic wrap or plastic freezer bags. Seal tightly, then place in a larger freezer bag.

You may cut *large fish* into steaks, fillets, or boned strips before freezing; package in meal-size quantities, separating pieces with double layers of freezer wrap or wax paper. Or store the fish whole, first glazing them for extra protection. To glaze, freeze the fish unwrapped, then dip it quickly in ice water to form a film of ice over the surface. Continue to dip until the ice glaze is ⅛ inch thick; if necessary, place the fish in the freezer between dippings to get a hard glaze. Package in a large plastic freezer bag and store in the coldest part of the freezer.

To prevent fatty fish such as tuna and salmon from darkening and turning rancid, dip the pieces in an ascorbic acid solution (2 tablespoons ascorbic acid to 1 quart water) for 20 seconds. Then package the fish in meal-size portions, separating pieces with double thicknesses of freezer wrap or wax paper; freeze quickly.

Shellfish is easy to freeze. For *shrimp*, remove heads, but do not shell; or remove entire shell, then devein. Freeze in a single layer on trays until solid, then package in plastic freezer bags.

Shuck or open *clams* and *oysters* and place in a colander to drain; reserve juices. Remove meat and rinse thoroughly and quickly in a solution of 1 tablespoon salt to 1 quart water; drain well. Pack meat in freezer jars or rigid freezer containers; barely cover with reserved juices (and more of the salt solution, if needed), leaving headspace. Freeze quickly. (Keep in mind that freezing changes the texture and flavor of oysters; they're best used in stews or casseroles.)

Prepare *crab* and *lobster* as soon as possible after purchase. Rinse the shellfish well and cook for 20 minutes; drain and let cool slightly, then pick meat from shells while still warm. Tightly pack meat in freezer jars or rigid freezer containers, removing as much air as possible. Leave headspace.

Scallops are usually purchased ready for freezing. Pack them in rigid freezer containers; barely cover with a solution of 1 tablespoon salt to 1 quart water, leaving headspace.

For recommended storage times at 0°F for various fish and shellfish, check the chart below.

Fish	
Fatty fish (tuna, salmon)	2 to 3 months
Lean fish (haddock, sole, trout)	6 to 8 months

Shellfish	
Crab & lobster, cooked	2 to 3 months
Oysters	4 to 6 months
Clams & scallops	4 to 6 months
Shrimp	6 to 8 months

Freezing Glossary

Antidarkening agent. Any antioxidant used to keep light-colored fruits (and some vegetables) from browning after cutting. Antidarkening agents commonly used on fruits to be frozen include ascorbic acid, citrus juice, and commercial products containing ascorbic and/or citric acids (and often sugar).

Blanching. The process of heating food quickly in boiling water or steam (or, in small amounts, in a microwave oven) to inactivate enzymes that can cause loss of color, flavor, and nutritive value. Most vegetables are blanched before freezing.

Dry pack. *See* Sugar pack.

Freezer burn. Damage caused by dehydration; often found in improperly packed frozen foods. Freezer-burned food is spotted with dry, grainy-textured, whitish or brownish areas.

Freezer wrap. Any moisture- and vaporproof wrap, including plastic wrap, coated or laminated paper, and heavy-duty foil.

Headspace. The unfilled space between the top of the food or liquid in a freezer container and the lid of the container.

Liquid pack. Fruit or vegetables packed for freezing in syrup or other liquid.

Moisture- and vaporproof packaging. Choices include both containers and wraps. You may use rigid plastic containers with tight-fitting lids; wide-mouth dual-purpose glass freezer/canning jars; plastic freezer bags with reclosable tops (or bags sealed with wire twist-ties or freezer tape); plastic wrap; coated or laminated paper; and heavy-duty foil.

Sugar pack. Fruit packed for freezing with sugar but without added liquid. Also called *dry pack*.

Syrup pack. Fruit packed for freezing with a syrup of sugar and water (or juice).

Freezing Fresh Herbs

Freezing is a good way to preserve tender herbs such as dill, chives, and tarragon. Simply rinse freshly picked herbs, carefully pat them dry, and freeze in small plastic freezer bags in amounts you'll use at one time. Because frozen herbs darken and become limp upon thawing, add them still frozen to the food you're seasoning.

Dried foods are marvelous to have on hand for snacking and for use in cooking. Shown on the tabletop are (clockwise from left) bell peppers (page 117), apples (page 112), plums (page 113), Dried Fruit Trail Mix (page 109), tomatoes (page 117), Barbecued Jerky (page 120), Teriyaki Turkey Jerky (page 121), peaches (page 113), mushrooms (page 117), apricots (page 112), and a plate holding Dried Fruits with Blue Cheese and High-energy Trail Logs (both on page 109). On the shelf above are fragrant dried herbs (see page 118).

Drying

Sweet dried fruits,
colorful vegetables,
hearty jerky

*T*hough recent years have seen a surge in the popularity of home drying, this method of food preservation is hardly new. Early American settlers made it through the winter on dried foods, as did the pioneers who traveled across the country to settle on the Western frontier. Sailors, too, relied on dried food supplies during long ocean voyages. ● Home-dried food is economical and easy to store. And with the advent of modern electric dehydrators, it's easy to prepare: you can dry food under sanitary conditions 24 hours a day, in any weather, with little watching or turning. Though dehydrators aren't inexpensive, in a few summers they often pay for themselves—with delicious dried fruits, fruit leathers, tomatoes, vegetables, and other foods for snacking and backpacking. ● Of course, if you live in a hot, dry climate, you may prefer to dry your food naturally out of doors. Many foods can also be dried successfully at very low temperatures in conventional or convection ovens. ● Home drying isn't as exact a science as canning or freezing; your results may vary depending on the weather, the type of pretreatment, and the particular drying method you choose. But with help from this book—and a little trial and error—you'll soon find the techniques that suit you best.

What Happens in Drying?

When you dry food, you remove moisture from it to inhibit the growth of microorganisms that might cause spoilage. Enzyme activity also slows, though it doesn't stop entirely. Keep in mind, however, that drying *doesn't* sterilize food: as soon as it has been rehydrated, microorganisms begin growing again.

Dried fruits retain only 15 to 20 percent of their original moisture, dried vegetables about 5 percent. As a natural consequence of this moisture loss, dried foods are much lighter in weight and take up far less space than do their fresh counterparts.

Drying Basics

To dry food, you need two things: increased temperature and dry, moving air.

The optimal drying temperatures given in this chapter are high enough to remove moisture from foods, yet not so high that the foods begin to cook. In general, vegetables are dried at 125° to 130°F, fruits at 135° to 140°F, and meats at 140° to 150°F. Be sure the temperature doesn't fall below the suggested level: if the air is overly cool, food dries too slowly and may spoil. Nor should you try to hurry things along by using higher temperatures, since foods (especially fruits) may "case harden"—cook and harden on the outside while remaining moist on the inside. Case-hardened food is low in quality and tends to turn moldy.

Dry, moving air first absorbs, then carries away the water released by drying food. The drier the air and the greater the airflow, the faster the food will dry. Calm, humid conditions, on the other hand, retard the drying process and increase the likelihood of spoilage.

Three Drying Methods

You can dry foods in the sun, in an electric dehydrator, or in a conventional or convection oven. Each method has its advantages and drawbacks; when you decide which technique to use, consider the amount of time and money you have to invest as well as the quantity of food you plan to dry. And remember: for successful results by any method, you'll need a combination of warm temperatures, low humidity, and good airflow.

Sun Drying

Sun drying is the earliest known form of food preservation, and most commercial dried fruits—apricots, prunes, raisins, and figs, for example—are still prepared in this age-old way. In fact, fruits are probably the best choice for drying outdoors, since they're high in sugar and acid (both natural preservatives) and thus less prone to spoilage. Vegetables, low in sugar and acid, are more likely to spoil; and meat's high protein content favors the growth of microorganisms unless heat and humidity can be strictly regulated. These foods are better dried inside, under the controlled conditions of a dehydrator or oven.

Where climate permits, sun drying is the least expensive of drying methods, and it lets you prepare large quantities at one time. It does require a fair amount of time and effort, though, and the food must be protected from insects and birds and covered at night. Sun drying is most feasible in regions where the humidity is low, air pollution is minimal, and the weather is sunny and hot (temperatures of 85°F or higher) for many days in a row.

To sun dry, use racks or screens safe for contact with food, such as those made from stainless steel or plastic with a nonstick coating. Do *not* use screening made of aluminum or copper; aluminum tends to corrode, discoloring the food, while copper increases oxidation of the food and destroys vitamin C. Also avoid galvanized metal screens coated with cadmium or zinc; these can leave harmful residues on food.

To ensure good air circulation, place your racks or screens on blocks, then cover them with a second screen or nylon netting as protection against birds and insects. (Don't let the top screen touch the food.)

For more detailed information on sun drying, contact your local Cooperative Extension office.

Drying in a Dehydrator

An electric dehydrator offers you the easiest, most reliable means of drying foods. A dehydrator is a box-shaped or cylindrical appliance that maintains a low, even temperature and circulates heated air (either horizontally or vertically, depending on the model) with a blower or fan. Most dehydrators are equipped with a thermostat and several trays. Some types are expandable, and those with many shelves allow you to dry more food at one time than an oven can handle.

Dehydrators generally yield excellent results, and they can be used all day long, in any weather, for any kind of food. They aren't cheap, though; prices range from $50 to $350, with $100 to $200 the average cost. But if you eat dried foods regularly and often take them along while backpacking and camping, you'll probably make up your investment in short order.

Sources for dehydrators include some hardware and department stores, mail-order and seed or garden supply catalogs, and natural food stores. You might also check the Yellow Pages of your telephone directory under "Dehydrating Equipment"; or call your Cooperative Extension office.

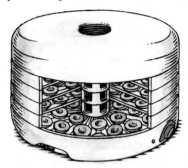

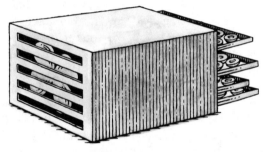

Electric dehydrators with vertical airflow (left) and horizontal airflow (below)

Dehydrator shopping tips. If you decide to buy a dehydrator, keep these questions in mind as you shop.

■ How well is the dehydrator constructed? Is the heating element enclosed for safety, and does it provide sufficient wattage for the entire drying area (about 70 watts per tray)? Are the walls insulated and easy to clean? Does the appliance have an enclosed thermostat? Is there a temperature control adjustable from 85° to 160°F? Is there a timer that can turn the dehydrator off to prevent scorching?

■ Does the fan or blower circulate heated air evenly over all of the food—and is it quiet? (Remember that you may be operating your dehydrator for long periods of time.)

■ Are the trays and inserts made of materials safe for contact with food, such as nylon, stainless steel, or plastic with a nonstick coating? Are there four to ten trays that can accommodate ample quantities of food? Are additional trays available? Can the trays be easily pulled forward or entirely removed? Are they easy to keep clean?

■ Is there a UL seal of approval? A 1-year warranty? Convenient service?

Oven Drying

If you can set your oven at a temperature between 120° and 150°F, you can use it for drying food. Unfortunately, many ovens have minimum settings of 200°F—too high for drying fruits and vegetables—but some modern conventional ovens may offer sufficiently low temperatures. Modern convection ovens can also be used for drying, and dehydrating accessories are often available for them; follow the manufacturer's advice. *The discussion below concerns conventional ovens only.*

Foods dry more rapidly in an oven than in the sun, but usually not as quickly as in a dehydrator, since most ovens lack a built-in fan to circulate air and carry away moisture. Oven drying also consumes more energy (and thus costs more) than dehydrator drying—and it can tie up your oven for hours at a time. Finally, oven-dried foods require a great deal of checking and tending as they dry.

Trays for oven drying should be 3 to 4 inches shorter than the oven from front to back, and narrow enough to clear the oven sides; you may use wire cooling racks placed on top of baking sheets or shallow baking pans. To permit proper air circulation, position the oven racks holding the trays 2 to 3 inches apart.

When you use a conventional oven for drying, you'll need to leave the door propped open by 2 to 6 inches; if you have an electric oven, make sure the upper (broiling) element is turned off. Because oven temperature varies when the door is open, place an oven thermometer next to the food; then adjust the oven temperature dial until the proper temperature is reached.

To improve air circulation, you can set a fan outside the oven door to one side, directing the airflow towards the oven opening. **Caution:** If you use a fan, be sure the oven and fan are attended throughout the drying period. If small children are present, don't use a fan at all; it can be dangerous.

One final note: *Never* oven-dry sulfured foods. Sulfur dioxide produces extremely irritating fumes and can also discolor the inside of your oven. You may, however, oven-dry foods dipped in a sodium bisulfite solution. (For more on sulfuring and sulfite dips, see pages 102 to 104.)

Equipment You'll Need

If you plan to use an electric dehydrator, you'll obviously need to start by buying that (see "Dehydrator shopping tips," at left). But almost all the other equipment you'll use is probably already in your kitchen: a scale for weighing ingredients, a colander for rinsing produce, a steamer (or a large pot and colander or wire basket) for blanching, a sharp knife or mandolin (or a food processor) for slicing, measuring cups and spoons, and a food processor or blender for puréeing fruit for leathers and dehydrated jams.

Packaging & Storing Dried Foods

Before packaging dried foods, make sure they're completely cool: warm food sweats, producing enough moisture for mold to grow. Dried fruits must be conditioned for 3 to 7 days before storage; see "Conditioning" (page 105).

Sun-dried foods in particular are susceptible to insect contamination, but dehydrators and oven-dried foods cooling indoors also attract flies and other pests. It's wise, therefore, to freeze all dried foods in plastic freezer bags for 48 hours to kill any insects or eggs that might be present. Once the food has been frozen, place it in clean, dry, insectproof containers, packing it as tightly as possible without crushing. Glass jars, metal cans or boxes, and rigid plastic containers with tight-fitting lids are all good choices—but don't place sulfured fruit in a metal can unless you've first enclosed it in a plastic bag (sulfur fumes react with metal and may cause the fruit to change color).

It's convenient to store dried foods in small heavy-duty plastic bags in amounts you'll use at one time. This kind of packaging is sensible from a freshness standpoint, too, since air and moisture enter each time you reopen packaged dried food, with a resulting decrease in quality. Just be sure to store bagged foods in one of the containers mentioned above (or in the refrigerator or freezer), since insects and rodents can penetrate plastic bags.

If stored in a cool, dry, dark area, dried foods will generally keep from 3 months to 1 year, depending on the particular food. Higher temperatures decrease maximum storage times; for example, most dried fruits store well for a year at 60°F, but only for 6 months at 80°F. Vegetables usually have about half this shelf life. Of course, refrigerated or frozen dried foods keep well longer.

Even foods that are very dry when stored can spoil if they reabsorb moisture, so check frequently to make sure your dried foods are still dry (glass jars make it easy to tell if there's moisture in the container). If the food looks at all moist, use it immediately; or redry and repackage it.

Drying Fresh Fruits

Naturally sweet and flavorful, nutritious dried fruits are delicious snacks and wonderful additions to cereals and baked goods. And when rehydrated, they're marvelous in sauces and toppings.

Preparing the Fruit

Assemble all the equipment you'll need for drying. Select fully ripe fruit in top condition, and prepare only as much as you can dry at one time. Just before processing, rinse the fruit well in cold water to remove dirt, insects, and insect eggs (you can't see the eggs, but if they're not washed away, they may hatch during storage).

As noted in our "Guide for Drying Fruits" (pages 112 and 113), most fruits dry more evenly and rapidly when sliced. When you cut them, keep in mind that lengthwise slicing yields fewer, larger pieces than crosswise slicing. If you like, you can dry peaches, nectarines, pears, plums, and apricots as halves; to shorten drying times, flatten the halves ("pop the backs") by pressing in the rounded side with your thumb to expose more surface. Dry the fruit skin side down, so juices will collect and dry in the cavity.

Some kinds of fruit can successfully be dried whole; be sure to pit them to hasten drying. Small whole fruits such as cherries, blueberries, cranberries, grapes, figs, and prune plums will dry faster if you first dip them in boiling water just long enough to crack ("check") the skins.

Many kinds, however, are best if pretreated to prevent *oxidation*: a chemical reaction that makes fruit darken when cut, diminishes flavor, and causes loss of vitamins A and C. A number of different pretreatments are described below; for advice on specific fruits, consult the chart on pages 112 and 113.

Pretreating Fruit

If you're drying fruit for long-term storage, you'll find that sulfuring it outdoors is the best way to preserve its color and flavor. Dipping fruit indoors in a sodium bisulfite solution is another excellent treatment. If you wish to avoid sulfur compounds, choose an alternative such as ascorbic acid, citric acid, or citrus juice; these often do a good job, though they're not as effective as sulfur.

Sulfuring. A very old and highly effective method, sulfuring preserves the fresh, natural appearance of

*Scandinavian Dried Fruit Soup (page 110) offers a delicious blend of flavors. Start by
simmering your favorite dried fruits with lemon slices, orange juice, and cinnamon;
then add fresh pineapple chunks, honey, and a little rum. Serve the dessert hot or cold,
topped with spoonfuls of vanilla yogurt and a sprinkling of cinnamon or nutmeg.*

light-colored fruits, helps repel insects, inhibits mold growth, and speeds drying time. There are drawbacks, though. The process is time consuming and demands special care—and in addition, sulfured fruit may cause an allergic reaction in some asthmatics.

Fruit to be sulfured is usually placed on wooden trays in a "sulfur box"—often just a large cardboard box with two vents—set on concrete blocks over a shallow pit containing a pan of flowers of sulfur. (Also sold as "sublimed sulfur," flowers of sulfur are available in some pharmacies and in many garden supply stores.) The sulfur is burned briefly; then the box vents are closed and the fruit is exposed to the sulfur fumes for several hours. Finally, the sulfured fruit is dried outdoors in a dehydrator or in the sun. Because sulfur dioxide fumes are harmful when inhaled, sulfuring—as well as the drying of the treated fruit—must *always* be done outside, in an area with good air circulation. *Never dry sulfured fruit indoors in an oven or dehydrator.*

For detailed instructions on making a sulfur box and sulfuring fruit, contact your local Cooperative Extension office.

Sulfite dip. Sulfite dipping isn't as effective as sulfuring, but it's an excellent pretreatment nonetheless—and it can be done safely and easily indoors. Sulfite-dipped fruit can be dried indoors or out: in a dehydrator or an oven, or in the sun.

To prepare a sulfite dip, start by purchasing food-grade sodium bisulfite, sodium sulfite, or sodium metabisulfite from a wine-making supply store, pharmacy, or hobby shop. Dissolve ½ teaspoon sodium bisulfite, 1 teaspoon sodium sulfite, or 2 teaspoons sodium metabisulfite in a quart of cold water. (Sodium sulfite is half as strong as sodium bisulfite, sodium metabisulfite a fourth as strong.) Add the fruit to the solution; soak slices for up to 10 minutes, halves for up to 30 minutes. Then remove the fruit, rinse it lightly under cold running water, drain, and dry.

Ascorbic acid. Though less effective than sulfuring in preventing browning, pretreatment with ascorbic acid (vitamin C in powder form) yields nutritious, good-tasting fruit.

To prepare the dipping solution, dissolve 1 tablespoon pure crystalline ascorbic acid (sold in pharmacies and most health food stores) in a quart of cold water. Add the fruit and soak it for a few minutes; then drain well and dry. After using the solution two or three times, discard it and mix up a new batch.

Commercial antidarkening agents. Commercially marketed antidarkening agents are mixtures of ascorbic and/or citric acids (and often sugar) sold for use on fresh fruits to be canned or frozen. They're not as effective as ascorbic acid.

To prepare the dipping solution, dissolve 1½ tablespoons antidarkening agent in a quart of cold water. Add the fruit and soak it for a few minutes; then drain well and dry. After using the solution two or three times, discard it and mix up a new batch.

Citrus juices. Lemon and lime juices help prevent oxidation and preserve color, but they're only a sixth as effective as ascorbic acid.

To prepare the dipping solution, mix 1 cup lemon or lime juice with a quart of cold water. Soak the fruit for no more than 10 minutes; then drain well and dry. (You may use unsweetened pineapple juice in place of lemon or lime juice, but it doesn't enhance the fruit flavor as much as the other juices do.)

Citric acid. Citric acid is just an eighth as effective as ascorbic acid, and its tart taste may mask the fruit's flavor.

To prepare the dipping solution, dissolve 1 tablespoon citric acid in a quart of cold water. Add the fruit and soak it for a few minutes; then drain well and dry. After using the solution two or three times, discard it and mix up a fresh batch.

Honey-lemon dip. Honey is a natural preservative; lemon juice helps fruit keep its color. To prepare the dip, mix ½ cup honey with ½ cup water and the juice of one lemon. Heat slightly to dissolve the honey. Dip the fruit in the mixture, then drain well and dry.

Honey dip. Many store-bought dried fruits are honey dipped. To make the solution, dissolve 1 cup sugar in 3 cups hot water; let cool, then add 1 cup honey. Dip fruit in small batches; drain well and dry.

Blanching. Steam or water blanching slows oxidation and helps fruit retain its color—but it gives a less flavorful product than other methods, and the fruit has a slightly cooked taste and texture. For details on blanching techniques and times, contact your local Cooperative Extension office.

Drying the Fruit

Regardless of the drying method you use, it's important to arrange the fruit on trays or racks in a single layer, without letting the pieces touch or overlap.

To sun dry, start by reading "Sun Drying" (page 100). Arrange racks or screens in direct sun. Check the fruit frequently; move the racks when they become shaded. Unless you live where nights are relatively clear and evening temperatures remain within 20 degrees of midday highs, you'll need to take the drying racks to a porch or other sheltered place at night to keep the fruit from being dampened by dew. (Even if you can leave your racks out overnight, be sure to cover them loosely.)

After the fruit has dried for 2 or 3 days, place it in the shade for the remainder of the drying time; it will have a better flavor and color and retain more nutrients than it would if left in the sun throughout the drying process.

To dry fruit in a dehydrator, follow the manufacturer's instructions. In general, fruit should be dried at 135° to 140°F.

To dry fruit in a conventional oven, consult "Oven Drying" (page 101). Set the oven temperature at 140°F.

To dry fruit in a convection oven, follow the manufacturer's instructions.

Determining Dryness

The "Guide for Drying Fruits" (pages 112 and 113) gives specific dryness tests for a number of fruits. If you're preparing apricots, prunes, apples, or other types that you'll often eat without rehydrating, it's important not to dry them so long that they turn hard or brittle. To avoid overdrying, check the fruit frequently as it becomes drier: let a piece cool to room temperature, then cut it in half. Most types should remain pliable, but they shouldn't be sticky or show any visible pockets of moisture.

Conditioning

Dried fruit should always be "conditioned" to distribute any remaining moisture more evenly, reducing the possibility of mold.

To condition fruit, cool it to room temperature; then pack it loosely in plastic or glass containers with tight-fitting lids and let stand for 3 to 7 days. Over this period of time, the excess moisture in some pieces will be absorbed by drier fruit. Each day, shake the containers to separate the pieces, then check for condensation. If you see droplets or a mist of moisture on the container sides, the fruit should be redried.

After conditioning the fruit, package and store it as directed on page 102.

Using Dried Fruits

Dried fruits are superb "as is" for snacks, though you may wish to soften them slightly before eating. If the fruit is to be stewed or served as a sauce or topping, though, you'll need to reconstitute it in liquid (wait until it's as plump as you like before adding sugar, since sugar tends to hinder water absorption). And remember: the longer a fruit takes to dehydrate, the more time it will require to rehydrate.

To soften dried fruit for snacks. If the fruit is too firm for your taste, place it (in 1-cup quantities) in a plastic bag, sprinkle it with several drops of water, close the bag tightly, and refrigerate overnight.

To soften dried fruit for use in bread, cookie, and cake recipes. Steam for several minutes, then cut or slice as the recipe directs.

To rehydrate dried fruit. Spread the fruit in a shallow container and barely cover it with liquid, using about 1 cup liquid for each 2 cups fruit. The liquid you use may be water, fruit juice, fruit liqueur, wine, or brandy. Fruit usually rehydrates within a few hours; if more time is needed, cover the dish and refrigerate it to keep the fruit from fermenting. Add more liquid if necessary—but for best flavor and texture, keep the liquid you add to a minimum.

To cook rehydrated fruit in liquid. If you want to cook fruit after it has been rehydrated, simmer it, covered, in any remaining soaking liquid (the liquid contains vitamins and other nutrients from the fruit). If necessary, add a small amount of water or juice to keep the fruit from scorching. Sugar should be added only when the fruit is nearly done.

To cook dried fruit in liquid. Un-rehydrated dried fruit can be cooked on the rangetop, in an electric slow cooker, or in a microwave oven. The amount of liquid you'll need depends on how you plan to use the fruit. If you'll be serving it in a compote or topping, use about 1 cup liquid to 1 cup fruit; if it's going into a pie, cobbler, dough, or batter, start with ⅔ to ¾ cup liquid per cup of fruit, then add more liquid as needed to achieve the desired consistency.

To cook dried fruit on the range, bring the liquid to a boil and add the fruit; then reduce heat, cover, and simmer until fruit is tender (usually 10 to 15 minutes).

To cook dried fruit in a slow cooker or microwave oven, follow the manufacturer's instructions.

It's easy to make sweet leathers from puréed fresh fruits—especially if you have a dehydrator. Shown here are strawberry, raspberry, peach, apricot, plum, and pear-pecan fruit rolls, all prepared according to the recipe on the facing page.

Fresh Fruit Leather

Pictured on facing page

Sweet fruit leathers are especially easy to dry in a dehydrator, but sun drying also works well—as long as the temperature is 85°F or higher and the relative humidity 60 percent or lower. Our recipe makes 10-inch squares of leather; if you'd like to make larger pieces or prepare several leathers at a time, just increase the amount of purée proportionately.

Fruit Purée (choices and directions follow)
Finely chopped nuts or shredded coconut (optional)

Prepare drying surface for dehydrator or sun drying.

Dehydrator drying. If your dehydrator has special trays for leather, prepare them according to the manufacturer's instructions. Or cover each drying tray with a sheet of plastic wrap, extending it over tray edges; secure with tape. Preheat dehydrator.

Sun drying. Start early in the day. Cover rimmed 10- by 15-inch baking pans or other shallow pans with plastic wrap (one continuous sheet per pan), extending it over tray edges; secure wrap to underside of pans with tape. Set pans in full sun, on a level surface such as a table.

Once drying surface has been prepared, prepare purée (or purées) of your choice. To make each leather, pour 1 cup purée onto prepared surface and spread to about 10 inches square. (You may need to double the amount of purée for some dehydrator trays intended especially for leathers.) Layer of purée should be about ⅜ inch thick; make it slightly thicker around edges to ensure that leather dries evenly, without brittle edges. If desired, lightly sprinkle purée with nuts or coconut.

Dry purée until leathery, pliable, and no longer tacky to touch; it should peel off drying surface with no sticky spots. Dehydrator-dried purées are usually ready in 5 to 10 hours; sun-dried purées take 1 to 2 days. To keep purées clean during sun drying, suspend cheesecloth over them, supporting it with 2-by-4s on each side. If purées aren't dry by day's end, bring them indoors; return to sun the next day.

While leather is still warm, roll it up jelly roll style in plastic wrap, enclosing the wrap. Or cut it into snack-size strips and wrap each piece in plastic wrap; store pieces flat or roll up. Store in an airtight container; for longer storage, place in plastic freezer bags or rigid freezer containers and refrigerate or freeze.

Makes 1 (10-inch-square) leather (2 servings) from each cup of purée.

Fruit Purée. It's not necessary to peel most fruits, but peeled fruits make smoother leather. Rinse all fruit well; pat dry (drain berries on paper towels). To purée, whirl fruit (plus lemon juice, spices, and/or sweetener) in a blender until very smooth, scraping down sides of container as needed.

Because the drying process concentrates natural sugars, many fruits don't need sweetening. If you do use a sweetener, sugar is fine—as long as you plan to freeze your leathers or eat them within a few weeks. But if you intend to store them at room temperature (or in the refrigerator) for over a week or two, sweeten them with honey or corn syrup, since sugar-sweetened leather may become grainy.

Each fruit choice below yields 1 cup purée.

Apple. In a 1½- to 2-quart pan, combine 2½ cups cored, sliced **apples** with ⅓ cup **apple juice** or water. Bring to a boil; reduce heat, cover, and simmer until apples are soft when mashed (about 10 minutes). Let cool slightly. Purée with 1 tablespoon **lemon juice**, about 2 tablespoons **honey,** light corn syrup, or sugar, and ¼ teaspoon **ground cinnamon** (optional); add a few tablespoons **apple juice,** if needed, to give purée the consistency of cake batter.

Apricot. Purée 1½ cups halved, pitted **apricots** with 1 tablespoon **lemon juice** and about 3 tablespoons **honey,** light corn syrup, or sugar.

Cherry. Pit about 1½ cups **sweet cherries**. Purée with 1 tablespoon **lemon juice**.

Peach or nectarine. Purée 2 cups sliced **peaches** or nectarines with 1 tablespoon **lemon juice** and about 2 tablespoons **honey,** light corn syrup, or sugar.

Pear. Juicy Bartletts are best. Purée 2 cups cored, sliced **pears** with 1 tablespoon **lemon juice**.

Plum. Purée 1½ cups sliced **plums** with 1 tablespoon **lemon juice** and about 2 tablespoons **honey,** light corn syrup, or sugar.

Raspberry or blackberry (blackberries include boysenberries, olallieberries, and loganberries). Purée about 2 cups **berries** with 1 tablespoon **lemon juice** and about ¼ cup **honey,** light corn syrup, or sugar. Press through a fine strainer; discard seeds.

Strawberry. Hull 1¼ to 1½ cups **strawberries** and purée with 1 tablespoon **lemon juice** and about 2 tablespoons **honey,** light corn syrup, or sugar.

Storage time. Up to 2 months at room temperature; up to 6 months in refrigerator; up to 1 year in freezer.

Per serving (approximate): 134 calories, 1 g protein, 35 g carbohydrates, 1 g total fat, 0 mg cholesterol, 3 mg sodium

Naturally Sweet No-cook Jams

Naturally sweet dehydrated jams are easy to make. Just purée your choice of fruit, then let it dry in a dehydrator or an oven—or in the sun, provided the temperature is 85°F or higher and the relative humidity 60 percent or lower. As moisture evaporates from the purée, it thickens to a jamlike consistency. The process usually takes 2 to 4 hours in a dehydrator or oven; sun drying requires a day or two.

Dehydrated Jam

Fruit Purée (choices and directions follow)

Sugar, honey, and/or lemon juice (optional)

Following the directions below, prepare a drying tray or container for dehydrator, oven, or sun drying. Then prepare purée and proceed as directed for each method. Once an hour, carefully scrape jam from edges of tray or pan with a rubber spatula and stir well; then spread evenly again. Let dry until jam is almost as thick as you prefer; it will thicken further as it cools. Spoon jam into a container and stir in a little more sugar, honey, and/or lemon juice, if desired. Cover; freeze or refrigerate.

Dehydrator drying. If your dehydrator has a door and removable drying trays, place a pie pan or other shallow baking pan on tray. Or make a container to fit the dimensions of your dehydrator tray, using a double thickness of heavy-duty foil; pinch foil container together at corners to secure. Spray pan or foil container with vegetable oil cooking spray before adding purée.

If your dehydrator has drying trays that stack over a heat source on the bottom and includes a special tray for fruit leathers and sauces, prepare tray according to manufacturer's instructions.

Pour purée onto tray and spread to a thickness of ⅜ inch. Use temperature recommended for drying fruit in your dehydrator (usually 135° to 140°F).

Oven drying. Lay a continuous sheet of parchment paper in a shallow baking pan (about 10 by 15 inches); paper should extend beyond pan edge.

Pour purée into pan and spread to a thickness of ⅜ inch. Heat oven to 120° to 130°F; place pan in oven. Prop oven door open several inches to allow moisture to escape; check oven temperature periodically with an oven thermometer.

Sun drying. Use a glass, metal, or plastic pan (about 9 by 13 inches). Pour purée into pan and spread evenly. Cover pan with plastic wrap, leaving about 1 inch along one long side uncovered. Place pan in full sun, on a level surface such as a table. If purée isn't sufficiently thickened by day's end, cover and refrigerate it overnight; return to sun the next day.

Purées dried by any method make about 1 cup apricot, berry, peach, or plum jam, ½ cup melon jam.

Fruit Purée. For best flavor, start with fully ripe, top-quality fruit. Rinse all fruit well; pat dry (drain berries on paper towels). To purée, whirl fruit (plus any lemon juice, sugar, or honey) in a blender until smooth, scraping down sides of container as needed. Each fruit choice below yields 2 cups purée.

Apricot. Purée 3 cups halved, pitted **apricots** with 1 tablespoon **lemon juice** and 2 to 4 tablespoons **sugar** or honey.

Melon. Cut peeled, seeded **cantaloupe,** Persian, or honeydew melon into chunks; purée enough melon to make 2 cups. Blend in 2 tablespoons **lemon juice** and 1 to 2 tablespoons **sugar** or honey.

Peach or nectarine. Purée 4 cups sliced peeled **peaches** or unpeeled nectarines with 1 tablespoon **lemon juice** and 2 to 4 tablespoons **sugar** or honey.

Plum. Purée 3 cups sliced **plums** or prune plums with 2 to 4 tablespoons **sugar** or honey. Pour purée into a 2-quart pan. Bring to a simmer, stirring occasionally; cover and simmer for 2 minutes. Let cool slightly.

Raspberry or blackberry (blackberries include boysenberries, olallieberries, and loganberries). Purée 4 cups **berries;** press through a fine strainer and discard seeds. Blend in 1 tablespoon **lemon juice** and 4 to 6 tablespoons **sugar.**

Strawberry. Hull 3 cups **strawberries** and purée with 1 tablespoon **lemon juice** and 2 to 4 tablespoons **sugar.**

Storage time. Up to 1 week in refrigerator; up to 6 months in freezer.

Per tablespoon (approximate): 27 calories, 0 g protein, 6 g carbohydrates, 0 g total fat, 0 mg cholesterol, 1 mg sodium

Dried Fruit Trail Mix

Pictured on page 98

A handful of this fruity mix is great on the trail or any time you want a treat. You can substitute other favorite fruits, either home-dried or purchased at a supermarket or health food store, for the selections below. Try dried cherries or cranberries in place of raisins or use mango slices instead of papaya.

- 1 cup *each* dried papaya slices and banana chips
- 1 cup unsweetened shredded coconut
- ½ cup *each* dark and golden raisins
- ⅔ cup chopped pitted dates
- ½ cup chopped dried apricots

Cut papaya slices into bite-size pieces; break banana chips into bite-size pieces. Place in a large bowl and add coconut, raisins, dates, and apricots. Toss gently until well blended. Package in airtight containers; or place in serving-size plastic bags, then in an airtight container. Makes about 5 cups.

Storage time. Up to 2 weeks at room temperature; up to 4 months in refrigerator; up to 1 year in freezer.

Per ½ cup: 207 calories, 2 g protein, 44 g carbohydrates, 5 g total fat, 0 mg cholesterol, 7 mg sodium

High-energy Trail Logs

Pictured on page 98

Backpackers will applaud these hearty little nuggets of energy. They're great as at-home snacks, too; stored airtight, they'll keep in the refrigerator for several weeks.

- 1¼ cups walnut pieces
- ¼ cup dry-roasted cashews
- 6 dried black figs
- ½ cup pitted dates
- ½ cup golden or dark raisins
- ¼ cup dried apples
- ½ teaspoon lemon juice
- 1 tablespoon dark or light rum
- 2 tablespoons powdered sugar or about ½ cup sweetened flaked coconut

Using a food processor or a food chopper fitted with a fine blade, grind walnuts, cashews, figs, dates, raisins, and apples. Turn into a bowl and mix thoroughly. Blend in lemon juice and rum.

To shape logs, scoop out mixture in 1-tablespoon portions; roll each portion into a ¾- by 2-inch log. Roll logs in sugar or coconut, arrange in a single layer, and let stand, uncovered, for 1 to 2 days to dry. Then cover airtight and refrigerate. To carry on the trail, wrap logs individually in foil or plastic wrap. Makes about 2½ dozen logs.

Storage time. Up to 3 weeks in refrigerator.

Per log: 68 calories, 1 g protein, 9 g carbohydrates, 4 g total fat, 0 mg cholesterol, 2 mg sodium

Dried Fruits with Blue Cheese

Pictured on page 98

The simplest of appetizers, these fruit treats are a great contribution to a buffet table or a nice beginning for a casual get-together. Top each piece with a cashew, walnut, or pecan; or sprinkle with minced fresh mint.

- 32 dry-roasted cashews, walnut halves, or pecan halves; or about 3 tablespoons minced fresh mint
- 5 ounces blue-veined cheese such as cambozola or Gorgonzola
- 1 small package (about 3 oz.) cream cheese, at room temperature
- ½ teaspoon ground white or black pepper
- 32 pieces dried fruit (use apricot, peach, or pear halves, whole pitted prunes, or some of each fruit)

Toast nuts in a small frying pan over medium heat until golden brown (about 4 minutes), stirring occasionally. Pour out of pan and let cool.

In a small bowl, beat together blue cheese, cream cheese, and pepper (or whirl in a food processor). Spread cheese mixture evenly over fruit pieces. (At this point, you may cover and refrigerate until next day.)

To complete appetizers, press a nut into cheese on each piece of fruit or sprinkle cheese with mint. Arrange fruit, cheese side up, on a platter. If made ahead, cover and refrigerate. Makes 32 appetizers.

Storage time. Up to 1 day in refrigerator before topping with nuts; up to 4 hours in refrigerator after topping.

Per appetizer: 39 calories, 1 g protein, 3 g carbohydrates, 3 g total fat, 6 mg cholesterol, 70 mg sodium

Scandinavian Dried Fruit Soup

Pictured on page 103

Dried fruits and chunks of fresh pineapple combine with orange juice in this refreshing Scandinavian-style dessert.

2½ **cups mixed dried fruit, such as apples, apricots, peaches, and prunes, cut into bite-size pieces**

½ **cup raisins or dried cherries**

½ **lemon, thinly sliced and seeded**

1 **cinnamon stick (about 3 inches long)**

3½ **cups water**

2 **cups orange juice**

1½ **cups fresh pineapple chunks; or 1½ cups pineapple chunks packed in their own juice, drained**

⅔ **to ¾ cup honey**

⅛ **teaspoon salt (optional)**

⅓ **cup rum or brandy**

1 **tablespoon cornstarch blended with 2 tablespoons cold water**

Vanilla yogurt or sour cream

In a 3-quart pan, combine dried fruit, raisins, lemon slices, cinnamon stick, water, and orange juice; bring to a boil over high heat. Reduce heat to medium-low, cover, and simmer for 10 to 15 minutes. Then remove from heat and stir in pineapple, honey, salt (if desired), and rum. Let stand for 10 minutes to blend flavors and let fruit soften.

Return pan to heat; then blend cornstarch mixture into soup. Cook over medium-low heat, stirring, until liquid is bubbly, clear, and thickened. Remove cinnamon stick and lemon slices. Serve soup hot; or cover and refrigerate to serve cold. Top with spoonfuls of yogurt. Makes 10 servings.

Storage time. Up to 2 days in refrigerator.

Per serving: 247 calories, 2 g protein, 61 g carbohydrates, 0 g total fat, 0 mg cholesterol, 9 mg sodium

Chopping Dried Fruit

To chop dried fruit more easily, occasionally dip your scissors or knife in hot water or coat the blades lightly with salad oil. Freeze dried fruit before chopping it in a food processor or blender.

Fettuccine with Dried Tomatoes & Mushrooms

Pictured on facing page

Intensely flavored dried tomatoes and mushrooms lend zest to this colorful pasta dish. You can use any kind of dried mushrooms; we suggest button or shiitake.

1 **ounce (about 2 cups lightly packed) dried sliced mushrooms, such as button or shiitake**

2 **ounces (about 1½ cups) dried sliced beefsteak-type tomatoes; or 2 ounces (about 1½ cups) dried pear-shaped (Roma-type) tomatoes, coarsely chopped**

1 *each* **medium-size zucchini and crookneck squash**

8 **ounces dry fettuccine**

2 **tablespoons olive oil**

2 **cloves garlic, minced**

¼ **cup dry white wine**

1 **tablespoon chopped fresh basil or 1 teaspoon dry basil**

1 **tablespoon chopped fresh tarragon or ½ teaspoon dry tarragon**

¼ **teaspoon *each* crushed red pepper flakes and salt**

½ **cup grated Parmesan cheese**

Place mushrooms in a medium-size bowl; place tomatoes in another medium-size bowl. Add cold water to cover each vegetable; let stand until vegetables are soft (about 1 hour). Drain off any liquid; set vegetables aside. Cut zucchini and crookneck squash into ¼-inch-thick slices; then cut each slice into thirds. Set aside.

In a 6- to 8-quart pan, cook fettuccine according to package directions just until tender to bite. Meanwhile, heat oil in a wide frying pan over high heat; add mushrooms, zucchini, crookneck squash, and garlic. Cook, stirring, until zucchini is tender-crisp to bite (2 to 3 minutes). Mix wine, basil, tarragon, red pepper flakes, and salt; pour over vegetables and toss to heat through.

Drain pasta; return to cooking pan. Add vegetable mixture and tomatoes and toss to mix. Transfer to a large platter; sprinkle with cheese. Makes 6 servings.

Storage time. Best when served immediately, but you may cover and refrigerate for up to 1 day, then reheat (add cheese just before serving).

Per serving: 262 calories, 10 g protein, 36 g carbohydrates, 8 g total fat, 41 mg cholesterol, 233 mg sodium

*Dried tomato slices and shiitake mushrooms bring vibrant and earthy flavors to
a combination of tender pasta strands, fresh summer squash, and herbs. For a satisfying
lunch or supper, you might serve Fettuccine with Dried Tomatoes & Mushrooms (facing page)
with a crisp salad, warm bread, and dry white wine.*

Guide for Drying Fruits

For details on sulfuring and other pretreatments, see "Pretreating Fruit" (page 102). When treating fruits with sulfite or other dip, don't soak them for more than a few minutes; oversoaking causes a decrease in nutritional value. If you're drying fruit halves, keep in mind that they'll take longer to dry than slices do.

Fruit & best types for drying	How to prepare	Treatment before drying	Test for dryness*
Apples Firm varieties such as Granny Smith, Gravenstein, Jonathan, Newtown Pippin, Rome Beauty	Rinse, peel, cut off both ends, core, and cut into ¼- to ⅜-inch-thick slices.	Dip in sulfite solution, ascorbic acid solution, or citrus juice dip. Or sulfur fruit, using 2 teaspoons sulfur per pound of cut fruit.	Soft, leathery, pliable
Apricots Royal-Blenheim, Tilton	Rinse, halve, and pit. If drying fruit as halves, press halves to flatten. Otherwise, cut halves into ¼-inch-thick slices.	Dip in sulfite solution, ascorbic acid solution, or citrus juice dip. Or sulfur fruit, using 1 teaspoon sulfur per pound of cut fruit.	Pliable, with no areas of moisture
Bananas	Choose fruit that's solid yellow or slightly speckled with brown. Peel; cut into ¼- to ⅜-inch-thick slices.	Treatment optional; may dip in honey-lemon or honey dip.	Pliable to crisp
Berries	Blackberries, boysenberries, huckleberries, and raspberries are not recommended for drying; they're too full of seeds and take too long to dry. They do, however, make good fruit leathers; see page 107.		
Blueberries	Choose large, firm, fully ripe berries with deep blue color. Rinse and remove stems.	Dip in boiling water until skins crack. Dip briefly in ice water; drain on paper towels.	Leathery and pliable
Cherries, all varieties *Sweet:* Bing, Lambert, Royal Ann *Sour:* Early Richmond, Montmorency	Rinse and remove stems. Pit fruit and leave whole; or halve and pit.	Treatment optional; may dip in boiling water until skins crack.	Leathery and pliable, with no areas of moisture
Citrus peel Peels of grapefruit, kumquat, lemon, lime, orange, tangerine	Peel from thick-skinned navel oranges is better than that from thin-skinned Valencias. If fruit is marked "color added," do not dry its peel. Rinse well to remove surface residues. Pare off colored part of peel only, avoiding bitter white pith beneath.	No treatment necessary.	Crisp
Coconut	Choose fresh coconut, heavy for its size. Pierce eyes and pour out milk; crack nut with a hammer. Remove meat; discard outer skin. Grate or slice thinly.	No treatment necessary.	Crisp
Cranberries	Rinse.	Treatment optional; may dip in boiling water until skins crack.	Shriveled, with no areas of moisture
Figs Black Mission, Kadota, Calimyrna	Use tree-ripened figs; when fully ripe and ready for drying, they fall to the ground. Rinse; halve or leave whole.	Treatment optional; may dip in boiling water until skins crack.	Leathery outside, but still pliable. Slightly sticky inside, but not wet

* Cool a piece before testing

Fruit & best types for drying	How to prepare	Treatment before drying	Test for dryness*
Grapes (for raisins) Green or red seedless varieties	Rinse and remove stems; leave whole or halve.	Treatment optional; may dip in boiling water until skins crack.	Leathery, with wrinkled, raisinlike texture; no areas of moisture
Melons, all varieties	Avoid overripe fruit. If using watermelon, cut lengthwise into quarters. Cut quarters into ¼- to ⅜-inch-thick slices; then cut slices into 2-inch pieces as you remove rind and seeds. If using other melons, halve, seed, and peel; cut into ¼-inch-thick slices, then into 2-inch pieces.	No treatment necessary.	Soft and pliable, with no areas of moisture (very sweet melons will be slightly sticky)
Nectarines Flamekist, Flavortop, Red Diamond	Rinse; no need to peel. Halve and pit. If drying fruit as halves, press halves to flatten. Otherwise, cut halves into ⅜-inch-thick slices.	Dip in sulfite solution, ascorbic acid solution, or citrus juice dip. Or sulfur fruit, using 2 teaspoons sulfur per pound of cut fruit.	Soft and pliable, with no areas of moisture
Peaches Elberta, Flavorcrest, O'Henry, Redtop	Rinse and peel; halve and pit. If drying fruit as halves, press halves to flatten. Otherwise, cut halves into ⅜-inch-thick slices.	Dip in sulfite solution, ascorbic acid solution, or citrus juice dip. Or sulfur fruit, using 2 teaspoons sulfur per pound of cut fruit.	Soft and pliable, with no areas of moisture
Pears Bartlett	Rinse, peel if desired, halve, and core. If drying fruit as halves, press halves to flatten. Otherwise, cut halves into ¼-inch-thick slices.	Dip in sulfite solution, ascorbic acid solution, or citrus juice dip. Or sulfur fruit, using 2½ teaspoons sulfur per pound of cut fruit.	Soft and pliable, with no areas of moisture
Pineapple	Use only fully ripe fruit. Rinse; peel, then cut out eyes and core. Cut crosswise into ½-inch-thick rings.	No treatment necessary.	Leathery but not sticky
Plums, most varieties	Rinse. Do not peel; do not dry fruit whole. Halve and pit. If drying fruit as halves, press halves to flatten. Otherwise, cut halves into ¼- to ⅜-inch-thick slices.	No treatment necessary.	Leathery and pliable, with no areas of moisture
Prune plums (for prunes) French, Italian	Rinse. Do not peel. Halve and pit; press halves to flatten. Prunes may also be dried whole, but will take 4 times as long as halved fruit. If you are sun-drying whole fruit, pit it; then dip it in boiling water until skins crack.	No treatment necessary.	Leathery and pliable, with no areas of moisture
Strawberries	Choose red, fully ripe berries. Rinse gently and hull. Cut into ½-inch-thick slices.	No treatment necessary.	Leathery and pliable, with no areas of moisture

* Cool a piece before testing

Drying Vegetables

Vegetables are easily dried at home in a dehydrator. Oven drying is acceptable, too, though it's more complicated and time consuming than dehydrator drying. Sun drying is best avoided—because vegetables are low in sugar and acid, they tend to spoil under uncontrolled outdoor conditions.

Preparing the Vegetables

If possible, get vegetables ready for drying immediately after harvesting, preparing only as much as you can dry at one time. Rinse vegetables thoroughly in cold water, but don't soak them—that depletes minerals and vitamins. Peel vegetables, then cut out any woody, fibrous, decayed, or bruised areas. Cut or slice each type of vegetable as directed in the chart on pages 116 and 117, keeping pieces uniform in size so they'll dry at the same rate.

About Blanching

Many vegetables must be blanched before drying. *Blanching*—quick heating to inactivate enzymes—prevents deterioration during drying and storage; it also sets color and shortens drying and rehydrating time by relaxing cell walls, allowing moisture to escape and re-enter more rapidly.

To blanch vegetables, you may dip them in boiling water or steam them briefly. Steam-blanched vegetables retain more nutrients than do those treated in boiling water, but water blanching is faster and generally more effective in removing surface residues and microorganisms.

To blanch vegetables in boiling water, you'll need an 8-quart or larger pan filled with about 1 gallon of rapidly boiling water (for leafy greens, use 2 gallons of water). A blanching pot with a perforated basket and lid is ideal. Place about 1 pound of prepared raw vegetables at a time in a wire basket or metal colander (or in blanching pot basket); then immerse in the boiling water. Let the water return to a boil; then cover the pan and begin timing as directed in the chart on pages 116 and 117.

To blanch vegetables in steam, use a steam blanching pot or an 8-quart or larger pan with a tight-fitting lid and a wire or perforated basket that will hold food at least 3 inches off the pan bottom. Pour 2 inches of water into the pan, cover, and bring to a boil over high heat. Place 1 to 2 pounds of prepared raw vegetables in a single layer in the basket; cover. When steam begins to escape from pan, begin timing as directed in the chart on pages 116 and 117.

To cool blanched vegetables, lift them from the pan and immediately plunge into a large quantity of cold (60°F or lower) water. Cool them just long enough to stop the cooking action; *do not* cool to room temperature (the heat remaining in the vegetables allows them to start drying faster). If you plan to dry the vegetables in a dehydrator, pour them directly onto a dehydrator tray held over a sink; wipe any excess water from the tray underside. If you're oven-drying the vegetables, pour them onto paper towels to drain, then quickly transfer to trays or baking pans.

Drying the Vegetables

Whatever drying method you use, it's important to arrange the vegetables on trays in a single layer, without letting the pieces touch or overlap. Don't dry strong-flavored vegetables such as garlic, onions, and chiles with milder kinds; you'll end up with onion-flavored celery, garlicky green beans, and so on. Also avoid drying onions or garlic in the house, since the odor will permeate upholstery, draperies, and clothing. Instead, place the dehydrator on a covered porch or patio or in a garage.

To dry vegetables in a dehydrator, follow the manufacturer's instructions; a temperature of 125° to 130°F is recommended for most vegetables. Drying time will vary from about 4 to 14 hours.

To dry vegetables in a conventional oven, consult "Oven Drying" (page 101). Preheat oven to 120° to 140°F (temperatures above 140°F will reduce tenderness and cause loss of nutrients).

To dry vegetables in a convection oven, follow the manufacturer's instructions.

Determining Dryness

As the vegetables become drier, check them often to avoid scorching. When ready to store, most types are crisp and brittle; check the chart (pages 116 and 117).

Packaging & Storage

Store your dried vegetables as directed in "Packaging & Storing Dried Foods" on page 102. At cool room temperature, they'll keep well for about 6 months.

Chips, Flakes & Powders

When chopped or ground into flakes or powder, dried vegetables make flavorful bases for soups and sauces—and super seasonings for salads, cooked vegetables, and other foods. You can enjoy dried vegetable slices whole, too, as crisp and nutritious snacks.

Vegetable Chips

Wholesome and low in calories, vegetable chips are a tasty alternative to commercial deep-fried potato and corn chips. To prepare them, slice vegetables thinly before drying, using a food processor, mandolin, or sharp knife. Then serve them as is or with a favorite dip.

Beets, carrots, summer squash, tomatoes, and zucchini all make great chips. Zucchini and other squash chips are especially flavorful if dipped in barbecue sauce or sprinkled with seasoned salt before drying. Or try sprinkling ¼-inch-thick firm-ripe tomato slices with a little salt and, if you like, a bit of dry basil before drying.

Vegetable Flakes

Crushed or chopped into flakes, dried vegetables make excellent soup bases and seasonings. To prepare the flakes, use a blender, rolling pin, or wooden mallet. The vegetables must be really crisp before chopping, and the chopping equipment (particularly if you're using a blender) must be very dry. Because flaked vegetables have a shorter shelf life and lose nutritional value more rapidly than do sliced or whole dried vegetables, prepare them in small amounts—only as much as you'll use within a month. Then store them in small airtight containers such as empty spice bottles or baby food jars.

To use your vegetable flakes, try these ideas:

- Sprinkle the flakes over green salads to add color and crunch. Tomato and carrot flakes are especially good served this way.
- Create your own soup and dip mixes by combining a variety of vegetable flakes.

Vegetable Powders

Vegetable powders are finer than flakes. To prepare them, simply grind dried vegetables in a blender, food processor, or food mill until powdery; make sure the vegetables are crisp and the grinding equipment very dry. Store as for vegetable flakes (at left).

To use vegetable powders, try these ideas:

- Use homemade onion and garlic powders in place of commercial products.
- Make seasoned salts by mixing herb and vegetable powders with table salt. Equal parts of celery powder and salt make celery salt; one part garlic powder to four parts salt gives you garlic salt.
- Use vegetable powders to flavor sauces and cream soups. For each cup of soup or sauce, mix about 1 tablespoon vegetable powder and ¼ cup boiling water; let stand for about 15 minutes, then add to soup or sauce.
- Use tomato powder to make tomato sauce and paste. (Tomato powder is very concentrated: just 1 tablespoon is equivalent to about 1 medium-size fresh tomato.) To make tomato paste, mix 1¼ cups water and 1 cup tomato powder in a blender; whirl until smooth. For tomato sauce, use 1¾ cups water to 1 cup tomato powder.
- Make your own single-serving instant soups: mix about 1 tablespoon of your favorite vegetable powder with 4 teaspoons instant nonfat dry milk. Stir in 1 cup boiling water, then season to taste with salt, pepper, and herbs. You can prepare the soup in a large mug or small bowl; or, for more flavor, mix it in a small pan and simmer for a few minutes before serving.
- Keep vegetable broth mix on hand to use as a seasoning and for quick, nourishing snacks. Just powder any combination of vegetables, such as carrots, celery, green beans, peas, peppers, spinach, tomatoes, mushrooms, onion, garlic, and/or parsley; include favorite dry herbs, too. To make each cup of broth, combine about 1 tablespoon vegetable powder with 1 cup of boiling water.

Guide for Drying Vegetables

For details on blanching methods, see "About Blanching" (page 114).

To rehydrate dried vegetables, soak them in cold water, vegetable juice, or broth; most will rehydrate within an hour or two. If they need over 2 hours (or if you plan to soak them overnight), refrigerate them.

To speed up rehydration, you can soak the vegetables in boiling water. Or omit soaking and add the vegetables directly to stews and soups (they'll be a bit less tender than if they'd been soaked).

Vegetable	Best for drying	How to prepare	Test for dryness*
Artichokes	Tender hearts only	Rinse hearts and cut into ⅛-inch-wide strips. To blanch, heat in boiling solution of 3 cups water and ¼ cup lemon juice for 6 to 8 minutes.	Brittle
Asparagus	Tender tips, slender green stalks	Rinse stalks well; break off tough ends and halve large tips. Cut stalks into 1-inch pieces. Blanch for 3½ to 4½ minutes in boiling water, for 4 to 5 minutes in steam.	Leathery to brittle
Beans, snap	Tender varieties with crisp, thick walls and small seeds	Rinse. Cut off ends; then cut beans diagonally into short pieces. Blanch for 2 minutes in boiling water, for 2 to 2½ minutes in steam. (You may freeze beans for 30 to 40 minutes after blanching for better texture.)	Very dry, brittle
Beets	Small, tender beets	To keep color from bleeding, leave root ends and 1 inch of tops on beets. Scrub well; don't peel. Cover with boiling water and boil gently until tender when pierced (25 to 35 minutes). Cool. Remove skins; trim off stems and roots. Cut beets into ⅛-inch-thick strips. No further blanching required.	Tough, leathery
Broccoli	Young, fresh stalks	Trim off outer leaves and tough stalk bases. Rinse broccoli. Quarter stalks lengthwise. If desired, soak for 30 minutes in salt water (¼ cup salt per gallon of water) to help remove insects; drain. Blanch for 2 minutes in boiling water, for 3 to 3½ minutes in steam.	Brittle
Cabbage		Remove outer leaves. Rinse cabbage; then quarter and core. Cut into ⅛-inch-wide strips. Blanch until wilted: 1½ to 2 minutes in boiling water, 2½ to 3 minutes in steam.	Tough to brittle
Carrots	Crisp, tender carrots only	Rinse and peel. Cut into ⅛-inch-thick slices or strips. Blanch for 3½ minutes in boiling water, for 3 to 3½ minutes in steam.	Tough, leathery
Cauliflower		Rinse and break into small flowerets. If desired, soak for 30 minutes in salt water (¼ cup salt per gallon of water) to help remove insects; drain. Blanch for 3 to 4 minutes in boiling water, for 4 to 5 minutes in steam.	Tough to brittle
Celery	Crisp, tender stalks relatively free from strings	Rinse and slice. Blanch for 2 minutes in boiling water or steam.	Brittle
Corn	Young, tender ears in milk stage	Discard husks and silk; rinse corn. Blanch until milk does not exude when kernels are cut: 4 to 5 minutes in boiling water, 5 to 6 minutes in steam. Cut kernels from cob after blanching.	Dry, brittle
Eggplant *See* Squash, summer (& eggplant)			
Garlic		Peel and finely chop garlic cloves. No blanching required. Odor is pungent; dry outdoors in protected area in dehydrator.	Brittle
Greens (including spinach)	Young, tender leaves of chard, kale, spinach, and turnip	Rinse carefully. Drain; continue to rinse until water is clear and free of grit. Cut tough stems from leaves. Blanch for 1½ minutes in boiling water, for 2 to 2½ minutes in steam.	Brittle

* Cool a piece before testing

Vegetable	Best for drying	How to prepare	Test for dryness*
Horseradish		Rinse; remove all small rootlets and stubs. Peel or scrape roots. Grate. No blanching required.	Very dry and powdery
Mushrooms	*Commercial mushrooms only. Do not dry mushrooms gathered in the wild, which may be poisonous*	Use young, medium-size mushrooms with small closed caps. Rinse well, but quickly. Trim off tough stems. Cut tender stems into short sections. Do not peel small mushrooms or "buttons"; you may peel and slice large mushrooms. Blanch for 3 minutes in boiling water, for 3 to 4 minutes in steam.	Very dry and leathery
Okra		Rinse; trim ends. Cut pods crosswise into ⅛- to ¼-inch-thick slices. No blanching required.	Tough to brittle
Onions	Onions with strong aroma and flavor	Rinse and peel onions; cut into ⅛- to ¼-inch-thick slices. No blanching required. Odor is pungent; dry outdoors in protected area in dehydrator.	Brittle
Parsley		Rinse well. Separate clusters. Discard long or tough stems. No blanching required.	Brittle, flaky
Peas, green	Young, tender peas of a sweet variety (mature peas become tough and mealy)	Shell. Blanch for 2 minutes in boiling water, for 3 minutes in steam.	Crisp, wrinkled
Peppers, bell or chile		If preparing chiles, wear rubber gloves. Rinse. Remove stems and seeds. Cut bell peppers into ½-inch squares or ⅛-inch-wide strips. No blanching required. Cut chiles into ½-inch squares; or dry whole outside if you live in a hot, sunny, dry climate. No blanching required. Do not dry hot chiles with other vegetables in a dehydrator.	Brittle
Potatoes, white		Rinse well; peel. Cut into ¼-inch-thick julienne strips or ⅛-inch-thick slices. Blanch for 5 to 6 minutes in boiling water, for 6 to 8 minutes in steam.	Brittle
Spinach *See* Greens (including spinach)			
Squash, summer (& eggplant)	Crookneck, zucchini, pattypan; eggplant	Rinse squash or eggplant and trim ends. Cut into ¼-inch-thick slices. Blanch for 1½ minutes in boiling water, for 2½ to 3 minutes in steam.	Brittle
Squash, winter (including pumpkin)	Banana, Hubbard, pumpkin	*For banana squash,* rinse and peel; cut into ¼-inch-thick strips. Blanch for 2 minutes in boiling water, for 3 minutes in steam. *For Hubbard squash and pumpkin,* cut into pieces. Scrape out all seeds and fibrous material. Cut into 1-inch-wide strips; peel strips and cut crosswise into ⅛-inch-thick slices. To blanch, steam until tender when pierced.	Tough to brittle
Tomatoes	Firm-ripe tomatoes with good color, no green spots	*For beefsteak-type tomatoes,* rinse and core. If desired, peel: dip in boiling water until skins crack (30 to 60 seconds), then dip in cold water and slip off skins. Cut crosswise into ¼-inch-thick slices; using a salt shaker, sprinkle with a tiny amount of salt to set color. No blanching required. *For small pear-shaped (Roma-type) tomatoes,* rinse and peel (see above). Halve; or, for large tomatoes, quarter or cut into ¼-inch-thick slices. Using a salt shaker, sprinkle with a tiny amount of salt to set color. No blanching required. Dry all tomatoes in a dehydrator for best results.	Slightly leathery

* Cool a piece before testing

Drying Fresh Herbs

If your garden has provided you with more herbs than you can use fresh, you may want to dry some for later use. The process is simple: you just expose leaves or seeds to warm, dry air until their moisture is gone. We give instructions for drying herbs in open air or in a microwave or convection oven; don't try to use a conventional oven, since you're almost certain to end up with scorched herbs.

In most cases, you should harvest herbs for drying when the flowers first open.

Bunch drying is an easy way to dry long-stemmed herbs such as marjoram, sage, savory, mint, parsley, basil, and rosemary. Cut long stalks and rinse them in cool water; discard any dead or yellowed leaves. Then tie small bunches of herbs together by the stem ends. To keep dust from collecting on the leaves, place each bunch inside a paper bag before hanging; gather the top of the bag and tie the herb stems so the leaves hang freely inside the bag. For ventilation, cut out the bottom of the bag or punch air holes in the sides. Then hang the herbs—leafy ends down—in a warm, dry place (either inside or outdoors) not exposed to direct sunlight.

An even temperature in the range of 70° to 90°F is best for drying. Be sure there's good air circulation around the drying herbs—don't hang them against a wall. If you dry herbs outside, bring them in at night so the dew won't dampen them.

After a week or two, the herbs should be crackling dry. Carefully remove the leaves without breaking them; they retain flavor longer if left whole until ready to use. Store airtight.

Tray drying works well for seeds and large-leafed herbs; it's also the best choice for types with short stems that are difficult to tie together for hanging. Dry the herbs on shallow-rimmed trays covered with cheesecloth; or arrange them on wire racks set atop trays.

Rinse the herbs in cool water; shake off excess moisture.

To dry leaves, either remove them from their stems or leave them attached. Spread only one layer of leaves (loose or still on stems) on each tray: if you attempt to dry too much at once, air won't reach all the herbs evenly and they'll take longer to dry. Put the trays in a warm, dry, well-ventilated place not exposed to direct sunlight.

Every few days, stir or turn the leaves gently to assure even, thorough drying. Depending on the temperature and humidity, it should take the herbs a week or so to dry completely; if you're drying them outside, bring them in at night so the dew won't dampen them. When the leaves are crisp and thoroughly dry, take them off the trays and store airtight.

To dry seeds, spread them on trays in a thin layer and dry as for leaves. Once they're dry, carefully rub the seed capsules through your hands, gently blowing away chaff. Store airtight.

Microwave ovens let you dry herbs quickly. Rinse herbs in cool water; shake off excess moisture (if you put wet herbs in a microwave, they'll cook, not dry). Put no more than 4 or 5 herb branches in the oven, arranging them between 2 paper towels. Microwave on **HIGH (100%)** for 2 to 3 minutes; remove herbs from oven. If they're not brittle and dry, microwave on **HIGH (100%)** for 30 more seconds. Place herbs on a rack and let cool; then store airtight.

Convection ovens can also be used for drying herbs, though there is some flavor loss at higher temperatures. Use the lowest oven setting possible and leave the oven door ajar by about ½ inch. Rinse herbs in cool water; shake off excess moisture. Then prepare as for tray drying. Herbs usually dry in 1 to 3 hours; start checking after the first 45 minutes. To test for doneness, rub a few leaves to see if they crumble readily. Store airtight.

How to Make Jerky

Like other dried foods, meat jerky—tough, leathery strips of dried meat—was a staple for pioneers and "mountain men" in times past. Today, beef jerky is still a favorite among backpackers, skiers, and campers—and a popular snack for armchair sports fans, too. Modern jerky is prepared in an electric dehydrator or oven; sun drying, the technique favored in pioneer days, presents too great a risk of spoilage or contamination.

Though most of the following recipes call for beef, we also offer instructions for making turkey-breast jerky. Compared to jerky made with trimmed beef flank steak, it has less fat. It also has a more brittle texture, since poultry is fairly fibrous.

If you like, you can prepare beef jerky with game instead—but if you do, freeze the meat before drying for at least 30 days at 0°F as a precaution against disease.

The leaner the meat you use for jerky, the better: a lower fat content means a longer shelf life. As a first step for any jerky, trim and discard all visible fat and connective tissue from the meat; partially freeze it (to make slicing easier), then cut it into thin (⅛- to ¼-inch-thick) strips about 1 inch wide. Cut with the grain if you like a chewy jerky, across the grain if you prefer a more tender, brittle product.

Properly dried beef or game jerky should crack, but not break, when bent; turkey jerky, however, will crack and break.

Once the jerky has been dried, let it cool; then pack it in a rigid freezer container or plastic freezer bag and freeze for 72 hours at 0°F. Then store it in an airtight, insectproof container for up to 3 weeks in a cool, dark, dry place. Or, to maintain flavor and prolong shelf life, refrigerate or freeze.

Basic Jerky

You can use this recipe for lean cuts of beef such as flank steak, round steak, or brisket; it's good with venison, too.

- 1½ **pounds lean boneless meat (see recipe introduction, above), trimmed of all fat and connective tissue**
- ¼ **cup soy sauce**
- 1 **tablespoon Worcestershire**
- ½ **teaspoon onion powder**
- ¼ **teaspoon *each* pepper, garlic powder, and liquid smoke**
   Vegetable oil cooking spray

Freeze meat until firm but not hard; then cut into ⅛- to ¼-inch-thick slices.

In a medium-size glass, stoneware, plastic, or stainless steel bowl, combine soy sauce, Worcestershire, onion powder, pepper, garlic powder, and liquid smoke. Stir to dissolve seasonings. Add meat and mix until all surfaces are thoroughly coated. Cover tightly and refrigerate for at least 6 hours or until next day, stirring occasionally; recover tightly after stirring.

Drying the jerky. Depending upon the drying method you're using, evenly coat dehydrator racks or metal racks with cooking spray; if oven drying, place racks over rimmed baking pans.

Lift meat from bowl, shaking off any excess liquid. Arrange meat strips close together, but not overlapping, on racks.

Dehydrator drying. Arrange trays according to manufacturer's directions and dry at 140°F until a piece of jerky cracks, but does not break, when bent (8 to 10 hours; let jerky cool for 5 minutes before testing).

Oven drying. Set oven at 140° to 200°F (the lower, the better—the lowest your oven allows). Place racks at least 4 inches away from (above or below) heat source. Prop oven door open by about 2 inches. Dry until a piece of jerky cracks, but does not break, when bent (4 to 7 hours; let jerky cool for 5 minutes before testing).

Pat off any beads of oil from jerky. Let jerky cool completely on racks; remove from racks, place in a rigid freezer container, and freeze for 72 hours. Then store in airtight, insectproof containers in a cool, dry place; or freeze or refrigerate. Makes about ¾ pound.

Storage time. Up to 3 weeks at room temperature; up to 4 months in refrigerator; up to 8 months in freezer.

Per ounce: 94 calories, 12 g protein, 1 g carbohydrates, 4 g total fat, 28 mg cholesterol, 398 mg sodium

Barbecued Jerky

Pictured on page 98

If you love barbecue, you'll appreciate this jerky. It's great for taking along on a backpacking or camping trip; you'll also enjoy it for at-home snacking.

- 1½ **pounds flank or lean top round steak, trimmed of all fat and connective tissue**
- ½ **cup catsup**
- ⅓ **cup red wine vinegar**
- ¼ **cup firmly packed brown sugar**
- 1½ **teaspoons** *each* **dry mustard and onion powder**
- 1 **teaspoon salt**
- ½ **teaspoon garlic powder**
- ¼ **teaspoon ground red pepper (cayenne)**
  Vegetable oil cooking spray

Freeze meat until firm but not hard; then cut into ⅛- to ¼-inch-thick slices.

In a medium-size glass, stoneware, plastic, or stainless steel bowl, combine catsup, vinegar, sugar, mustard, onion powder, salt, garlic powder, and red pepper. Stir to dissolve seasonings. Add meat and mix until all surfaces are thoroughly coated. Cover tightly and refrigerate for at least 6 hours or until next day, stirring occasionally; recover tightly after stirring. Then proceed as directed in "Drying the jerky" for Basic Jerky (page 119). Makes about ¾ pound.

Storage time. Up to 3 weeks at room temperature; up to 4 months in refrigerator; up to 8 months in freezer.

Per ounce: 119 calories, 12 g protein, 8 g carbohydrates, 4 g total fat, 28 mg cholesterol, 345 mg sodium

Texas-style Jerky

Cayenne, black pepper, and chili powder give this jerky its slightly hot flavor.

- 1 **pound lean top round steak, trimmed of all fat and connective tissue**
- 1 **tablespoon salt**
- 1 **teaspoon** *each* **black pepper, chili powder, garlic powder, and onion powder**
- ¼ **teaspoon** *each* **ground red pepper (cayenne) and liquid smoke**
- ½ **cup water**
  Vegetable oil cooking spray

Freeze meat until firm but not hard; then cut into ⅛- to ¼-inch-thick slices.

In a medium-size glass, stoneware, plastic, or stainless steel bowl, combine salt, black pepper, chili powder, garlic powder, onion powder, red pepper, liquid smoke, and water. Stir to dissolve seasonings. Add meat and mix until all surfaces are thoroughly coated. Cover tightly and refrigerate for at least 6 hours or until next day, stirring occasionally; recover tightly after stirring. Then proceed as directed in "Drying the jerky" for Basic Jerky (page 119). Makes about ½ pound.

Storage time. Up to 3 weeks at room temperature; up to 4 months in refrigerator; up to 8 months in freezer.

Per ounce: 78 calories, 13 g protein, 1 g carbohydrates, 2 g total fat, 32 mg cholesterol, 857 mg sodium

Paniolo Beef Jerky

In Hawaii, a cowboy is called a *paniolo*—hence this jerky's name. Ginger and lime bring a taste of the islands to the marinade; crushed red pepper adds a little heat.

- 1½ **pounds flank steak, trimmed of all fat and connective tissue**
- ¼ **cup lime juice**
- 2 **tablespoons** *each* **reduced-sodium soy sauce and Worcestershire**
- 1 **tablespoon grated fresh ginger**
- 1 **teaspoon crushed red pepper flakes**
- ¼ **teaspoon coarsely ground black pepper**
- ⅛ **teaspoon liquid smoke**
  Vegetable oil cooking spray

Freeze meat until firm but not hard; then cut into ⅛- to ¼-inch-thick slices.

In a medium-size glass, stoneware, plastic, or stainless steel bowl, combine lime juice, soy sauce, Worcestershire, ginger, red pepper flakes, black pepper, and liquid smoke. Stir to dissolve seasonings. Add meat and mix until all surfaces are thoroughly coated. Cover tightly and refrigerate for at least 6 hours or until next day, stirring occasionally; recover tightly after stirring. Then proceed as directed in "Drying the jerky" for Basic Jerky (page 119). Makes about ¾ pound.

Storage time. Up to 3 weeks at room temperature; up to 4 months in refrigerator; up to 8 months in freezer.

Per ounce: 95 calories, 12 g protein, 1 g carbohydrates, 4 g total fat, 28 mg cholesterol, 170 mg sodium

Teriyaki Turkey Jerky

Pictured on page 98

For a modern twist on a very old tradition, try jerky made from lowfat turkey.

- 1 **pound boned, skinned turkey breast or turkey tenderloins, trimmed of all fat and connective tissue**
- ¼ **teaspoon *each* onion powder and garlic powder**
- ½ **cup water**
- ¼ **cup reduced-sodium soy sauce**
- 2 **teaspoons Worcestershire**
- 2 **tablespoons firmly packed brown sugar**
- 1 **teaspoon pepper**
- ½ **teaspoon liquid smoke**
  Vegetable oil cooking spray

Freeze turkey until firm but not hard; then cut into ⅛- to ¼-inch-thick slices.

In a medium-size glass, stoneware, plastic, or stainless steel bowl, combine onion powder, garlic powder, water, soy sauce, Worcestershire, sugar, pepper, and liquid smoke. Stir to dissolve seasonings. Add turkey and mix until all surfaces are thoroughly coated. Cover tightly and refrigerate for at least 6 hours or until next day, stirring occasionally; recover tightly after stirring.

Drying the jerky. Depending on the drying method you're using, evenly coat dehydrator racks or metal racks with cooking spray; if oven drying, place racks over rimmed baking pans.

Lift turkey from bowl, shaking off any excess liquid. Arrange strips close together, but not overlapping, on racks.

Dehydrator drying. Arrange trays according to manufacturer's directions and dry at 140°F until a piece of jerky cracks and breaks when bent (4½ to 6 hours; let jerky cool for 5 minutes before testing).

Oven drying. Set oven at 140° to 200°F (the lower, the better—the lowest your oven allows). Place racks at least 4 inches away from (above or below) heat source. Prop oven door open by about 2 inches. Dry until a piece of jerky cracks and breaks when bent (4 to 6 hours; let jerky cool for 5 minutes before testing).

Pat off any beads of oil from jerky. Let jerky cool completely on racks; remove from racks, place in a rigid freezer container, and freeze for 72 hours. Then store in airtight, insectproof containers in a cool, dry place; or freeze or refrigerate. Makes about ½ pound.

Storage time. Up to 3 weeks at room temperature; up to 4 months in refrigerator; up to 8 months in freezer.

Per ounce: 85 calories, 15 g protein, 5 g carbohydrates, 0 g total fat, 35 mg cholesterol, 557 mg sodium

Drying Glossary

Antidarkening agent. Any antioxidant used to keep light-colored fruits from browning after cutting. Antidarkening agents commonly used on fruits to be dried include sulfur, sulfite dips, ascorbic acid, citric acid, commercial formulas containing ascorbic and/or citric acids (and often sugar), and citrus juice.

Blanching. The process of heating food quickly in boiling water or steam to inactivate enzymes that can cause loss of color, flavor, and nutritive value. Most vegetables are blanched before drying.

Case harden (usually used to describe fruit). To form a hard shell on the outside, trapping moisture inside and resulting in deterioration. Case hardening often results from drying fruit at too high a temperature.

Dehydrating (drying). Removing moisture from food by exposing it to warm temperatures and moving air. The term is often used to refer to the process of drying foods in an electric dehydrator.

Dehydrator. An electric appliance, usually relatively small, used for drying foods at home. It maintains a low, even temperature and circulates heated air with a blower or fan.

Oven drying. Drying foods in a conventional or convection oven set at a low temperature.

Oxidation. A chemical reaction to oxygen that makes fresh produce darken when cut, diminishes flavor, and causes loss of vitamins A and C.

Sulfiting. Pretreating fruit by soaking cut pieces in a solution of water and sodium bisulfite, sodium sulfite, or sodium metabisulfite.

Sulfuring. Pretreating fruit by exposing cut pieces to the fumes of burning sulfur.

Sun drying. Drying foods (primarily fruits) by exposing them, usually in cut pieces, to the sun.

Syrups, Toppings & Cordials

Refreshing syrups, unique toppings, dried fruit cordials

*H*ome-canned fruits and jewel-bright jams let you enjoy summertime flavors all year long. But there are other ways to capture the essence of summer, too—with mellow cordials, luscious toppings, and brilliant-hued Italian fruit syrups. ● The syrups make refreshing drinks when mixed with sparkling water or wine; or you can freeze them to make sorbetlike *granitas.* ● To make our fabulous toppings, use your boiling water canner. You'll find that the fruity sauces, some lightly spiked with liqueur, are wonderful with ice cream, sorbet, waffles, and pancakes. And don't pass up our rich Caramel Pecan Topping—it's great to have on hand in the refrigerator, ready to use in tempting sundaes or to spoon over French toast. ● If you have dried fruit in your cupboard, try mixing it with a little wine, brandy, and sugar; let the mixture mellow for a few weeks, then sip the liqueur and enjoy the spirited fruit on ice cream or cake.

Italian Fruit Syrups

The summery sweetness of ripe berries, plums, or citrus fruits comes through with flair in these enticing syrups. Mix a few spoonfuls with sparkling water or white wine for a refreshing drink, or freeze a half-and-half blend of water and syrup to make sorbetlike *granita*.

Because the syrups are fermented, their flavors are especially intense. The yeast-fruit mixture, which bubbles and froths for several days, looks dull at first; but when you cook it before bottling, it brightens and takes on a jewel-like clarity.

> 2 **pounds ripe strawberries, raspberries, blueberries, peaches, or plums; or 2 cups orange, lemon, or lime juice**
> 2 **packages active dry yeast**
> 1 **teaspoon sugar (if using lemon or lime juice)**
> **Sugar, water, and lemon juice (amounts for each fruit or juice choice follow)**

Choose fruit or juice from the list above. Hull strawberries; pit (do not peel) and slice peaches or plums. Whirl fruit in a food processor or blender until puréed. Press raspberry purée through a fine strainer to remove seeds. Measure purée; the amount you need for each fruit is listed at right.

Pour purée or juice into a 3-quart or larger glass, ceramic, or stainless steel bowl. Sprinkle with yeast; if using lemon or lime juice, add 1 teaspoon sugar. Stir to moisten yeast. Cover bowl with a dishtowel or paper towel and set aside at room temperature to ferment, stirring occasionally. Mixture will bubble and rise in bowl; when bubbles no longer appear when mixture is stirred, fermentation is complete. The process takes about 2 days for juices, 3 to 4 days for purées.

Line a colander with 3 or 4 thicknesses of moistened cheesecloth, making sure squares of cloth are large enough to hang over sides of colander. Set colander over a 6- to 8-quart stainless steel or unchipped enamel pan. Pour purée or juice through cheesecloth; bring together corners of cloths and twist to extract juice. (You may have to scrape purée from cloth in order to force out as much juice as possible.) Discard pulp and any seeds; remove colander from pan.

To pan, add sugar, water, and lemon juice as specified for each fruit purée or juice. Bring to a boil over high heat; boil, uncovered, until reduced to amount specified for each fruit or juice (15 to 20 minutes).

Let syrup cool completely, then pour into a 1- to 2-quart glass container. Cover tightly and refrigerate for up to 6 months. A harmless sediment may form at bottom of container; to keep syrup clear, do not shake container. Makes 3½ to 7 cups, depending on fruit or juice used.

Fruit Purée or Juice. Check the listings below to see how much purée you need for each fruit and to find out how much sugar, water, and lemon juice each choice requires.

Strawberry. You should have 2½ to 2¾ cups purée. Use 6 cups **sugar**, 4 cups **water**, and 1½ cups **lemon juice**; boil down to 7 cups.

Blueberry, plum, or peach. You should have about 2 cups purée. Use 4½ cups **sugar**, 3 cups **water**, and 1 cup plus 2 tablespoons **lemon juice**; boil down to 5¼ cups.

Orange, lemon, or lime juice (2 cups). Use 4½ cups **sugar** and 3 cups **water**. *For orange juice only,* also add 1 cup plus 2 tablespoons **lemon juice**. Boil down to 5¼ cups.

Raspberry. You should have 1½ cups strained purée. Use 3 cups **sugar**, 2 cups **water**, and ¾ cup **lemon juice**. Boil down to 3½ cups.

Storage time. Up to 6 months in refrigerator.

Per tablespoon (approximate): 46 calories, 0 g protein, 12 g carbohydrates, 0 g total fat, 0 mg cholesterol, 1 mg sodium

Water Cooler

Partially fill an 8- to 10-ounce glass with **ice**. Fill glass with **sparkling or plain water** and ¼ cup (or to taste) **Italian Fruit Syrup**. Makes 1 serving.

Per serving: 184 calories, 1 g protein, 47 g carbohydrates, 0 g total fat, 0 mg cholesterol, 4 mg sodium

Italian Wine Cooler

Add 2 tablespoons (or to taste) **Italian Fruit Syrup** to ½ to ⅔ cup chilled **dry white wine**. Makes 1 serving.

Per serving: 182 calories, 0 g protein, 25 g carbohydrates, 0 g total fat, 0 mg cholesterol, 9 mg sodium

Granita

Combine equal parts **water** and **Italian Fruit Syrup**. Freeze until almost hard. With an electric mixer or a food processor, beat to a coarse slush; serve as a dessert or between courses.

Per ½ cup: 184 calories, 0 g protein, 47 g carbohydrates, 0 g total fat, 0 mg cholesterol, 4 mg sodium

Garden Lemon Syrup

This sweet, lemony syrup is delicious on pancakes, waffles, or ice cream; you can also stir it into chilled sparkling water for a refreshing beverage.

> 2 **cups lemon juice**
> 3 **cups sugar**

In a heavy-bottomed 6- to 8-quart pan, combine lemon juice and sugar. Bring to a boil over medium heat, stirring until sugar is dissolved. Then reduce heat and simmer, uncovered, for 6 minutes, stirring often. Remove from heat and let cool. Pour into freezer jars or freezer containers, leaving ½-inch headspace; apply lids. Freeze or refrigerate. Makes about 3 half-pints.

Storage time. Up to 1 month in refrigerator; up to 6 months in freezer.

Per tablespoon: 50 calories, 0 g protein, 13 g carbohydrates, 0 g total fat, 0 mg cholesterol, 2 mg sodium

Blackberry-Peach Topping

Pictured on page 10

Fresh blackberries and peaches combine in this luscious, homey topping. If you like, you can also use unsweetened frozen fruit; let it stand just until thawed before adding it to the sugar mixture.

> 3 **cups sugar**
> ½ **cup water**
> 2 **tablespoons lemon juice**
> ¼ **teaspoon ground cinnamon**
> 4 **cups crushed blackberries (about 2 quarts whole berries)**
> 4 **cups peeled, pitted, crushed peaches (about 2¾ lbs. peaches)**

In a heavy-bottomed 8- to 10-quart pan, mix sugar, water, lemon juice, and cinnamon. Bring to a boil over medium heat, stirring constantly (about 8 minutes). Add blackberries and peaches; increase heat to medium-high and return to a boil, stirring constantly (about 12 minutes). Then boil, uncovered, for 5 more minutes, stirring constantly. Mixture should be slightly thinner than the consistency you prefer at room temperature.

Ladle hot topping into prepared, hot jars, leaving ½-inch headspace. Gently run a narrow nonmetallic spatula between topping and jar sides to release air bubbles. Wipe rims and threads clean; top with hot lids, then firmly screw on bands. Process in boiling water canner for 10 minutes. Or omit processing and ladle into freezer jars or freezer containers, leaving ½-inch headspace; apply lids. Let cool; freeze or refrigerate. Makes about 10 half-pints or 5 pints.

Storage time: *Processed:* Up to 1 year. *Unprocessed:* Up to 1 week in refrigerator; up to 10 months in freezer.

Per ¼ cup: 84 calories, 0 g protein, 22 g carbohydrates, 0 g total fat, 0 mg cholesterol, 0 mg sodium

Raspberry-Peach Topping

Pictured on page 2

Follow directions for **Blackberry-Peach Topping**, but substitute 4 cups crushed **raspberries** (about 2 quarts whole berries) for blackberries. Makes about 10 half-pints or 5 pints.

Per ¼ cup: 81 calories, 1 g protein, 21 g carbohydrates, 0 g total fat, 0 mg cholesterol, 0 mg sodium

Plum-Marnier Topping

This delectable fresh plum sauce, flavored with a hint of orange liqueur, makes a superb topping for ice cream, sorbet, or fresh fruit.

> 8 **cups pitted, chopped unpeeled plums (about 5 lbs. plums)**
> 3 **cups sugar**
> ½ **cup water**
> 1 **tablespoon grated orange peel**
> ¼ **cup orange-flavored liqueur**

In a heavy-bottomed 8- to 10-quart pan, mix plums, sugar, water, and orange peel. Bring to a boil over medium heat, stirring constantly; boil, uncovered, for 5 minutes. Transfer mixture to a blender or food processor, a portion at a time; whirl until smooth. Return to pan and bring to a boil over medium-high heat, stirring often. Continue to boil until thickened (5 to 10 more minutes). Add liqueur and boil, stirring often, for 3 more minutes.

Ladle hot topping into prepared, hot jars, leaving ½-inch headspace. Gently run a narrow nonmetallic spatula between topping and jar sides to release air bubbles. Wipe rims and threads clean; top with hot lids, then firmly screw on bands. Process in boiling water canner for 10 minutes. Or omit processing and ladle into freezer jars or freezer containers, leaving ½-inch headspace; apply lids. Let cool; freeze or refrigerate. Makes about 6 half-pints or 3 pints.

Storage time. *Processed:* Up to 1 year. *Unprocessed:* Up to 1 week in refrigerator; up to 10 months in freezer.

Per ¼ cup: 135 calories, 0 g protein, 33 g carbohydrates, 0 g total fat, 0 mg cholesterol, 0 mg sodium

Easy Cherry-Amaretto Topping

Pictured on page 2

Lots of plump sweet cherries go into a topping that's a snap to make at any time of year. You don't even need to thaw the cherries before you begin.

- **4 pounds frozen pitted dark sweet cherries**
- **3 cups sugar**
- **1 tablespoon lemon juice**
- **¼ cup amaretto liqueur**

In a heavy-bottomed 8- to 10-quart pan, mix cherries, sugar, and lemon juice. Cook over low heat, stirring occasionally, until cherries thaw (10 to 15 minutes). Then bring to a boil over high heat, stirring occasionally (about 15 minutes). Reduce heat to medium-high and continue to cook until syrup is slightly thickened and mixture has the consistency of a thick sauce (about 35 minutes). Add liqueur and cook, stirring often, for 3 more minutes.

Ladle hot topping into prepared, hot jars, leaving ½-inch headspace. Gently run a narrow nonmetallic spatula between topping and jar sides to release air bubbles. Wipe rims and threads clean; top with hot lids, then firmly screw on bands. Process in boiling water canner for 10 minutes. Or omit processing and ladle into freezer jars or freezer containers, leaving ½-inch headspace; apply lids. Let cool; freeze or refrigerate. Makes about 6 half-pints or 3 pints.

Storage time. *Processed:* Up to 1 year. *Unprocessed:* Up to 1 week in refrigerator; up to 10 months in freezer.

Per ¼ cup: 154 calories, 1 g protein, 38 g carbohydrates, 1 g total fat, 0 mg cholesterol, 0 mg sodium

Caramel Pecan Topping

Pictured on page 2

Ideal for spooning over ice cream, this topping is just as good with waffles, pancakes, and French toast. If you like, you can add a little light or dark rum before stirring in the nuts.

- **3 cups firmly packed brown sugar**
- **1½ cups light corn syrup**
- **1 cup water**
- **¼ cup light or dark rum (optional)**
- **2½ cups coarsely chopped toasted pecans**

In a heavy-bottomed 6- to 8-quart pan, mix sugar, corn syrup, and water. Bring to a boil over medium heat, stirring constantly; reduce heat to medium-low and simmer for 5 minutes. Add rum, if desired, stirring well; then stir in pecans.

Ladle hot topping into prepared, hot jars, leaving ½-inch headspace. Gently run a narrow nonmetallic spatula between topping and jar sides to release air bubbles. Wipe rims and threads clean; top with hot lids, then firmly screw on bands. Process in boiling water canner for 10 minutes. Or omit processing and ladle into hot jars; apply lids. Let cool; then refrigerate. Makes about 6 half-pints or 3 pints.

Storage time. *Processed:* Up to 1 year. *Unprocessed:* Up to 1 month in refrigerator.

Per ¼ cup: 237 calories, 1 g protein, 43 g carbohydrates, 8 g total fat, 0 mg cholesterol, 38 mg sodium

Dried Fruit Cordials

Dried apricots, peaches, pears, or prunes soaked in a mixture of sweetened white wine and brandy make fruity cordials that mellow with age. Because the fruit softens any harshness, you can use inexpensive wine and brandy. Sip the liqueur; serve the soaked fruit over ice cream or pound cake.

- **1 pound dried apricots, prunes (with pits), pears, or peaches**
- **1 bottle (750 ml.) or 3⅓ cups dry white wine**
- **1 cup brandy**
- **2 cups sugar**

Place fruit in a 2-quart glass, ceramic, or stainless steel container. Stir in wine, brandy, and sugar until well blended. Cover tightly. Let stand for at least 1 week at room temperature to allow flavors to develop; stir occasionally during the first few days to dissolve sugar.

After 1 week, apricots, prunes, and pears should be soft; peaches should still be slightly firm. After 3 to 4 weeks, the cordial's fruit flavor will reach maximum intensity. After about 6 weeks, fruit should be removed if it has become too soft. (If you'd like to give a cordial as a gift, transfer it to 1 or 2 decanters or other attractive glass containers.) Makes about 6 cups fruit-cordial mixture.

Storage time. Up to 6 weeks at room temperature for fruit-cordial mixture; indefinitely for cordial alone.

Per ½ cup fruit-cordial mixture: 312 calories, 1 g protein, 57 g carbohydrates, 0 g total fat, 0 mg cholesterol, 7 mg sodium

Index

About Our Nutritional Data

For our recipes, we provide a nutritional analysis stating calorie count; grams of protein, carbohydrates, and total fat; and milligrams of cholesterol and sodium. Generally, the analysis applies to a tablespoon or cup amount, based on the total yield for each recipe and the amount of each ingredient. If a range is given for the yield and/or the amount of an ingredient, the analysis is based on an average of the figures given.

The nutritional analysis does not include optional ingredients or those for which no specific amount is stated. If an ingredient is listed with a substitution, the information was calculated using the first choice.